Burcu Şentürk graduated from Boğaziçi University with a BA in Political Science and International Relations before going on to complete an MSc in Sociology from the Middle East Technical University in Ankara. She holds a PhD in Politics from the University of York. She is currently a faculty member of the Department of Business Administration at Ege University in Turkey.

'By looking at the urban poor, *Urban Poverty in Turkey* offers a new perspective on modernisation in Turkey. It is a well-researched overview of the relevant and current research in the field, but through its focus on the group that has not been previously studied the work offers valuable and unexpected insight on the impact of modernisation on the poor; in particular the analysis of the different experiences of different generations of slum dwellers and the process of growth and development of the slums are both original and enlightening.'

Professor the Baroness Afshar OBE AcSS, University of York

'This is an important and original piece of work, on a topic on which there has been very little recent literature. In preparing the book, Burcu Şentürk lived with her parents in the squatter settlement of Ege, in Ankara, and thus acquired unique first-hand acquaintance with the community. This is reflected in a lively and engaging story. She adds depth to this account by describing the process of migration, outlining the rural backgrounds of the migrants, as well as the motives for their move. The development of the community, with a second wave of immigrants, is described and analysed with skill and understanding. Burcu Şentürk thus makes a valuable contribution to the global literature on urban transformation in developing societies.'

William Hale, Emeritus Professor, School of Oriental and African Studies, London

URBAN POVERTY IN TURKEY

Development and Modernisation in Low-Income Communities

Burcu Şentürk

I.B.TAURIS
LONDON · NEW YORK

Published in 2016 by
I.B.Tauris & Co. Ltd
London • New York
www.ibtauris.com

Library of Modern Turkey 21

ISBN: 978 1 78453 653 4
eISBN: 978 1 78672 056 6
ePDF: 978 1 78673 056 5

A full CIP record for this book is available from the British Library
A full CIP record is available from the Library of Congress

Library of Congress Catalog Card Number: available

Typeset in Garamond Three by OKS Prepress Services, Chennai, India
Printed and bound by CPI Group (UK) Ltd, Croydon, CR0 4YY

MIX
Paper from responsible sources
FSC
www.fsc.org
FSC® C013604

To all slum dwellers, who surprise the rest of the world with their amazingly creative survival strategies

To the lovely memory of Güven Aydoğan, who always follows the wind and silently passed away one midnight in Ege

CONTENTS

LIST OF FIGURES

PREFACE

This book is based on lived experiences of squatter dwellers and attempts to understand the transformation of squatter areas in Turkey. My research on the strategies and transformation of squatter dwellers in Turkey went far beyond an academic work and turned into a personal adventure that forced me to question my middle-class values, which I had never previously noticed, and to change them. I am no longer who I was before starting my research. People of Ege, where I stayed with my parents to conduct my fieldwork, warmly welcomed me and my parents, opened their doors wide and let me in by telling their invaluable stories, sharing what they have and also what they do not have. Without their contributions, this work would never have been completed. So, this book belongs to them more than to me.

Living in a squatter neighbourhood reminded me and my parents how to light a stove, as we had done ten years before in our family house, how to find wood and coal, cut the wood and store it. From our storage we took an old copper vessel, large basins and buckets which were quite useful for boiling water on the stove, carrying and storing coal and keeping water in the bathroom. From the fact that half of our conversation was about heating and cleaning away the coal dust, we understood from practical experience how vital the distribution of coal by the municipality was for the people living in squatter areas and why women complain about the difficulties of living in them. Moreover, after living in a multistorey apartment block for ten years, we appreciated the community support in Ege where the neighbours helped us in cutting wood and finding furniture and shared food with us. For me and my parents, this was a life journey through which we came to question our recent middle-class life in the multistorey apartment block and our middle-class values and approach to people in squatter areas. This enabled me to take a critical perspective towards the literature on the residents of squatter settlements, all of which is written by middle-class researchers. In this way, I suppose I was able to abstain from both romanticising and looking down on life in *gecekondus*. As well as myself, this fieldwork also touched my parents; my father still keeps in touch with his contacts from Ege and my mother, who is a feminist activist, wrote her memoirs and published them in a feminist journal.[1] My parents were devoted enough to live in Ege with me. They lit the stove, cooked for me and put up with all my caprices, which were reflections of my worries about my fieldwork. Without my father, I would not have been able to contact the local men so easily. My mother's observations, questions and concerns about Ege enriched this study. I would like to present my deepest gratitude and apologies to them.

Professor the Baroness Haleh Afshar not only supervised me in my research but also became a role model with her modesty and hardworking, generous and wise personality. She patiently taught me how to understand politics and power relations from the bottom rather than from the top and to challenge the mainstream understanding of politics. Looking back, I realise it has been a privilege to be a researcher under her supervision. I am grateful to Professor Dr William Hale for his mind-opening questions and insightful suggestions to my work and his continuous support. Special thanks to my friend and colleague Erman, who supported me throughout the ups and downs of writing my study and my life in York. Despite their limited time, my friends in Ankara and my brother and his wife all visited me in Ege to encourage me to hold out against my worries and fears. I would also like to thank Anıl Gökpek, who not only shared my enthusiasm of my work but also carefully read and patiently edited my book. I enjoy expressing my gratitude to all those who accompanied me throughout this journey and made this study possible.

INTRODUCTION

What is a *Gecekondu?*

'Squatter and uncontrolled settlements appear under a variety of names reflecting the local culture and the specific circumstances of their establishment' (Karpat 1976:11), such as favela in Brazil, barrios in Mexico, bustee in Bangladesh, bidonville in Algeria, chawls in Bombay and *gecekondu* in Turkey. *Gecekondu* literally means 'built overnight' and refers to poor quality houses built by migrants, mostly on public land in large cities without planning permission. In this sense, the name reflects the spontaneity of the squatter houses. *Gecekondu* can refer to individual shanty houses, illegal housing or a squatter area in Turkish; however, in this work, the term denotes shanty house in order to avoid possible confusion. *Gecekondus* first appeared in the large cities of İstanbul, Ankara and İzmir in the 1930s and spread to other cities during the following decades. These houses first entered the agenda of public and political debate in the 1940s and were denoted by their publicly recognised name, *gecekondu*, in Gecekondu Law No. 775 in 1966.

Although *gecekondu* areas have similarities with squatter and slum areas all over the world in their lack of basic services, unhealthy living conditions and illegal and inadequate building structures (see UN Human Settlements Programme 2003), there are also a variety of differences among them. There are many differences between *gecekondu* areas and shanty towns in developed countries in terms of population density, the ratio of house owners to tenants, the level of temporality of residents, their aspirations about being a part of and visible in cities and their upward mobility (Keleş 2010:481–484, Zürcher 2004:269–270). On the other hand, when they are compared to squatter areas in developing countries,[1] it can be argued that *gecekondu* areas can be classified as transition areas rather than squatter areas. In the context of these differences, in Turkey *gecekondu* areas are not densely populated and only a few people live in each small house (see Mahmud and Duyar-Kienast 2001). They are not people without hope in the sense that they are a part of both city life and the political and economic system. Because of these important differences, in order to be specific about what is being discussed, rather than the notion of slums or squatters, the term *gecekondu* will be used throughout this study.

Gecekondus were built by the pioneer rural migrants who came to the cities as a result of rapid urbanisation and changes in the government's development strategy. In the absence of affordable housing, they occupied and demarcated the available land, which mostly belonged to the state, as early as the 1930s. While the pioneer rural migrants formed the nucleus of the *gecekondu* neighbourhoods, large *gecekondu* communities first appeared in the 1950s when the first wave of mass migration took place. By the time of the second wave of mass migration in the 1980s, there was no available land remaining for occupation in existing *gecekondu* areas and the newcomers searched for new areas on the outskirts of the city to build houses. This resulted in increasing numbers of *gecekondu* areas.

During the developmentalist period between the 1950s and the 1980s, migration to urban areas and *gecekondu* communities were mostly dealt with in the framework of industrialisation, the housing problem, development and urbanisation both in academia and at the policy making level. Field surveys and empirical research, which mostly underlined the deprived physical space, lack of infrastructure and the inadequacy of social services and equipment, dominated. A number of studies and pieces of research undertaken by the Turkish Statistical Institute, the Ministry of Health and Welfare and academics (Karpat 1976, Kıray 1970, Öğretmen 1957, Yasa 1966, Yavuz et al. 1978, Abadan 1963) can serve as examples of these approaches. During this period, the common tendency among researchers was to aim for an understanding of the reasons for internal migration and they mostly relied on the idea that, if the reason was properly understood, the migration could be prevented (Yıldırmaz 2010:399). The overlapping concerns of the academic and public approaches were shaped by a modernist/elitist perspective in which the *gecekondus* were considered to be backward, rural and inferior spaces that should be erased immediately. This reflected the discomfort felt by the elite about the presence of *gecekondu* dwellers, whom they considered to be a threat to modernity, while 'some proposals went as far as suggesting restricting access to large cities or granting visas for entering İstanbul and Ankara' (Demirtaş 2009:75).

Attempts at preventing migration failed and *gecekondu* residents consolidated their permanence, especially with the second wave of mass migration during the 1980s. This was mostly why discussion about the prevention of migration gradually disappeared and had vanished altogether by the 1980s. While *gecekondus* first appeared as spontaneous and irregular housing built by rural migrants for their own use, in due course the social and physical context of *gecekondus* changed. By the second half of the 1980s, when the new development policy was based on integration with global markets and liberalisation of the national economy, most of the *gecekondus* were transformed into multistorey apartment blocks on the build-sell (*yap-sat*) model. This was based on increased development rights at the parcel level to build apartment blocks on individual parcels of land. Therefore, the term *gecekondu* lagged behind in describing the spontaneous, low-income housing that was built to shelter rural incomers and *gecekondus* lost their 'innocence' for the public at large during the 1980s. This change is reflected in the studies on *gecekondus* as well as the urban policies and the way in which politicians addressed *gecekondu* communities. The concept of 'illegal construction' increasingly replaces the term *gecekondu* in academic approaches, in order to reflect all aspects of the phenomenon (Akbulut and Başlık 2010:26). Starting in the 1980s, as Demirtaş and Şen suggest, a serious rupture emerged between the academic discourse and public debate; academic works focused on developing an in-depth approach to migrants' lives while the term *gecekondu* retained its pejorative and exclusionary connotation in public debate and the media (2006:90). The academic literature increasingly referenced urban poverty, social exclusion and marginalisation during the 1990s, when the extensive poverty could no longer remain untouched by the politicians (see Erdoğan and Bora 2007, Buğra 2007, Erman 2001, Işık and Pınarcıoğlu 2002, Özyeğin 2001, Eroğlu 2011, Keyder 1987, Çınar 1993, Dedeoğlu 2008, Özyeğin 2002, Buğra 1998, Çelik 2010, Buğra 2007, Murakami 2011). The gentrification process of *gecekondu* neighbourhoods started in the 1990s and accelerated during the 2000s so a great deal of current research on *gecekondu* communities takes place within the framework of urban transformation and urban movements against gentrification (see Güzey 2009, Turan 2007, Dündar 2001, Dinçer 2011, Aslan 2010).

A Brief Note on the Research

This book is based on a research about the life story of one particular *gecekondu* community which appeared during the second half of the 1970s in Ege neighbourhood in Ankara. I chose Ege for the fieldwork on the basis of previously conducted pilot fieldwork in Ege, Harman and Çinçin neighbourhoods in Ankara in 2010. I started this research by thinking about the historical process of *gecekondu* building and went into my fieldwork in Ege neighbourhood to discover what my research questions should be. In this sense, this study is based on grounded theory. My research questions, as well as the main themes discussed in this study, emerged out of my open-ended interviews and daily discussions and conversations during the fieldwork. In 2011, I started the fieldwork in Ege, where I was able to find both first settlers and newcomers. This enabled me to discuss the emergence and development process of the *gecekondu* community as well as the process of dissolution of community ties and integration. I rented a local house and stayed there with my parents for three months (see Figure 1). In 2012, I returned to Ankara for a month and made regular visits to Ege to hold more interviews and make further observations. In addition, I visited some of my interviewees in Ege in 2013 and I remained in contact with some of the participants via e-mails and phone calls. As a researcher, I tried to function as a mirror, to reflect what *gecekondu* residents think about, who they were and who they are now. In order to be able to reflect the dynamic and flexible nature of *gecekondu* dwellers, I preferred to use multiple methods in a flexible manner. My gender and class position created some barriers in contacting local men, but thanks to my parents' presence during my fieldwork I was able to gain access to them. On the other hand,

I would not have been able to meet female *gecekondu* dwellers if I had not been a woman.

Outline of the Book

The first chapter of the book discusses the research field, the power relationship between researcher and researched and the obstacles and advantages created by being a female researcher in a *gecekondu* area. It is followed by a historical discussion of the dynamics of internal migration and of the emergence process of *gecekondu* communities. Since migration is not an isolated issue, internal migration will not be the focus for its own sake, but will be detailed in order to understand the foundation of *gecekondu* communities. Considering the fact that the movements of people have always been strongly related to the movements of capital and commodities (Castles and Miller 2003:77), migration will be taken both as a cause and a consequence of a series of changes in rural and urban population composition, economic strategies and the labour market. The heterogeneity of *gecekondu* settlers will not be overlooked; rather, the different effects of migration will be discussed through an exploration of differences between migrants. In this context, *gecekondu* dwellers will be categorised based on the period during which they arrived in Ankara, their gender and whether or not they were born or brought up in Ankara.

The dynamics of the building of *gecekondu* neighbourhoods and communities will be examined in terms of the history of Ege. A brief discussion of *gecekondu* dwellers' lives in rural areas before their migration reveals the reasons for migration and the hidden dynamics of solidarity networks within the *gecekondu* communities. This will be followed by an account of the faith, ethnicity and diverse locations of origin of Ege people in order to disentangle the political identities and left-wing leaning character of some *gecekondu* communities. The history of building *gecekondus* in Ege not only provides a deeper understanding of the construction process of migrant communities but also shows that the community is built up through solidarity, which is a result of common needs, problems and expectations.

The possible dynamics of *gecekondu* identity will be unpacked step by step from the point at which the residents arrived in cities in relation to the socioeconomic and political atmosphere of Turkey. Since it was a chain migration, initial networks were based on place of origin. First-comers found jobs and *gecekondus* and learnt about opportunities in the city through their *hemşehri* (fellow countrymen), so these networks were the primary base on which their identity was built. There was a relatively powerful left-wing movement during the 1970s and this movement's emphasis on *halk* (the people) and the working class built a bridge between the identities of rural migrants and the urban working class. At this point, *gecekondu* people combined their working-class features with their rural backgrounds. However, during the physical production of *gecekondu* neighbourhoods, rural migrants' social relations were denser with the people in their neighbourhood with whom they had common problems and with whom they collectively struggled to resolve those problems. Their neighbourhood provided them with a residence-based informal economy in which people helped one another and mutual trust was deployed for the purpose of information and work exchange. This resulted in breaching the boundaries of political polarisation, faith and ethnic differences. This informal economy was their main tool for survival in the cities. Therefore, social relations within their community became a dominant element in determining their identity.

The increase in the number of *gecekondu* dwellers during the 1980s with the second wave of mass migration also increased the *gecekondu* people's negotiating power with politicians. The legalisation process is important in terms of understanding *gecekondu* ownership and the relationship between politicians and *gecekondu* dwellers. Their determination to obtain legal title deeds was combined with the policies of rapid liberalisation that began immediately after the coup d'état in 1980, which saw a series of Gecekondu Amnesties being passed in the 1980s that legalised the *gecekondus* built before 1985. The *gecekondus* of second-wave migrants were not legalised since the last amnesty did not cover the *gecekondus* built after 1985. This created a major division between *gecekondu* dwellers in terms of ownership of their homes. In Ege, this separation did not become the determining element in local people's solidarity and sense of community until the Ege Urban Transformation Project, which was based on property ownership, started in 2001. This transformation process creates confusion in the people's self-perception. Since the legal title deed owners benefit from this project and are given one or more flats, they start to feel as though they belong to the middle class even though their regular income, main consumption practices and position in the labour market have not changed. On the other hand, due to the future cost of maintaining these buildings, their desire to provide homes for their children, the low level of incomes and significant cultural and class differences with their future neighbours, most of Ege's people cannot live in these luxury apartments. Not all the people possess formal title deeds for their *gecekondus* since some of them were built after the last Gecekondu Amnesty that legalised the existing *gecekondus* had passed. The dispossessed struggle for the amelioration of their neighbourhood and fight against the demolition of their *gecekondus*. Local people have different interests in the face of the urban transformation process depending on their *gecekondu* ownership status and people with formal title deeds do not collaborate with the dispossessed in their struggle against the demolition of their houses. During the urban transformation project the disparities in terms of legal ownership of *gecekondus* divided the local people and this gradually dissolved the sense of community in Ege.

Urban reforms are not the only reason for the breakdown of social cohesion in *gecekondu* areas. Through the case of Ege, elements of the collapse of social cohesion, such as an increase in crime, the individualisation of society and the weakening of the left-wing movement and of the sense of community will be discussed. Since these are not specific to Ege district alone, these discussions will include changes in the state structure generated by the implementation of neoliberal policies during the 1980s and the intensification of these policies throughout the 1990s and 2000s, the political pressure resulting from the military intervention in 1980 and social assistance programmes. It will be suggested that decreasing formal employment opportunities for the younger generation, the gradual breakdown of the community and the younger generation's higher expectations generated by their familiarity with the urbanites have pushed many young *gecekondu* men into illegal activities and the gangs through which they attempt to become empowered and develop a new sense of belonging.

The results of my fieldwork suggest that the duration of their residence in urban areas affects the lifestyles, values and living conditions of *gecekondu* dwellers. Increasing levels of education among younger generations and women's participation in paid employment, which are among the main pillars of the transition to modernity, are among the most visible changes in *gecekondu* neighbourhoods. The longer rural migrants stay in the city, the better the educational attainments of their children compared to migrants of previous generations, although they do not always have the same opportunities as their urban peers. Working in paid employment was not common among the first-generation women due to their low level of income, absence of education, skills and knowledge about the city, as well as community values that did not permit women to work outside the home. Over decades, younger women gradually acquired more education and skills and the values of the community changed in favour of women's employment. Moreover, decreasing incomes among the working class due to the neoliberal policies of the 1980s made women's employment necessary for *gecekondu* households to survive. The dynamics of women's participation in paid employment and the younger generations' greater opportunities in higher education as well as the conflicts created by these issues between the generations will be discussed.

CHAPTER 1

A FEMALE RESEARCHER IN A *GECEKONDU* NEIGHBOURHOOD

Before starting the field research, I focused on the available literature on *gecekondus* in Turkey and slums and squatter settlements in other countries. Previous work on *gecekondu* areas in Turkey has mostly dealt with residents' political participation, criminality, urban regeneration, welfare policies, unemployment, level of education and poverty in these areas and the government's policies on *gecekondus.* Although these issues are closely linked to the emergence, development and integration of *gecekondu* communities, there is a clear gap as there has been very little research focusing on these issues throughout the lifespan of a *gecekondu* community. I thought that listening to the life stories of people in *gecekondu* districts, talking with them and seeing their living conditions and neighbourhoods might help me to get closer to my topic and reveal more about the dynamics of the lives of *gecekondu* dwellers. I thought that the notions of what to look for would come in part from what I learnt from the data (Ramazanoğlu and Holland 2002:160). Therefore, a fieldwork study was inevitably important to investigate the lifespan of a *gecekondu* community. Although the number of *gecekondu* neighbourhoods is larger in İstanbul, I chose Ankara since it was at the core of the new modern Turkish Republic's plan to impose a western lifestyle and it became the capital city in 1923. The appearance of *gecekondu* neighbourhoods, as early as the 1940s, conflicts with the modernist claims of the Turkish Republic. Existing studies about the *gecekondu* areas of Ankara are mostly about housing problems, legal procedures relating to *gecekondus*, social policies and the participation of residents in politics. Therefore, I suggest that exploring the *gecekondu* areas of Ankara through the narratives of *gecekondu* dwellers and the life story of a *gecekondu* neighbourhood might be a useful contribution. After a pilot study, I conducted pilot fieldwork in Ege neighbourhood, where the first settlers were contactable as well as the younger generation.

Initial Reflections on Fieldwork

For my main fieldwork, I went to Ege in August 2011 and visited Ali, *muhtar* of Ege, whom I already knew. I asked him to kindly help me find a *gecekondu* in Ege where I could live with my parents for several months. On the same day, he showed me a *gecekondu* just opposite the *muhtar*'s office. The owner of this *gecekondu*, Mr Mahmut, had returned to his village for the summer. Ali called him and told him that 'one of my nieces' needed a *gecekondu* for some months. He also bargained about the price although I was ready to pay anything that was suggested. Finally, Mr Mahmut reduced the rent from 300 liras to 200 liras, which was less than one third of the rent for an average middle-class flat in Ankara at that time. Mr Mahmut's *gecekondu,* where he lived in the winter, and the empty *gecekondu* that I wanted to rent were next to each other. The *gecekondu* opposite these two also belonged to Mr Mahmut, his mother and nephew lived there. Since the empty *gecekondu* was very close to the others, he wanted to rent it to a trustworthy person to protect his and his relatives' safety. I was introduced as Ali's niece, which denoted Ali's trust in me rather than a blood relation, therefore Mr Mahmut did not hesitate too much in accepting me as his lodger. Ali and I visited them and Mahmut's nephew gave me the key without any contract, deposit or rent in advance. This was very different from the house renting process in middle-class areas where a deposit, a contract, one month's rent and sometimes a guarantor are a necessity. I needed a few days to organise some furniture so I told them that I would return and move in with my parents in a few days. Moreover, since I had not expected to find a *gecekondu* on my first visit after a year of my pilot work, I did not have enough money to pay the first month's rent in my pocket at that time. I offered to pay Onur online or to meet the next day to pay in cash. Both Onur and Ali, although Ali was neither the owner nor a relative of the owner of that *gecekondu*, rejected this and advised me to feel free in terms of paying the rent. In spite of their attitudes, I felt uneasy until I had paid it due to my middle-class habits. Thus, my first day in Ege enabled me to see the moral economy and the mutual trust that it created among *gecekondu* people.

Moving into Ege and Starting the Fieldwork

Gecekondu neighbourhoods were not areas that non-locals visited regularly. So, they were not very familiar with non-locals and easily recognised who was local and who was not. Since I was an educated, professional woman who lives alone and studies in the UK, I was an outsider to the *gecekondu* community from their point of view. I was quite careful with my clothes and appearance during my visits to the *gecekondu* areas. I wore modest clothes, which were mostly loose, long-sleeved shirts and baggy, dark-coloured trousers. I abstained from sustaining my stranger position and seeking the attention of the residents. I did not wear makeup. I did not wear accessories or fashionable clothes and high heels, which might seem 'arrogant'. In fact, I did not dress too differently from my usual style. In daily life, I do not wear formal or fashionable clothes, high heels or makeup. So, I did not pretend to be a person that I was not; what I did was to try to eliminate the basic factors that might create more barriers between my respondents and myself and, as Letherby (2003:110) discusses, my aim was not to access the best data but to allow both myself and my respondents to feel comfortable.

Considering the patriarchal formation of this society and the high rates of violence against women, living alone in a *gecekondu* neighbourhood that I did not know well would create worries about my own security and these worries would be the biggest obstacles in making contact with local people. Besides, a woman who is a stranger living alone in a *gecekondu* neighbourhood to carry out research would be awkward for the local people and they might feel uncomfortable. Living with my parents both decreased my worries about security and normalised my existence in Ege. Since I was part of a family, we were invited for evening teas and breakfast by the other families and we could invite them to our home for similar reasons (see Figure 2). It was a big opportunity for me to develop my relations with the local people away from our interviews.

In fact, in the case of this study, it would have been possible to prepare a randomly selected sample of Ege people instead of using a snowball technique, since I could have easily obtained a list of Ege's inhabitants from the *muhtar* and prepared a randomly selected sample. However, this would have felt too formal for *gecekondu* people and I might have seemed like a state officer coming to check on them. Since this perception might be the biggest obstacle to reaching the local people, I chose informal ways of engaging with them. So, the best way to reach them seemed to be to go to the districts where they lived, approach the households and politely ask them – and also the *muhtars* – to introduce me to their relatives, friends and neighbours.

I explained my aim to my interviewees by saying that I was trying to understand the lifestyle of *gecekondu* dwellers and I would like to interview them about this. But I realised that although people were quite eager to participate in the interviews they got a bit anxious because they thought that their 'intellectual capacity' might not be enough for this. I answered all these hesitations by explaining that I was not going to test their knowledge and I would only try to understand their opinions, which were the most valuable thing for my study. I think their hesitation was due to my position as a person who comes from a university.

I asked their consent to participate in the research but I did not have a consent form since this would be seen as very formal and signing a consent form might induce a feeling that they were engaging in an activity that was organised by the state or a formal institution. All the interviews, except two, were recorded. Before we began, I did not directly ask for permission to record. Instead, I said, 'Now, let's talk about your experiences and life story and let me start the recorder.' I showed them the recorder and put it between me and the interviewee. It might sound strange but, based on my previous fieldwork experience, I knew that if I directly asked: 'Would you mind if I record your voice?' at the very beginning, the idea of 'recording their voice' would seem to them to be something very serious, they were likely to feel uncomfortable and the interview would be a very formal one.

For my fieldwork, I conducted 83 in-depth interviews with local people, some of which were in the form of informal conversations. I talked to most of the interviewees more than once since I met them regularly around the area. I conducted one prearranged focus group with seven local high school students in the classroom at the *muhtar*'s office where they were given extra classes by volunteer left-wing activists and one spontaneous focus group with seven local women while they were both baking and chatting in a local woman's backyard. I conducted three in-depth interviews with socialist activists who were active in Ege and another one with the city planner on Mamak council. I also used participant observation techniques, I participated in a protest meeting with local people, accompanied them while they were visiting Mamak municipality and the district governorate (*kaymakamlık*), I joined in with local women while they prepared bread and tomato sauce for the winter and so on, I frequently visited local public places such as the *muhtar*'s office, coffee house, local primary school and market. The data was not collected by conventional qualitative methods; what I did was to use the most appropriate way to reflect the richness and to fit into the flexible nature of *gecekondu* dwellers' lifestyle. Since I met the local people every day and we developed friendships, our relations were not limited to a researcher and researched relationship. Therefore, in our interviews there are moments when very personal exchanges of confidences take place. As a researcher, I respected all such information and did not reveal it. If this information was relevant to my research questions, I gave a general account and outline without mentioning any particular participant.

After each interview, I asked each of the interviewees whether they would like to conceal or reveal their names; the majority did not want to conceal their names. Especially for the men, revealing their names was a sort of pride and through letting me reveal their names they were trying to show that they were brave and proud of their life story. However, considering the fact that some of the men were engaged in illegal activities and were telling their stories frankly, using their real names might have put them in danger. Therefore, although they allowed me to use their names, I decided not to use their real names in order to protect them from any possible danger. To be consistent with the names, I used nicknames for all the interviewees except Sırrı Süreyya Önder, who is an MP, and Ali, who is the current *muhtar* of Ege. In addition to these considerations, there were some women who did not wish to conceal their names but who wanted to pick other names which they thought fit them better than their real names. I asked permission to take and use photos of people for this research.

One of my participants generously shared her personal photo archive and allowed me to use the images.

Since I lived in the district with them, I discussed my work with my interviewees whenever I found an opportunity during my stay in Ege *Mahallesi* (neighbourhood). I asked all my interviewees whether they would like to read the transcript or a summary transcript of our interview. Some of the men took this question to mean that I was testing their trust in me and told me that 'we trust that you will not change our words'. I mostly thanked them for their trust but also added that maybe we could talk more about the issues that we had discussed during the interview or that they might like to add more. Most of the people who wanted to read it preferred to read the summary since they thought the full transcript might take too long to read. When I gave the summary or the transcripts to the participants many of them, especially the women, asked me to read it slowly and loudly. Sometimes they asked me to pause and told me more about their life story. Some women cried when they saw that their life story was recorded and written down and they told me that they would keep that piece to read to their daughters or other family members. One day a local woman stopped me and said, 'I heard that when we talked about our life, you wrote it down, would you please do the same with me?' I feel that this lady's question, as well as the other women's attitudes about the written form of our interviews, showed that the women felt 'important' because their life story was recorded and written down.

Contacting Men

Contacting local men without an intermediary was not so easy. Unless my father was with me, inviting a male person to my *gecekondu* for an interview could have been misinterpreted. Yet, it is not unusual for feminist scholars researching in highly patriarchal societies to gain entry into privileged, male only areas through the connections of their male family members (Gupta 1979). My father, who is a very sociable person, made friends with local men, went shopping with them and visited the local coffee house and local market regularly. The coffee house was the main public place where many local men gathered daily. It was exclusive to men, so as a female researcher it was nearly impossible for me to gain access on my own. After gaining access through my father, I realised that my gender was an asset in the sense that I was harmless to the local men because I could not be a threat to the honour of local women. My outsider position and education could have aroused suspicion among the men in the local coffee shop where they usually gambled and smoked marijuana. However, since I was the daughter of an old retired teacher whom they knew, the local men accepted me there as an honorary man.

In Ege, all the men, even the older ones, called me *Abla* (older sister). In Turkish culture, especially in more traditional areas, it is not culturally welcomed for a man to call an unrelated woman only by her name. According to the age of a woman, men use words such as *Anne* (mother), *Yenge* (sister-in-law), *Bacı* (younger sister), *Abla* (older sister) and all these words denote a familial bond. In this way, men indirectly show that they do not consider the woman to whom they speak to be a sexual being. Being addressed as Burcu *Abla* indicated both distance and closeness between me and the local men. It was a sign of distance since the use of *Abla* does not refer to my age but to my hierarchical position. However, I was not called *Hanım* (Mrs/Miss/Ms), which is used among traditional communities for an unknown woman who is educated or middle class, in the way that they addressed female teachers at the local primary school as X *Hanım*. I lived there and all the men knew my father, therefore I was one step closer to them than other urbanite, middle-class, educated women. For me it would be culturally unacceptable to call men only by their name, except those who were obviously younger than me. My mother called the young men *Oğlum* (my son), but I was culturally too young to address someone as *Oğlum* except the kids. I had to address adult men either as *Abi* (older brother), *Amca* (uncle) or *Bey* (Mr), otherwise it would have been a sign of being too close and would have been misinterpreted. I did not choose to call any of them '*Bey*' since this was too formal for the social setting of Ege. I addressed the men, except those who were obviously younger than me, as *Abi* (older brother) and I said *Amca* (uncle) to those who were around or older than my father's age, which was 60. In most of my interactions with men, the gender hierarchy overcame the hierarchy based on class and educational background. This was most obvious in the interviews conducted in the local coffee house where men gathered to gamble and to smoke joints. Group discussions in this coffee house usually turned into a verbal competition among the men. Frequently, the men started a hot debate on an irrelevant issue such as soccer matches or horse racing and it was nearly impossible for me to persuade them to return to our discussion because nobody was listening to me.

Inventing 'Ms Useful'

Male researchers may have difficulties in accessing the world of women if 'there is a strong division between the sexes' (Hammersley and Atkinson 1995:93). I would not have gained any access to the local women if I had not been a woman since the local women spent most of their time either in their homes or at neighbours' houses. When I was introduced to them, either by the *muhtars* (the governor of a *mahalle*) or by their neighbours, they invited me to their houses. So I interviewed all the women either at their own or at their neighbours' houses.

Teenage girls called me *Abla* and I only used their names. I called older women, depending on their age, *Abla* or *Teyze* (aunt). However, most of the local women, even those who were much older than me, preferred to call me Burcu *Hanım*, meaning Mrs/Ms/Miss. While I aimed to minimise hierarchy, being *Hanım* clearly indicated a hierarchy between me and the Ege women since *Hanım* is used to superiors (Braun 1988:22). Sometimes I asked them not to call me *Hanım*. To older ladies I said: 'Aunt, I am one of your daughters, please only say my name,' and to the women around my age I said: 'We are friends now, no need for *Hanım*.' However, the women were not comfortable calling me Burcu and I thought this request might be another pressure placed on them and that this might deepen the hierarchy between us. Therefore, I stopped requesting them to call me just by my name. Rather, I tried to spend more time with them and gave them a hand in my visits and, in spite of their insistence I tried not to behave as a guest when I was in their homes. For example, when I was visiting, I helped them when they were serving tea, washing the dishes and so on. And, in due time, the women with whom I spent more time started to call me only Burcu, and for me this was a sign of the first step towards establishing more equal relations.

In due time, the local women discovered that I could be helpful and useful to them. For example, women who put much effort into their kids' education but did not have enough resources to provide them with additional help asked me to help their kids with their homework. Some weeks after I moved into Ege, I started to visit different households to help with children's homework. After every session, the women prepared a wide range of food to serve me. I was so embarrassed because the women worked hard to thank me with their food and there was no way to stop them. Moreover, if I requested them not to prepare anything for me, it might be understood that I was looking down on their food. So, I stopped asking them not to prepare food. Moreover, I could be useful in empowering them in terms of power relations within their family. Sometimes local women asked me to say things that they could not say to their husbands and sons. Since I was educated and not *cahil* (ignorant), which was how they put it, their husbands or teenage sons would listen to me. Actually, these women were challenging the men's authority through challenging the gender hierarchy by using the hierarchy based on education and class. In fact, I was hesitant about accepting these requests, because I was not a member of their families and therefore my attempts would be those of an outsider and my interference might exacerbate the power relations against the women. However, when women desperately asked for help, it was impossible for me to reject their requests.

All of the interviewees, when I visited their houses, behaved towards me as if I was a 'guest' rather than a researcher; and tried to make me feel comfortable. The local women gave me presents such as a scarf or *patiks* (a kind of handmade female sock), which is common, especially among families with a rural background. These presents might be considered a signal of being perceived as an ordinary girl rather than an urbanite expert researcher with a university degree. In this sense, I think that we succeeded in eliminating some of the traditional hierarchy between researchers and researched. Although this did not change my outsider position, at least I was perceived as a woman whose life expectations and plans were similar to those of the daughters of the women who gave me these presents. It seemed that my female interviewees and I could interact on the basis of being women. However, since there were other factors, such as our age, skin colour, class, ethnicity and accent, which were all likely to have an effect on how we were seen by respondents, being a woman was not in itself enough to be perceived as an insider. On the other hand, 'it is not necessarily the case that matching interviewers with interviewees in terms of race, class, age and gender' (Kelly, Burton and Regan 1994: 35) will be beneficial and in any case this kind of matching might be very difficult and rare

(Mellor 2007:59–60). Moreover, the researcher and the researched might interpret differences and similarities quite differently from each other (Ramazanoğlu and Holland 2002:113–115).

The Question of Translation

Despite the fact that we all spoke Turkish, it did not take long to realise that, in fact, we were speaking different languages. Our vocabularies and accents were quite different from one another. During my time in the *gecekondu* districts, I felt that our language was the most distinctive and obvious feature that drew a significant line between me and the *gecekondu* dwellers. The other problem in terms of language was that, although I spoke in Turkish to Ege people, I had to write in English. I am not a native speaker of English and only started to live in an English-speaking country at the age of 26, therefore it was quite hard for me to reflect the colourful life and diversity of *gecekondu* people in English, which sounds to me very formal due to the fact that I spoke it only on formal occasions before moving to the UK. Considering the fact that language is 'one of many elements that allow us to make sense of things, of ourselves' (Spivak 2004:369), it was not just a matter of difficulty in translating the words. Since any language is closely interlinked with its culture (Gal and Irvine 1995) and in some ways reflects it, this difficulty is about a translation from one culture to another. I used both direct translations and the adaptation method. If the narrative does not have culturally specific references and is based on parallel categories/concepts, I translated word by word. However, the word order and syntax is completely different in Turkish and English, which are not languages of the same family, therefore I had to change the word order. When using this method it is possible that 'the cultural embeddedness and mediating function of language is overlooked' (Maclean 2007:787) and this reduces the readability of the text (Birbili 2000). If the narratives convey an incomprehensible message to the English-speaking audience and refer to culturally specific social settings, as suggested by Vinay and Darbelnet, I had to 'create a new situation that can be considered as being equivalent' (2004:135). Under such circumstances, like many other researchers, I run the risk of misrepresenting the conversations and underestimating different perspectives and priorities. For example, when my participants talked about bribery they mostly used the phrase 'to see someone' (*görmek*) which is a slang term for bribery. However, I had to translate it merely as 'to bribe'. Furthermore, in some cases, I needed to combine these translation methods by borrowing the original version of some concepts and explaining them and giving the sociohistorical background of the meaning. Even the use of all these approaches could not entirely eliminate the loss in translation, but they did minimise this loss. Moreover, the participants' accents could not be reflected in the translation of their words into English. So, the reader is not able to understand the difference between the participants' Turkish and literary Turkish. As a researcher, I am accountable for the understandings (Ramazanoğlu and Holland 2002:102) that I produce.

CHAPTER 2

INTERNAL MIGRATION AND *GECEKONDU* COMMUNITIES IN TURKEY

The rural-to-urban migration experience within Turkey started as early as the 1930s; however, the population distribution was significantly changed by two large-scale mass migrations during the 1960s and 1980s. *Gecekondu* dwellers comprised 4.7 per cent of the urban population in 1955 and 16.4 per cent in 1960, but this ratio reached 22.9 per cent in 1965, 26.1 per cent in 1980 and 35 per cent in 1995 (Keleş 2010:494). The two waves of mass migration from rural to urban areas in Turkey can be considered as a response of the rural population to the transformation in both rural and urban areas as well as an increasing hierarchy between them in terms of quality of life, economic conditions, job opportunities and public services (Ataay 2001:62, Hemmasi and Prorok 2002:400–401). This chapter will discuss the historical context of the internal migration in Turkey by focusing upon the migrants' survival strategies and the interlinked relationship between their strategies and state policies.

Historical Background for the First-Wave Migration

The period following World War II was marked by high rates of economic growth around the world. Beginning in the second half of the 1940s, Turkey gave up closed, self-sufficient, state-led industrialisation based on domestic resources as its main strategy and shifted to a model which aimed at the mechanisation of agriculture based on foreign resources (Boratav 2004:94, Aydın 2005:28–30). Under the guidance of the Truman Doctrine of 1947 and the Marshall Plan of 1948, Turkey had a role as a 'bulwark' against communism and was expected to be an agricultural goods supplier, link its markets by road and increase agricultural productivity via mechanisation.

Marshall Aid contributed to the large-scale transformation of agricultural production and rural structure during this period. With the loans provided by Marshall Aid, tractors, fertilizers, irrigation systems and new agricultural products were introduced into Turkey. Marshall Aid also contributed to the development of transportation in terms of building more roads linking rural and urban areas (Şenyapılı 2004:119, Yıldırmaz 2010:408). Turkey focused on the Road Project with the support of the US and much of the aid was invested in road construction. In 1950, the General Director of Highways was established and an extensive programme for the improvement and construction of roads started. The total of surfaced roads went up from 14,961 to 21,266km from 1948 to 1957 while asphalt roads increased from 816 to 4,123km (Coşar and Demirci 2009:31).

The 1960s were marked by dramatic changes, in terms of the transformation not only of rural areas, but of urban areas as well. After a brief experiment with agriculture-led growth in the 1950s and the failure of Import Substitution Industrialisation (ISI), urban production began to be implemented during the 1960s (Altuğ et al. 2008:400, Aydın 2005: 90). Within the import substitution period, the aim was to scale up national production through montage industry. Turkey, as with many other less developed countries, would not only provide raw materials but would also integrate into the world economy by initiating a process of industrialisation based on import substitution Ataay 2001: 59–63). Turkey returned to a state-led economy during these years (Zürcher 2004:264–7, see Boratav 2004, Chapter 7). Within this framework, national capital owners were supported to produce for the internal market and invest in industrial production and were subsidised by the government; they did not need to compete with foreign investors. As a result, they increased their profits and throughout the 1960s Turkey witnessed a vigorous economic recovery and high growth rates in GNP (Çeçen et al. 1994:38).

The new system was based on a negotiation between social classes, with the state taking on the role of arbiter as well as the guardian and manager of national development (Pınarcıoğlu and Işık 2008:1356, Aydın 2010:150). This inclusiveness was apparent in the new constitution of 1961, which enlarged the rights of workers. Trade unions were quite powerful and capable of keeping workers' wages high, although their influence was limited to the employees of large enterprises, while the wages of the rest of the workforce were not so high (Zürcher 2004:272). A social security organisation for workers in the formal economy was introduced in 1964. Considering the fact that social security was based on formal employment at that time, being a worker in the formal sector appeared to be a very big opportunity for upward social mobility and generating security in their lives for the rural settlers.

The urban population was not large enough to supply the cheap labour required by the newly emerging industries. The migrant population was needed by the urban markets, which were searching for cheap labour. So, increasing industrial job opportunities was the prominent factor that pulled the rural population to urban areas. However, besides this, other factors such as the 'education skill and information level of potential rural migrants, transportation and communication facilities and existence of previous migrants' (Gedik 1997:171) also played a decisive role in the migration process.

It was mostly the young, the most educated, skilled and shrewd male member of the family who left home. In addition, some rural families (especially those who could not access the loans for tractors) even rented or sold their small land holdings in their village and decided to migrate to urban areas together. So, the personal qualifications of the potential rural migrants were no less significant than the other push and pull factors. For married men, the usual pattern was to leave their family in the village, because of the lack of accommodation or a definite job in the urban destination. Although the general pattern was the migration of one male member of the family, there were families who migrated together. So, for the migrating nuclear family within an extended family with a small landholding, the nuclear family who had some connections with the urban areas migrated, since the risk of being homeless and jobless was relatively lower for them compared to families who did not have any kind of contacts. As Todaro states, migrants had to balance the probabilities and the risks of being unemployed or underemployed for a considerable period of time against the positive urban-rural real income differentials (1992:241).

It should be borne in mind that only people who could afford the cost of transportation and the period of time required to search for a job and accommodation could migrate. Rural people either sold their animals or rented out their small farms to afford the migration costs of the migrating family. In most cases, they did not sell their farms but kept them so that, if they could not survive in the city, they could return to their villages and continue with rural production.

First-Wave Migrants in Ankara

The rural migrants searched for some time before securing appropriate accommodation for their stay in the cities. They could not afford to buy or rent a house in the city centre. *Bekar Odaları* (bachelor rooms), which were rented by as many as ten men or sleeping at their workplaces (for the ones who found a job) were the alternatives. Due to the lack of any social policies to provide the newcomers with accommodation, in Turkey as in many other places, rural migrants had to solve their own problems and the only option for new rural arrivals was illegal occupation of land and spontaneous self construction (Amis 1987:252, Gilbert 1994:96, Keleş 2010: Chapter 10, Ward 1976, Lloyd 1979:23–7). So, after staying temporarily in these places, pioneers built *gecekondus* quickly and without legal permission in the same way as the early arrivals had done. They built *gecekondus* either with a loan from extended family members or with savings from selling or renting land in their village. First-wave migrants typically hired craftsmen to teach them how to build the house and some less qualified workers to assist the craftsmen (Duyar-Kienast 2005:148). While most constructed these *gecekondus* for their own use, a few *gecekondu* dwellers built them to sell. The occasional production of *gecekondus* for exchange value began in the 1960s (Duyar-Kienast 2005: 41–6, Keleş 2010: 502, 520, Şenyapılı 2004: Chapter 4).

Initially, *gecekondus* were poor residences without any electricity, water or sewerage (Tas and Lightfoot 2005:268), on the outskirts of the city where they did not even have any public transportation or proper roads into the city centre. But it was the only option if they were to have affordable accommodation. In the beginning, like many slum dwellers in Latin America, *gecekondu* people only built the basic elements (Gilbert 1994:96–97, Ward 1976:340) to give the impression of a finished house since the demolition teams needed to get permission from the courts before they were allowed to demolish this kind of *gecekondu* (Duyar-Kienast 2005:152). Using this strategy, the migrants could delay or even prevent the eventual demolition of their *gecekondus*, so they did not complete the whole *gecekondu* at once, rather they added or developed some parts gradually, so the *gecekondu* dwellers had to 'discover spatial and architectural tactics of survival' (Nalbantoğlu 1997:206). According to Keleş, the gradual establishment of *gecekondus* demonstrates that rural migrants found a solution to the accommodation problem without placing a burden on the shoulders of either the state or the market (2010: Chapter 10).

The internal migration had been a chain migration, with the result that many families from the same village or region had clustered in the same neighbourhood (*mahalle*). As a result, the squatter houses of the 1940s, which were the nucleus of the *gecekondu* areas, turned into established and more permanent *gecekondu mahalle*s (Şenyapılı 2004: Chapter 3). *Gecekondu* areas and communities were quite important for their role of welcoming newcomers and decreasing the risk of being socially excluded as a result of problems such as temporary unemployment, cultural adaptation or lack of accommodation (Işık and Pınarcıoğlu 2002:117).

After the 1950s, the population of *gecekondu* areas was much larger than the labour force required by the industrial sector. Turkish industry failed to absorb many of the migrant job seekers (Hemmasi and Prorok 2002:401) and many could not find jobs in the formal sector. The informal sector was the only option for the rest since it required little capital input, few qualifications and there was a lack of legal barriers to enter it and so they struggled on as well as they could within the informal sector (Pınarcıoğlu and Işık 2008:1355, Koray 1993:18, Tekeli 2008:122). The arrival of migrants in large numbers created a growth in the informal economy in Turkey after the first half of the 1950s (Ataay 2001:62).

As surplus labour transforms people into informal initiators (Davis 2007:182), many used their limited savings to set up their own businesses in the marginal sector; this mostly involved street selling, the marginal service sector – which included creative jobs such as shoe painters, luggage and market bag carriers – and artisanship. Through these self-initiated businesses, some migrants became quite successful and even started to control a sector both in the formal and informal sense. For example, being the driver of a *dolmuş*[1] (shared taxi), selling clams in the street, parquet making and the construction business are among the jobs and businesses that were controlled by migrant groups and clientelism based on area of origin was a crucial determinant in finding a job in these areas (Erder 1996:266–272, Pınarcıoğlu and Işık 2008:1362–3).

By the 1960s, although most of the new migrants were working in the marginal sector, they were no longer at the margins of the economy (Şenyapılı 2004:186–7). Moreover, by the first half of the 1960s, 59 per cent of Ankara's population and 45 per cent of Istanbul's population lived in *gecekondus* (Buğra 1998:307). Their labour was needed for the running of the economy and their role could not be ignored in fulfilling the national goal of developing Turkish industry. At this point, it can be suggested that these changing circumstances empowered the position of newcomers to city life. *Gecekondu* districts, with their increasing population, who had gradually become the main workforce, and their affordable immediate needs, seemed to political parties to be areas where they could act as vote-hunters and *gecekondu* communities were targeted by the political parties. The distribution of title deeds and the provision of infrastructure facilities were used as instruments by politicians to get the support of *gecekondu* areas, especially during the periods immediately before elections. Their empowered situation can be read through the Gecekondu Act, passed in 1966. This law was crucially important in the sense of naming the squatter houses as *gecekondus* and the reorganisation of the status of *gecekondus* (Erman 2001:989) for the first time since the beginning of *gecekondu* building. This law attempted to improve *gecekondus* as well as to stop more *gecekondu* construction and established the gradual distribution of title deeds for *gecekondus* to residents for very low prices. In Article 3, it was stated that the *gecekondu* dwellers would be provided with long-term credit in order to be able pay the cost of these title deeds. In Article 2, a *gecekondu* was defined as a settlement that had been constructed by violating the legislation on improvement and construction and general laws, on land which belonged to someone else without the permission of the owner. The distributed land's value rose with unforeseen speed due to the new demands directed towards land and rapid urbanisation. The title deed distribution of the 1960s was a *fait accompli* and Gecekondu Amnesties followed throughout the 1970s (Keleş 2010:504). However, in the absence of a formal approach to the problem of low-income housing, the Gecekondu Amnesties had a moral legitimacy in the sense of satisfying the need for accommodation for the lower class (Buğra 1998:306–7, Işık and Pınarcıoğlu 2002:113). *Gecekondu* dwellers who were provided with title deeds secured their accommodation. In addition, during election campaigns, some *gecekondu* districts were provided with water and sewerage facilities even before they had a title deed or a legal status.

The *gecekondu* settlers cannot be considered as passive objects in their relations with politicians and local governors and in the transformation of *gecekondu* areas. When they lived in their villages, they engaged with the state through the village elders or *muhtar*[2] or larger landowners, on whom they were commonly economically dependent and they used to vote according to the instructions of local leaders. However, once in the city, their passive role was transformed and they realised their electoral power (Karpat 1976:198–200, Özler 2000:42). The larger the number of *gecekondu* dwellers in a district, the greater was their power in their negotiations with politicians and local governors. The newcomers tried to find new opportunities through negotiations with local as well as central state institutions and a reciprocal relationship between these institutions and *gecekondu* dwellers, 'the mythical *devlet baba* [father state] authoritarian semi-deity' transformed 'into a living government – into a human organisation that could be manipulated to do or undo certain acts, especially with regard to the *gecekondu*' (Karpat 1976:198) for *gecekondu* dwellers.

During the 1960s and 1970s, people in *gecekondu* areas established *hemşehri dernekleri* (hometown organisations), which comprised people from the same village or town. So, in a *gecekondu* area, it was (and still is) quite usual to see associations like 'The Association of People of Yozgat'. *Hemşehri dernekleri* were instrumental in communicating with local governors and politicians. Additionally, through these organisations, migrants not only made contact with other migrants from the same region but also maintained close relations with their friends from the same village (Kurtoğlu 2005, Fliche 2005, Hersant and Toumarkine 2005). *Hemşehri dernekleri* were used when entering into communication with local and central authorities and also stood for the institutional aspect of *hemşehrilik* (a social link between migrants from the same place of origin) networks for migrants, which were based on helping each other to find a job, finding a contact in a hospital, school or any other state institution (Kurtoğlu 2005, Erder 1999:165–6). Coffee houses in *gecekondu* districts were another important public venue in which male migrants came together and built social networks which could provide solidarity to cope with local people's problems when the family and kinship support network was insufficient.

Gecekondu dwellers contacted politicians and local government officials in order to make their needs and demands known. Municipal governors and *muhtars*, who were the elected headmen/headwomen governing the smallest administrative unit, played key roles in the provision of infrastructure and the distribution of social necessities to the *gecekondu* settlements. Municipalities were responsible for the construction and repair of streets and the installation and operation of water, electricity, gas and light rail services. *Muhtars* were also intermediaries in the relationship between *gecekondu* dwellers and municipal governors as well as other state institutions and politicians.

Most *gecekondu* dwellers in the first wave returned to their homes during the holidays to harvest and work on their land or to help their extended families. In contrast to perceiving their existence in cities as a temporary one, most of them did not return to their home villages since their children had settled in the cities and they also had got used to the lifestyle in the outskirts of large cities. Maintaining their relationship with their homes should not be understood as meaning that they did not get used living in cities or that they wanted to turn back. Rather, they successfully built up a new life and new social environment in the cities. Kurtoğlu (2005) affirmed this claim by giving the examples of *hemşehri dernekleri* and *hemşehrilik* and argued that these associations and these relationships between migrants were proof of their visibility and their persistence in continuing their lives in the cities.

Women of the First Migrant Wave

Married women among the first-wave migrants usually came to the city after their husbands had found a job or a place to build a *gecekondu*. Despite the fact that rural-to-urban or international migration of single women is not unusual in many parts of the world, such as Iran (see Velayati 2011), Mexico (see Kanaiaupuni 2000) or the Philippines (see Parrenas 2001), it was not common in Turkey. Marriage between relatives or *hemşehri*s was a strong tradition (Özgür and Aydın 2012) so many single male migrants got married to women in their home villages. Therefore single women in the same category came to the city through their marriage, to a man from the same village as them, who was already there. Some migrant women who came to the city via marriage told me that their husbands had married them because they needed a woman to do the housework, take care of elders and sick members of the household and satisfy the needs of the newly built *gecekondu*. So, for previously single women, it was marital migration.

It was not considered proper for women, especially migrant women, to be visible publicly, so they could not be as active as men in *hemşehri dernekleri*. Furthermore, coffee houses were exclusive to men and there were no available special public areas in which women could gather and engage in social life. In order to compensate for this, women mostly designated the doorstep of the house as the public space in which they could gather with their neighbours and relatives. As Mahmud and Duyar-Kienast (2001:272) suggest, 'the intensive use of public spaces enables people to interact and to help each other'. In due course, first-wave migrant women started to meet and build friendships with the other migrant women in their *gecekondu* district. The doorsteps of the *gecekondus* were the equivalents of coffee houses for *gecekondu* women. In these areas, they could both do some housework, such as cleaning dishes and clothes, hanging up washing and baking seasonal bread and help each other and socialise with their neighbours at the same time. It can be claimed that this doorstep part of their houses was the first step for them to become visible in the public sphere. The longer they stayed in the cities, the more familiar they became with the public sphere through taking their children to school, shopping at local shops etc.

First-wave migrant women rarely worked in paid employment. When the family thought that the family income was enough for their well-being, working for female members of the family could seem to them to be unnecessary and improper. Their husbands and fathers might not allow them to work, since they were new in the city and male members of the family were anxious about their safety outside the house (Hemmasi and Prorok 2002:401). It could be suggested that male members of the family feared that they would lose their culture, that their daughters and wives would look like the urban women and they would lose control and power over them. As women are mostly constructed as the indicators of the borders of cultures (Yuval-Davis 2003: Chapter 3), male control over the migrant women implied keeping their culture under control and unchanged. Moreover, since it was traditionally men who were responsible for making money for the household as the main part of their gender role, the working of women outside might reduce the men's reputation in their neighbourhood since they might be perceived as being unable to fulfil their breadwinner role.

Although first-wave migrant women did not earn money directly, their contribution to the family budget cannot be ignored. Migrant women are mostly considered as dependants, both in economics and migration studies (Velayati 2011:18). However, women who moved to the city just after their husbands had found a plot to construct a *gecekondu* worked on their construction no less than male members of the family did. It was women's primary responsibility to make their scrappy houses into liveable places and to transform these hovels into 'homes'. Due to the lack of infrastructure and services, they organised their courtyards to clean the dishes and clothes and built primitive ovens or heaters in the garden for baking bread. Additionally, it was also their responsibility to find water sources and to carry the water for their daily needs to the house. These water sources might be the nearest mosque or water fountain. Thanks to their skills, they made jars, tomato pastes and breads and sewed for the family. As a result, less of the main family income was spent on food, clothes and construction. At this point, it should be noted that social networking among the migrant women played a crucial role in their subsistence production. Their close relations with their neighbours provided them with a supply of labour for demanding tasks such as making tomato paste, jam and seasonal bread (Eroğlu 2010:48).

Structural Adjustment Policies and Changes in *Gecekondu* Areas after 1980

In the late 1970s, Turkey's economy, like those of many other countries, was dramatically affected by the large imbalance of payments on its current account, the oil crisis of the 1970s, instability and a prolonged exchange rate crisis (Stewart 1992:14–5, Aydın 2010:150–7, Altuğ et al. 2008:400, Yalman 2009:227–37). Capital accumulation problems for capital owners were exacerbated. A number of developing countries applied for funds to the IMF and World Bank. Funds were made available after a series of agreements in which the countries agreed to apply an economic programme determined by the funding institution. Turkey also applied for funds and prepared a new package, known as the '24 January Decisions', which took the perspective of the IMF's stability policy and the World Bank's Structural Adjustment Policy (SAP) (Boratav 2004:147–9) during the early days of 1980. In the intention letter submitted to the IMF and in the letter of commitment presented to the World Bank, it was stated that an economic system based on free-market forces would be formed, the state would withdraw from various sectors and the sectors of industry, agriculture and oil would be opened up to foreign investors. In brief, this package of decisions aimed to shrink the state's share of the market and minimise its role in the regulation of the market and the economy.

Many Third World countries moved towards a contraction of public expenditure and a series of market-oriented development policies as a result of the implementation of SAPs (Afshar and Dennis 1992:3) and Turkey was no exception. The 24 January Decisions, which 'consisted almost entirely of macro policy instruments; and had not been concerned with the distributional effects on different groups within the country' (Stewart 1992:18), were a start and created a base for the SAPs in Turkey. Due to social unrest and the relatively powerful left-wing opposition to the implementation of neoliberal policies before 1980, these decisions could only be implemented after a coup d'état in 1980 which harshly subdued opposing voices. At this time, 650,000 people were arrested, 230,000 were tried, 50 were executed and 171 were killed, besides the thousands tortured. Moreover, the activities of 23,700 civil society associations were suspended and 927 publications banned (Hürriyet Dailynews 2008, Human Rights Watch 2012). In a series of public speeches, Kenan Evren, chief of the general staff and president after the coup d'état, listed the problems in the Turkish economy and accused the trade union movement and its struggle to increase the real wages of workers of exacerbating these problems. His speeches can be understood as attempts to justify both the coup d'état itself and the structural adjustment policies that were applied directly after this military invention. In this vein, the military rulers banned a large section of the trade unions.

After the suppression of organised left-wing opposition, the SAPs which marked the years after 1980 were adopted and put into action. These SAPs prepared Turkey to play its role as a developing country in the global marketplace and fulfil its prescribed task in the global division of labour. This new role for Turkey was about being engaged in labour-intensive production for global markets. As Elson (1991:169) has pointed out, 'the encouragement of the production of labour-intensive manufacture for export is an important component of the switch from nontradables in many countries'.

Turkey's economic policy shifted from a developmentalist, economically protectionist, closed economy with an import substitution based programme to an economic policy that aimed at integration with the global economy. Rather than focusing on production for the internal market, an export-oriented economic policy was adopted. So, after 1980, the aim was to narrow down domestic demand through a drop in real wages, while exports were promoted by incentives provided by the state. In the domestic sphere, these programmes notably brought about privatisation, devaluation, an expansion of the informal economy, deregulation, a shrinking of public expenses (Davis 2007:Chapter 7, Özar and Ercan 2004:193–8, Şenses and Taymaz 2003:2–10, Aydın 2005:43–8) and 'improving incentives for the production of goods which are internationally tradable and to switch resources away from production of goods which are not internationally tradable' (Elson 1991:164). In terms of foreign affairs, the reduction of trade barriers was the most important issue. In brief, the coup d'état of 1980 provided a base for the implementation of SAPs and the transformation of Turkey's economic policy. The implementation of the 24 January Decisions, in the framework of SAPs, effectively dismantled 'the constitutional framework and the redistributive institutions of the previous period' (Keyder 1987:228) and demonstrated that the existing development strategy had been abandoned.

Due to the attempts at integration with the global market, which highlighted cost competition, the capital owners needed a flexible and fragmented labour force and reduced labour costs. When the laws enacted over the last 20 years are considered, it is obvious that flexibility for employees has been greatly expanded whereas the laws that used to protect workers have been abandoned. The 1982 Constitution contained a number of restrictions on labour strikes and union activity. According to Article 52, unions may not join in political activities; Article 54 suggests that strikes and lockouts may be forbidden or postponed by law. Additionally, given the relative weakness of the trade unions, which had a downward effect on salaries, market flexibility is maximised. According to research by Petrol-İş, if the real wages of 1979 are taken as 100, they dropped to 79.89 in 1980. While increasing throughout the period 1982–84, they dropped to 79.3 in 1985 (Petrol-İş 1995:339). The share of wage incomes was 32 per cent of GDP in the 1970s whereas it decreased to 26.9 per cent in 1980 and 20.7 per cent in 1987 (DİE 1999:54–5).The scope of the informal sector was enlarged as a result of new profit-generating strategies which were supported by SAPs in the 1980s and the 1990s. According to estimations by Çetintaş and Vergil, the informal market increased its share of the economy from 18.01 per cent in 1975 to 23.07 per cent in 1988. It continued to increase and reached 31.29 per cent in 1995 (2003:28). As the object was to increase the flexibility and fragmentation of the labour market, the number of establishments based on employing more temporary, part-time and contracting employees and preferring to work with subcontractors grew (Özar and Ercan 2004:195). During the 1980s, the state also began to provide fewer subsidies and loans for small agricultural concerns as well as investing less in agricultural production than it had done previously (Boratav 2004:165). For example, the number of subsidised agricultural products decreased to ten in 1987 from 22 in 1980 (Turkish Development Bank 2012:13). So, for the rural population, the returns from agricultural production were diminished.

Second-Wave Migration

A sharp decrease in agricultural subsidies under the SAPs after 1980 caused more small and middle-scale agricultural rural producers to decide not to continue with agricultural production. It has been suggested by many scholars (Tekeli 2008, Şenses and Taymaz 2003, Ataay 2001:82–6, Kendir 2003) that these state interventions in agriculture were the prominent push factor for mass migration after the 1980s. In addition, because the new mode of production created by SAPs increased the need for cheap and unskilled labour in urban areas, this constituted the main pull factor for the second wave of mass migration, which started during the 1980s.

Expansion of telecommunication services and media instruments were viewed as a vital foundation to support a vibrant national economy integrated with global markets by Özal's austerity programme in the

1980s (Wolcott and Çağıltay 2001:135). This resulted in easier access of mass population to the telecommunication facilities. The number of telephone subscribers grew by 80 per cent and the number of villages having telephone service grew by 162 per cent and the total capacity of telephone exchanges increased by 83 per cent in 1982–86 (Wolcott and Çağıltay 2001:135). Thanks to the development of communication technologies during the 1980s, rural people could communicate with their friends and relatives by telephone more easily and this kept their relations closer. Their connections with their relatives, friends or family members who had already settled in urban areas were their primary source of information about their opportunities in the city. Therefore, compared to the first-comers, the migrants in the second wave knew more about city life, job opportunities and facilities in Ankara before their migration. Moreover, compared to the 1950s and 1960s, transportation facilities were much more advanced in the 1980s and afterwards, so it was easier for the second wave of migrants to move to Ankara. Since the accessibility of urban centres can be important as one of the factors in migration (Gedik 1997:171, Greenwood 1997:666–8, Lucas 1997:782), the advancement of communication and transportation infrastructures and facilities might have accelerated the migration to urban centres.

The introduction of general liberalisation policies during the 1980s also affected *gecekondu* appropriation and the *gecekondu* market and this resulted in less state control over *gecekondu* settlements. During the general election campaign in 1983, Turgut Özal, head of the Anavatan Party, promised to grant land title deeds and won the elections (Karpat 2004) by taking a significant proportion of the votes in *gecekondu* areas. A series of Gecekondu Amnesties were passed in 1983, 1984 and 1986, which legalised the *gecekondus* built before 1986. Like the previous title deed provisions, these were also a fait accompli. The main aim of the amnesties of the 1980s was to open up public land for the land market. The amnesties permitted construction in *gecekondu* areas. In the most advantageously located *gecekondu* areas, large construction firms were the main actors and transformed these areas into 'high-rise prestigious residential neighbourhoods' (Dündar 2001:392). In *gecekondu* areas that were not close to the city centres but were linked to them by main roads and were close to the prestigious residential areas, the main actors were small-scale developers. People who lived in nonadvantageously located *gecekondu* areas transformed their *gecekondu* houses into four-storey family apartments on their own, mostly using their family savings (Dündar 2001:393). So, these laws caused increasing population density and the transformation of *gecekondu* areas into low-standard residential areas with limited social services and green areas (Dündar 2001:393, Sat 2007:31). Legalisation of *gecekondus* could also be considered as compensation for unequal income distribution or, as Başlevent and Dayıoğlu say (2005:40), 'an informal redistribution process [...] where the state failed to provide social assistance to the poorer sections of society'. Two aspects of these amnesties throughout the 1980s are most commonly highlighted by scholars: the first is about the general orientation of the political system during the 1980s that left everything to market forces and individuals' limited choices (Duyar-Kienast 2005:46–50). The second, on the other hand, is about the state's attempt to compensate lower class people for the losses generated by the structural adjustment policies (Başlevent and Dayıoğlu 2005:40–2). Besides, this was why the early migrants whose *gecekondus* were legalised before 1985 could remain appeased during economic liberalisation, exacerbating working conditions and decreasing level of real incomes (Boratav 2004:153). From the state's perspective, it was also an instrument to prevent social unrest from dominating in squatter areas and integrating structurally urban periphery to the new economic system (Buğra 1998:309–10, Aslan 2009:960). However, since the period after 1980 was infamous for the commercialisation of *gecekondus*, they lost their legitimacy in public opinion and the *gecekondu* people were increasingly considered as undeserving beneficiaries of unfair privilege and invaders of public property by the urbanities (Pınarcıoğlu and Işık 2008:1356, Duyar-Kienast 2005:46–51, Keyder 2005:130).

If the second-wave migrants had close relatives or family members in the city, these allowed the second-comers to built *gecekondus* on the same plot as theirs. However building their own *gecekondu* on in-city neighbourhoods was no longer an option because there was no available land in existing *gecekondu* areas. At this point, they either bought or rented *gecekondus* that had already been built by the first-comers or searched for new districts at the outskirts of cities where they could find empty plots to occupy. Although some late comer migrants could find empty plots at the outskirts of the city, they could not find a place on in-city neighbourhoods and more importantly could not legalise their *gecekondus* built after 1985 since the latest gecekondu amnesty covered the *gecekondu* houses built before 1986. Following Harvey's suggestion that social groups who enter to urban land market late are less advantageous compared to early comers (2009:168), it could be suggested that people who built *gecekondu* houses after 1985 had less choices compared to the early comers. Therefore the early migrants gained higher positions in terms of ownership of *gecekondu* and the location of their *gecekondu*.

It can be said that *gecekondu* areas seemed to be more heterogeneous after 1980. While the liberalisation of markets through structural adjustment policies decreased the living standards of second-wave migrants, the early comers could enjoy limited places for upward mobility through their established networks which they could depend on in finding a job, developing their business and making deals on their *gecekondus* and through success in mobilising political contacts. In this sense, *gecekondu* dwellers became differentiated not only in terms of ownership of *gecekondus* but also in terms of their income levels and integration to the city life both economically and spatially. The number of migrant employees in the informal sector, which was mostly characterised by short-term, insecure and flexible employment relationships and little or no prospect of internal promotion, increased sharply, especially after the 1980s. Newcomers to the industrialised cities comprised a reserve labour force and this situation led the workers in the primary sector to become anxious about keeping their jobs and they began to regard the workers in the secondary sector as their rivals (İçduygu et al. 1998:210–3). In addition, even the unions considered the workers in the secondary sector to be rivals and were reluctant to reach out and organise them (Erendil 2003 cited in Bergan 2009:224). However, these secondary jobs were the only chance for the newcomers and they could not be included in the system at all unless these kinds of jobs were provided (Koray 1993:18). The informal economy was not the rescuer but, if there had not been any opportunities provided by the informal economy, people in *gecekondus* would have felt totally hopeless (Davis 2007:198). Despite the harsh working and living conditions during the 1980s, it can be suggested that both first- and second-wave migrants were content with their new status. On that point, Tekeli has argued that migrants did not feel a great deal of relative deprivation (2008:127) because they compared their new status with their previous one, which provided them with less access to public services and fewer opportunities for social mobility.

As well as solving accommodation problems, in their job seeking process their friends and relatives who already had networks helped them. It can be suggested that, compared to their town counterparts, *gecekondu* dwellers were much more helpful to each other. For Korte and Ayvalıoğlu, *gecekondu* dwellers' 'low income status and strong identification with a territorial area may also encourage local patterns of mutual aid' (1981:137). Sometimes their jobs were even ready before they came to Ankara because their relatives already had networks in the job markets or because people from their village controlled a sector as in many other cities (Erder 1996:268). This mutual relationship was mainly based on mutual trust, as was the case in helping each other in finding accommodation or finding a contact in schools, hospitals and other formal institutions (Kurtoğlu 2005). Although it seems as though it was a kind of 'favour' for the second-comers, their relationship was a reciprocal one. The first-comers found jobs for the second-comers or employed them in their businesses, however, the second-comers needed to show their loyalty to the first-comers. For example, if someone was employed in an enterprise by a person from the same village, it was not proper for him/her to ask for job security, to reject working for longer hours than others etc. Borrowing the term 'poverty in turn' (*nöbetleşe yoksulluk*) from Işık and Pınarcıoğlu (2002), it could be suggested that the migrants of pre-1985 era handed over the unprivileged status to the later comers. So, the migrants of the pre-1985 period were not the dispossessed anymore, they gained higher positions in the hierarchy due to the better locations and income generating opportunities (Keyder 2005:126). Their role was replaced by the later migrants in Turkish cities since they were not the only people who were constructing for their own use, but they were also selling the *gecekondus* and employers for the late comers (see Erder 1996, Işık and Pınarcıoğlu 2002: Chapter 2, Dubetsky 1976).

Women among the Second-Wave Migrants

With the economic liberalism which brought about high rates of unemployment, flexible and insecure working conditions and low incomes, accompanied by the shrinking of public expenditure, migrant households had to create their own survival strategy in order to deal with these conditions. Within this framework, it was nearly impossible for marginal groups to survive on one person's income. In many *gecekondu* homes, the male head of the household tried to find a second job. While Chant (1994) examined the situation of slum dwellers in Mexico City after structural adjustment policies she called the families' survival strategy as 'self exploitation of families' (p. 206). They cut down on expenditure and consumption and alongside the male's labour, child and especially female paid employment grew to be valuable for families in terms of survival strategies (Chant 1994:206, Latapi and Rocha 1995:66–9). This was the case in Turkey where women in large numbers in squatter areas had to work in paid employment due to the economic necessity of the household, which was not usually the case before the 1980s.

While the enlargement of the informal market due to the neoliberal economy increased women's participation in employment, they were mostly concentrated in low-status jobs (Ecevit 2007:15, Chant 1994:210). Due to market conditions, lack of education, required skill and language, their traditional housewife role, the lack of public childcare facilities, discrimination against women in the labour market and the patriarchal social formation, women mostly preferred to work in industrial home-based jobs such as piece-work. According to TUIK (Turkish Statistical Institute), in 1989 in urban areas the number of women in home-based employment was 66,000 which had increased to 100,000 by 1995 (Ecevit 1998:61).

When the state withdrew from social spending after the coup d'état of 1980, women's domestic labour, home-based production of fundamental necessities[3] and their caring responsibilities for children, the elderly and sick members within the family became more important. Women needed to increase their input to caring facilities (Elson 1991:177). Since the adjustment worsened the available health and educational facilities and the government started to devote lower budgets to these services, the time that women spent on these activities increased (Stewart 1992:34, Elson 1991:176). When women in *gecekondu* households started to work outside, other female members of the household as mothers, sisters and especially the elder daughters needed to spend more time on household chores.

The relationship between the *gecekondu* women's income-generating activities and the empowerment of these women is very problematic. As Erman (1997b) claims, these women who work in the informal labour market are aware of the fact that their economic contribution to the family is indispensable. According to Kümbetoğlu, in general *gecekondu* women's earnings comprise around one third of the total income of the family (1996:233). On the other hand, this income-generation does not provide them with more control over the family budget or more say in the decisions of the household.

Conclusion

The migrants have been among the most important components of Turkey's industrialisation and urbanisation story since the early 1960s. They were active agents whose survival strategies have marked the state's approach at different times and have influenced policies about *gecekondu* areas. Their movements and strategies also brought about changes, especially in the composition of the labour market, the distribution of land resources and the social formation of rural and urban areas. On the other hand, their movements were dramatically affected by the systematic economic changes and state policies.

Based on the historical context and background given in this chapter, the following chapters will discuss the formation of *gecekondu* neighbourhoods and communities, the change in the self-perception of *gecekondu* dwellers and in their survival strategies in the face of state policies and the dynamics of dissolving of community ties through the case of Ege district.

CHAPTER 3

BUILDING A *GECEKONDU* NEIGHBOURHOOD, COMMUNITY AND IDENTITY

When the rural migrants arrived in the cities, in the absence of affordable accommodation and social housing programmes they had to solve their own problems of accommodation. They occupied land that mostly belonged to the state on the outskirts of the cities. The first settlers of the *gecekondu* neighbourhoods had to solve the problems generated by the lack of infrastructure and struggle to get amenities. In this sense, the burdens of the market and the state were taken by the *gecekondu* people. Their efforts to find a roof overhead and to ameliorate their living conditions were the first step towards building *gecekondu* communities. This chapter will focus on the building of a community in Ege through the narratives of the Ege people themselves.

Village Life before the Migration and Deciding to Migrate

Until they migrated to Ankara, the migrants had lived in the rural hinterland where they grew up. As Lloyd (1979:101) wrote, 'the village community is by definition small and relatively isolated and self contained. Its members are bound together by multiple cross-cutting relationships,' and for them there was no life outside the village until their migration. In the villages, everybody used to know each other intimately and they always had contact with the same people. The population of Central Anatolian villages was homogeneous in terms of faith. The villages were either Alevi or Sunni. Therefore, the rural migrants did not have much experience of socialising with people of different faiths.

Rural people usually married people from the same village or from neighbouring villages. Endogamy was usual and marriage between patrilateral parallel cousins was the most common type of endogamy. These marriages strengthened the relations between families, ensuring that the community remained as close as possible and these relations were the social capital of the rural migrants, who used them to migrate to the city and get help in city centres. Delaney (1991:109) suggests that endogamy was an expression of mistrust of the outside world and a strong denial of separation among the community, as villagers take and give brides. Due to the patriarchal form of the family, new couples used to live together with the husbands' family and they worked together on the plot that belonged to the family of the husband. Living with their extended family was not easy for new couples. Young couples felt greatly oppressed by the mothers and fathers in the extended family. The father in the extended family was the head of the household and controlled the family budget. Married sons did not have as much control over the budget as their fathers; therefore they had to ask everything of their fathers and bow to their fathers. The mother of the extended family was usually in charge of arranging the division of labour among the female members of the family. This control over young couples affected young women more. Some of the female rural migrants told me that they wanted to leave the village just to escape from the extended family's control over them.

In the villages, life was based on collectivism in which people shared their work, problems and happiness with the rural community. Given the fact that the government made few investments to help them (Szyliowicz 1962:437), villagers usually solved their problems on their own. When their village needed something they resolved the problem through *imece* and *salma* practices. In *imece*, people do not contribute money, but they give their labour. *Salma* means collecting money from the villagers according to their income.

Additionally, rural life was based on less consumption. They were skilled enough to solve their problems without depending on money. A farming family could produce its own food and feed the family and could sell the small surplus for exchange and obligatory dues (Lloyd

1979:95). If they had animals such as cows, sheep or hens they could have dairy products and eggs. Since the climate of Central Anatolia is suitable for the production of wheat, they could produce flour and women baked their own bread and made *erişte* (a traditional type of noodle). If a village was rich enough, they could grow vegetables and fruit. So, women could make jams and tomato paste, which is the basic ingredient of many Turkish dishes. It can be suggested that the village community was self-sufficient.

The rural migrants used to work on agricultural production in their villages. The people of Ege had plots which belonged to their extended family. Although daughters were legal inheritors of their families' property equally with their brothers, they were not socially expected to claim a right to their families' land in rural areas. It was the sons who continued to work on the plot after their father's death. Brothers who shared their parents' inheritance with their sisters were appreciated and considered to have a good personality.

The interviewees told me that their plots were not sufficient for the whole family. Especially after the sons got married and had children, they started to worry about the future of their family. The plot was the same, but the number of male members in the family increased, so they needed to find some other solution for the family to survive. Nazım, who came to Ankara in 1972 when he was a child, explained their decision as follows:

> Why did we come? Well, we could not find a plot on which we could survive in Çorum. We lived in the village [of Çorum]. We were seven siblings [...] Four sisters and three brothers [...] Never mind the sisters, I mean, they would get married and leave the family. But, as a man, if you stayed in the village, there was no plot that could feed you. So, we said that there were more opportunities in large cities.

Considering the poor state of communication and transportation in villages, the low income levels of peasants and their hard work, it was not usual for them to visit other places. They used to go to the city centres or provincial districts at harvest time to sell their produce and to buy things and also when they needed to contact a government institution, e.g. when they needed to go to court, to hospital etc. It was only the men who visited the city centres. Some of the men became familiar with the cities (or other places apart from their villages) during their military service, seasonal work or visits to their *hemşehris* and relatives who lived in cities. Knowledge about Ankara was important in the migration decision process. At this point, based on the profile of my interviewees, I can suggest that, besides the villagers' concern about their future economic opportunities, their contacts with Ankara played a major role in the decision process about migration. For example, Sefer, who came to Ankara in the 1960s and moved to Ege in 1992, told me that he had nephews in Ankara before he migrated. He visited them regularly and this is why he was encouraged to move to this city. He knew about the opportunities and lifestyle in Ankara and had relatives who could help him.

Rural migrants did not sell their plots in their villages since they regarded them as security. Most of them told me that, if they sold their plots, the money would be shared among the brothers and the shares would not be much. So, they thought that it would not matter for them. Some *gecekondu* dwellers returned to their villages because they felt they could not survive in Ankara anymore and then came back to the city after spending some years in their villages. If all the members of the extended family had migrated to the city, they left their plots to relatives or neighbours in their villages. They worked on the plot and paid some of the income to the owner. In most cases, an adult son built a house in his family's home village after he had improved his living conditions and used it as a summer house.

The migrant who 'carries his mattress bundled upon his back along with his bag of food' (Şenyapılı 1982:238) was a typical figure of rural-to-urban migrants. At this point, when the first generation of migrants came to the cities, especially in the early years of migration, nearly all of them had nothing. Most of their migration stories were full of pain. For instance, Gül and Mahmut came to the city at the end of the 1960s with her husband. Gül told me that they did not have enough money even to buy a bus ticket. They found a person in their village whose job was transporting goods from Sivas's villages to Ankara and they got on the back of the van. There was nothing covering it although it was very cold. At the time of their migration, they had a seven-month-old baby. Gül started to cry when she told me that the baby contracted pneumonia during the migration and died a week after their journey to Ankara.

For Gül, it was not the pneumonitis, but their poverty which killed the baby. Others' stories of migration were similar. Most of my interviewees told me things like: 'we came to Ankara with only a spoon' or: 'when we came, we did not even have a blanket'.

First Settlers' Faith and Ethnicity

The majority of the population of Ege came from the villages of Sivas, Çorum and Yozgat. There are some first settlers who came from the rural areas of Gümüşhane, Kırşehir, Kırıkkale and Çankırı. There are many Alevis both in the city centre and in the villages of Çorum and Sivas. There are not so many Alevi people in the city centre of Yozgat, but some of Yozgat's villages are Alevi. So, the majority of first settlers in Ege were Alevi people. Among my interviewees, there were some Alevi-Kurdish people[1] who came from the villages of Sivas, Yozgat and Çorum.

Alevism vs. Sunnism is the main sectarian divide in Turkey. The majority of people in Turkey are Sunni Muslim and in the context of Turkey, Sunnism historically refers to the orthodox version of Islam. In a very general sense, Alevism is a branch of Shi'a and, in Turkey's sociohistorical context, it refers to heterodoxy in Islam and is known as a more liberal branch of Islam in Turkey. Alevis in Turkey believe in God, the Prophet Muhammad and Ali, the prophet's cousin. They place emphasis on Ali, which is not usually the case for Sunnis in Turkey. They do not build mosques and they do not follow *imam*, the Sunni religious leaders. Rather, their ceremonial gathering meeting (*cem*) is led by a *dede*, 'a member of a hereditary priestly caste' (Şahin 2005:466) and conducted in an assembly house (*cemevi*). So they do not go to mosque. *Namaz* (prayer) and *oruç* (fasting) in Ramadan, *zekat* (Islamic charity for the poor) and *hac* (pilgrimage to Mecca), which Sunnis are supposed to practice, are not commonly observed among Alevis. Despite this general framework of Alevi belief, Alevis in Turkey are allowed to combine this with Sunni beliefs. In this sense, many Alevi people in Turkey might fast during Ramadan, pray five times a day (*namaz*) and sacrifice animals during Eid. Because women and men worship together, there have been widespread rumours among Sunnis that communal sex is a part of Alevis' religious rituals (Şahin 2005:466). Alevis are labelled as *Kızılbaş* (red heads) by Sunnis and this Turkish word is a reference to the red bandannas of the followers of Caliph Ali. In most cases, it has a negative connotation. Bruinessen states that Alevi 'is a blanket term for a large number of heterodox communities whose beliefs and ritual practices differ significantly' (1996:7).

The estimated numbers of the Alevi population in Turkey in different resources ranges from 10 to 25 per cent (Erman and Göker 2000:99, Rittersberger-Tılıç 1998:99–100), Vorhoff 1998). The official statistics do not provide accurate information about the number of Alevis in Turkey because the official census does not ask for the ethnic backgrounds of the population. On the identity cards, there is a section for religion but if a person does not come from the Greek, Armenian or Jewish minorities, the only option for this section is 'Islam'. There is no separate category for Alevi people. Due to the long-term assimilative politics of the state since Ottoman times, Alevi people might tend to hide their identities (Erman and Göker 2000, Çelik 2003). For example, my mother and I met Ayşe, who came from a village of Çorum in 1970, in the park just opposite our *gecekondu* house. We invited her for a coffee to our home. She started to talk about her marriage. She did not say that she was Alevi, what she said was that her husband was Alevi. I asked whether their parents opposed their marriage because of the difference in faith and she said they did not. After ten minutes, she asked whether we prayed five times a day. It was obviously a question designed to discover whether we were Sunni or not. My mother replied no. We did not say anything about our faith but not praying five times a day does not mean anything about our faith since not all Sunni people pray five times a day. I realised that she felt relieved since she understood that we were either Sunni who were not very religious or Alevi. So, she said: 'I do not want to deny my background, I am an Alevi.'

Alevis have been the target of historical and recent oppression because of their heterodox beliefs and practices (Bozarslan 2007:3) since the time of the Ottoman Empire. Alevis' identity was shaped through oppression by the Sunni Islamic feature of the Ottoman State and their resistance against this. The Ottoman Empire was replaced by the Turkish Republic in 1923. This new state, founded by Mustafa Kemal Atatürk, was based on ethnic nationalism and was constitutionally secular. Since the Sunni feature of the state was abandoned by Atatürk, Alevis became emotionally attached to the new Turkish Republic, Atatürk and the CHP (the Republican People's Party), which was founded by Atatürk. The new modern republic strived to differentiate itself from the Ottoman Empire and a new Turkish identity, cleansed of its Sunni Islamic features, was the aim. In this sense, Alevi people were considered to be the original Turks who had been less affected by Sunni Islam and they were appreciated by the CHP (Ertan 2012). Moreover, the new Turkish state declared Alevis as Turks and 'regarded them as ardent supporters of secularism' (Çelik 2003:143). So, as a result of the elimination of all the major institutional obstacles to the Alevis' equality with the Sunni majority, such as the dissolving of the shari'a courts, the abolition of the sultanate and the caliphate, a new alliance appeared between Alevis and the modern Turkish Republic (Kehl-Bodrogi 2007:57). In this sense, it is not unusual to see a portrait of Mustafa Kemal Atatürk next to a portrait of Ali on the interior walls of Alevi houses, in *cemevis* or in political meetings of Alevi people.

Laicism failed to end the widespread Sunni prejudices against the Alevis (Bruinessen 1996:8). With the introduction of multiparty democracy in 1946, right-wing political parties that were inspired by Islamist perspectives started to be dominant. Kemalism could not sustain its laicism. There have been violent assaults by radical Islamist and fascist movements, some of which were implicitly supported by the right-wing parties and the government, against the Alevi population.[2] Considering right-wing parties' support for attacks on Alevis and their emphasis on Sunni creed on one hand and on the other hand the laicism discourse of Kemalism and its appreciation of Alevism, the majority of Alevi people support the CHP. Dubetsky's research on a *gecekondu* neighbourhood in İstanbul suggests that, while Alevi-Kurdish residences united in support of the CHP, the majority of Sunni Turks supported the right-wing Justice Party (1977:369).

Hemşehris as a First Step

Hemşehri was not a social category in the migrants' home villages since all the people were *hemşehri* to one another before coming to the city. However, *hemşehris* became very important for the migrants in the city centres in terms of feeling secure. The *hemşehri* relationship does not stand only for having the same interests; it is shaped by having the same emotions (Kurtoğlu 2005). *Hemşehris* were the people who came from a similar cultural background to the cities, where their needs were similar. Due to chain migration, the first settlers knew some of the other first settlers in Ege since they were relatives or *hemşehri*. The clustering of similar people in terms of origin gave a sense of familiarity and, as Halperin (1998:30) states, it 'permeates the community, especially if you know it well'. As Dubetsky (1976:444) suggests, people have more access to information about their *hemşehris*, so they 'can more easily obtain a reference about them or put pressure on them to behave properly via mutual acquaintance or, as is often the case [. . .] he just feels he knows their characters better owing to geographical proximity.' Because endogamy was the predominant form of marriage in villages, it was likely that *hemşehris* would have a kinship tie as well as the *hemşehri* bond. In this sense, it was usually hard to differentiate *hemşehri* relations from kinship relations. In the very beginning of their life in the city, *gecekondu* dwellers did not define themselves primarily through their position in labour relations. Their reference point for identity was their place of origin (*hemşehri* relations). As White, who researches on rural immigrant communities, says, these communities are oriented more by their place of origin than by urban geography (2004:43).

Willmott and Young (1976) argued that family and kinship networks could provide wider contacts rather than being limiting, enclosed and exclusive. These networks could be useful, especially in accessing economic and employment opportunities. Most of the first settlers of Ege found plots in Ege with the help of their relatives and *hemşehris* who lived in Ankara. Some villagers sent their sons to cities where they had relatives to provide the son with the chance of acquiring skills, finding a job or studying. Ege people helped their relatives and *hemşehris* to find a job. Often, jobs for later migrants from rural areas were ready before they came to Ege. As Tilly and Brown suggested, 'relations of kinship provide functional alternatives to personal skill, knowledge and power in dealing with the host community'. (1967:144)

Hemşehri relations made a significant contribution to the development of a sense of community in Ege. While 'special interest groups are relatively both more common and more important in larger communities' (Fischer 1976:111), people in Ege, like other rural migrants in large cities, established *hemşehri* associations. In this sense, it can be suggested that, while the *hemşehri* relationship emerged out of the necessity for trust and mutual assistance among migrants, it did not develop on its own. In order to survive this relationship, migrants institutionalised it. Ege people told me that these associations not only allowed them to socialise with their *hemşehris*, to organise social events and to solve the problems of city life, but they also helped them in regulating their relations with their villages.

A Brief History of Ege District

In the initial decades of the migration, in-city districts were the place for *gecekondu* communities. In due course, the number of rural migrants and so the number of *gecekondu* dwellers, increased and it became harder to find a plot in old *gecekondu* areas. Some early rural migrants who had spent several years in other *gecekondu* areas of Ankara wanted their own *gecekondu* and searched for new areas on the outskirts of the city. This resulted in the city expanding. Ege was discovered by the dwellers of central *gecekondu* areas in the 1970s and it became an entrance point for the rural migrants who came directly from the villages of Sivas, Çorum, Çankırı, Yozgat, Kırıkkale and Kırşehir, which were the cities in Central Anatolia and to the east of Ankara in the 1980s and 1990s. Additionally, there were many first settlers from the villages of Gümüşhane, which was a city in eastern Black Sea Region.

Ege neighbourhood is a part of Mamak district, which is one of the seven metropolitan districts of Ankara. Each one has a district municipality which is linked to Ankara (Metropolitan) Municipality and has a district governor (*kaymakamlık*), who is appointed by the central government and the district governors are linked to the Governor (*vali*) of Ankara. Mamak is a typical *gecekondu* settlement and is populated by low-income early Sunni and Alevi migrant families who came from the villages of Central Anatolia (Alpar and Yener 1991 cited in Eroğlu 2011:56–7). Mamak has a population of 549,585 according to the 2010 census and is composed of 66 neighbourhoods, which are governed by a *muhtar* elected by the local people every five years.

Before the 1970s, Ege was a part of İmrahor village. The government gave the tenure of this area to the villagers of İmrahor and they used it as a pasture for feeding their animals. This district was formally constituted in 1973 according to the state records. Until 1989, Ege Mahallesi[3] also included its neighbouring *mahalles*, namely Cengizhan, Boğaziçi, Akdere, Durali Alıç, Akşemsettin, Fahrikorutürk and General Zeki Doğan, in 1989 these areas were formally separated. Although Ege Mahallesi is the name of a specific area, in Ankara people still consider it to be the sum of all these *mahalles*. For example, currently 'Ege Mahallesi' is written on the buses that go to all these *mahalles*.

The rubbish dump area (*çöplük*) of Ankara was in the northern part of Ege and Ankara Municipality started to cover it in 1979. This ended in 1985. Özuğurlu, who conducted research on poverty in the *çöplük* area, claimed that the first settlers in the *çöplük* area of Ege came as a group of people who were mostly from Gümüşhane and built *gecekondu* houses nearby since they thought that the *çöplük* could not remain there forever (2001:45). So the northern part of the *mahalle* was built on a former solid waste dump. Before 1979, Ege district was identified with *çöplük*. Behzat came to Ege in 1974 and was among the first settlers there. He told me that 'This neighbourhood was *çöplük* [. . .] When people asked where I was going, I said I was going to *çöplük*.' Ege people still call the northern part of Ege *çöplük*, although this part of the *mahalle* is now full of *gecekondus*.

Building *Gecekondu* Houses

When the rural migrants came to Ege, the *muhtar* of İmrahor Village, Mr Fazlı, started to sell plots to the newcomers. I was told by the first settlers of Ege that Mr Fazlı was encouraged by his official position and he claimed the right to sell land in Ege since it was the common land of Imrahor Village. He did not provide any written documents that proved the sale and ownership of the plots. So, it was not a formal deal of selling. Constructing a *gecekondu* on this land was not legal and my interviewees suggested that Mr Fazlı took advantage of the illegality of this situation and if anybody refused to pay him, he reported them to the gendarmerie. Since Imrahor Village was not a part of Ankara city centre in the 1970s and the pasture that would become Ege district was a desolate place, there were no regular checks and controls by the gendarmerie unless there were reports or complaints.

When first settlers were asked for money by Mr Fazlı, they could not understand that he was doing so illegally. First-comers told me that it took around two months for them to understand that Mr Fazlı was not authorized to sell the plots and they did not need to give money to him in order to construct *gecekondus* in Ege. After paying some part of the required money to Fazlı, they came together and decided not to pay him anymore. Since all the people refused to pay him, he could not do anything. If they had not behaved as a community and had contacted Mr Fazlı individually, they would have continued to pay him. This implies that, through collective action, the people were able to discard Mr Fazlı. Nazım, who was one of the first settlers in Ege, narrated this process in this way:

> Do not think that the Ege district was like it is now. There was nothing around. There was not even a small shop or a proper road around. It was like countryside. So, there was no gendarmerie, police station, municipality, Yes, we could complain about Mr Fazlı. But to whom? And how? Then a group of people in the district came together and talked about this. We informed people around [. . .] No, we did not do it through an organisation; there was no need for it. We were seeing one another every day in those days. People were persuaded not to pay him anymore. Of course he could not do anything afterwards.

Nazım explained to me that they organised the land of Ege district. He said that the male settlers came together and decided where the roads and plots for *gecekondus* should be. They also shared a plot for a school. The account of Ali, the current *muhtar* of Ege, supported Nazım's narrative and he told me that Cevat, a person among the first settlers, drew up a draft plan for Ege and they decided where the roads should be according to this draft.

During the early years of migration, buying a plot for a *gecekondu* was not based on a formal contract. My interviewees told me that the seller asked for a little money or something in exchange such as a vacuum cleaner, washing machine or a bin of *bulgur* (a traditional type of wheat) and the seller did not provide a title deed or any document that showed the sale. It seemed as if the later comers were given informal permission by the earlier occupier of the plot to use it and the buyer gave something in return. As I learnt from my interviewees, the early comers occupied a plot, invited their extended family members, and then sold some of the plots that they occupied to the late comers. Trust between the people mattered in reserving plots next to their own. Kinship was the main source of trust. In that sense, people usually reserved the plots around their *gecekondus* for their kin. Moreover, the first-comers tried to show (or rent and sell) spare plots to their friends, *hemşehris* and relatives, in order to ensure that there were no strangers in the neighbourhood. So, knowing a person meant trust and this gave a sense of security to the *gecekondu* dwellers. As Wolf (1966:9) suggests, 'the private realm of trust may thus be translated into cooperation in the public realm'.

Due to economic hardship, the first generation tried to build their *gecekondus* step by step with materials that they bought from *ardiye* (literally meaning storage) and collected from demolished buildings (Duyar-Kienast 2005: Chapter 5). At least a week before the construction of a *gecekondu*, the rural migrants started to accumulate the material to be used in building it. They needed all the materials at once since they had to build the *gecekondu* overnight. They usually did not have enough money to afford all the materials at once so they asked *ardiye* to divide the price of all materials into small instalments that they could pay monthly. Since people in *ardiye*s were used to this kind of deal, they usually accepted. Abbas established an *ardiye* in Ege in 1986. He told me that if he asked for the cost of the materials all at once nobody would buy from him. They signed a contract which showed the monthly payments of the buyer.

When all the required materials were collected, they started to build the house overnight and finished it by the morning because the municipality demolition teams did not check *gecekondu* areas at night. Certainly, it was not possible to finish a *gecekondu* house in a night. What the *gecekondu* dwellers did during the first night of construction was to give the shape of a finished house to their structures to prevent the municipality demolition teams from destroying their houses since they were not allowed to destroy a finished building without special permission from the municipality. *Gecekondu* people helped one another, particularly during the first night of building, to speed up the construction of their neighbours' houses. Ali, the *muhtar* of Ege district explained to me that if the population of a place was large enough they could apply to be recognised as a district, which meant an administrative unit of the city. If a place was recognised as an administrative unit of the city, it became easier for the inhabitants to apply for title deeds and harder for the demolition teams to knock down the *gecekondus* and the municipalities – at least theoretically – were in charge of providing infrastructure and transportation service to these areas. So, mutual help was to the benefit of all. It could be suggested that helping one another in building houses was the basic activity that was inspired by the sense of community.

When the demolition teams came to Ege district, neighbours resisted them to prevent the *gecekondus* from being destroyed. Some of the local children and teenagers threw stones at the demolition team and blocked the path of their bulldozer. Women told me that they thought that if the women did not resist but cried quietly, the demolition teams might have mercy and delay the destruction. So, they told me that they tried not to resist but cried silently to attract the teams' attention. The interviewees whose *gecekondus* were destroyed told me that they could use various 'tactics' to be affected less by this destruction. Nazım told me that Ege people, although they were very poor, gave money to the demolition teams as bribes to prevent their houses from being demolished. Ferhat was one of these people whose *gecekondu* was destroyed several times. He came to Akdere, another *gecekondu* area of Ankara, in the 1960s from a village of Çorum when he was a teenager with his family. When he got married, he lived with his family for some years and then decided to move out with his wife. He sold one of his wife's golden bracelets and with this money bought a plot and constructed a *gecekondu* in Ege in 1983. His house was destroyed in the same year. He told me that if a person knew the people in the demolition teams or if someone had the same political view or a person was from the same ethnicity/religion, the demolition teams could do him 'a favour'.

If *gecekondu* dwellers realised that the demolition teams would certainly destroy their houses, they politely asked them to do the job with the minimum harm to the materials because they wanted to reuse the materials of their houses to rebuild them. This would reduce the cost of rebuilding. So, as well as Ferhat, many other people whose *gecekondu* houses were destroyed did not give up and they rebuilt their houses every time they were destroyed. 'They destroyed, we rebuilt and the *mahalle* was established' (*Onlar yıktı, biz yaptık, işte mahalle kuruldu*) was the motto that they narrated during the first decades of Ege. The neighbours who had helped in the first construction and in the development of the *gecekondu* usually helped when people needed to rebuild. However, some of my interviewees, who were among the first-comers, told me that the families whose houses were destroyed by the demolition teams sometimes spied on their neighbours to get their *gecekondus* demolished as well. So what I understood was that the relationship among the first settlers was not always an easy one. They were all helping each other, especially when this help was for the benefit of all, but if something directly happened to one family, this family might change its strategy. *Gecekondu* dwellers were in solidarity against the outside world (in this case against the demolition teams), but, as in other slum areas all over the world, there was also internal competition for the power and wealth (Lloyd 1979:164).

Since *gecekondus* were built overnight, they were in a very poor condition at first. Ege people developed their *gecekondus* step by step despite the danger from the municipality's demolition teams. Whenever they had some money, they bought more materials and added more rooms, a balcony or storage. In developing their *gecekondus*, they also used the materials that they found around them. For example, large banners from companies and political parties were used as balcony curtains and barrels were used as a chimney (see Figure 3). Ege people, like other *gecekondu* dwellers, shaped their *gecekondus* according to their needs. The marriage of their sons was the primary reason for adding extra rooms or building a smaller *gecekondu* next to their house. For example, Fadime, who came to Ege in the 1970s told that they built another *gecekondu* house for her newly married son next to their house. In order to maintain privacy for the new couple, they built the gate of the second house in the reverse direction from the first house. In this way, the new couple did not need to meet Fadime and her husband when they entered or left their house. Şehriban and her husband, who came to Ege in 1982 they bought a *gecekondu* from the first owner. They built a house for her married son in 1984 in front of their existing *gecekondu*. During the first night, they built only one room, which they currently use as a living room. Later they added two more rooms, a bathroom and a kitchen. Gülay was born in Sivas in 1977 and came to Tuzluçayır, which used to be an inner-city *gecekondu* area, in 1979. When her husband went bankrupt, they moved to her father-in-law's *gecekondu* house in Ege in 2009. The story of this *gecekondu* house shows how *gecekondu* people reshape their houses according to their needs and how people living in *gecekondus* change over the life course of a family (see Figures 6 and 7):

> When this house was built, there were only two rooms and they used the corridor as the kitchen. First of all, my older brother-in-law lived here. He added this living room and a children's room which is linked to the living room. Anyway, then, my older brother-in-law improved his economic situation and moved into a flat in Tuzluçayır. After that, my younger brother-in-law got

> married to a woman from their village. They moved into this house and lived here for ten years. When they improved their economic situation they got a loan from a bank and bought a flat in Tuzluçayır. My in-laws found a tenant for this *gecekondu*. The tenant lived here for several years and then moved out. My husband went bankrupt and we moved into this house. I like these rooms which were added later. It is good for keeping the house warm and paying less for heating. We light only the stove in the living room and open the door of the children's room. Since the rooms are connected, the children stay warm. Our bedroom is not connected with the living room. In order to economise on the heating cost, we do not light the stove there. In winter time my husband and I sleep in the living room.

Mahmut was skilled in constructing *gecekondus* since he used to come to Ankara as a seasonal construction worker before he moved to the city permanently. He built four *gecekondus* in Ege and added an additional room onto the house where he lived. He told me that he built this additional room for his children and added that:

> The children grew up. I thought that if they could not find a job, this small room could be used as a small market. All the children have good jobs now, so we use it as storage and my wife makes pasta there.

Hacer came to Ege directly from her village in 1986 to take her husband to hospital. In the beginning she was not planning to live in Ankara. However, her husband was seriously ill and she needed to take care of him. She told me that:

> I did not know Ankara. There was a nurse at the hospital where my husband stayed and had medical treatment. We became friends. She advised me to build a *gecekondu*, which I had never heard of before. She and her husband found us this area and we built a *gecekondu*. My husband died and we stayed here. In due course, I built 5 *gecekondus* on this plot. All of my children lived in these *gecekondus* for some time. I also found some tenants when all the children moved to other areas of Ankara.

Getting Infrastructure Facilities

There were no infrastructure facilities in Ege District in the 1970s. In Turkey, the municipalities are in charge of providing water, sewerage and electricity infrastructure facilities. Ege people regularly visited the Mamak Municipality and Ankara Municipality to ask for water and electricity. But when they began their visits, they could not get anything. They were in charge of solving their own problems. For water, they initially went to the fountain, which had been built by a 'beneficent' act, by the river downhill of the *mahalle* and carried water. Since the men were working elsewhere, it was mostly the women who carried the water and sometimes the men helped them in the evening when they returned from their work. This fountain was crucial in terms of getting to know one another since the first houses were built separately and far from each other. The first-comers met the people who were not their *hemşehri*s or relatives around the fountain. After some time, thanks to their visits to the municipality, another fountain was built by the Mamak Municipality in the middle of Ege. It became easier for Ege people to carry water since the fountain was closer.

Eventually, most people dug a well in their gardens. Some of them could not reach water and asked their neighbours who had reached water to share. The wells were not a sustainable solution for the water. During the 1980s, Ege became crowded and this combined with the regular visits of people to Mamak Municipality for water. Finally, in 1986, the municipality accepted their demand but told them that ASKİ (Ankara Water and Sewer Administration), which was a sub branch of the municipality, did not provide full service to Ege so they could only install water pipes along the main road. Since Ege residents needed water as soon as possible, they accepted this offer. People in Ege helped in digging the main road for ASKİ. Sıtkı, who came to Ege in 1981, told me that:

> In those times everybody knew who lived in which houses, so we knew about who could help or not. Anyway we planned like this, for example I would dig ten metres and my neighbour would dig 15 metres. The decision was announced by Vesile who became a *muhtar* in the second half of the 1980s. She visited every house. Suppose that I was not at home, she came and told my mother to ask me to dig ten metres. So everybody dug some parts. Then ASKI came and installed the pipes in the main road.

Installing water pipes in the main road did not mean that *gecekondus* had water. People needed to buy water pipes and install them on their own if they wanted to have water in their houses. As Sıtkı added:

> If your house was ten metres away from the main road, you were in the charge of digging these ten metres, buying water pipes and installing them.

In this sense, Ege people did not have the water facility in their houses at once. People who had a regular income got it first and others got it when they had saved enough money or found a regular job. In due course, all the households bought the necessary pipes and installed them between the main road and their houses. Having the water pipes was not enough to get the water in their houses. They needed to register with ASKİ and pay a registration fee. Registration meant paying bills. People who did not have a regular income yet did not apply in the beginning. They waited until they had improved their economic situation. People who got water before their neighbours shared it with their neighbours; they also shared the water bill. By the second half of the 1990s, every household had water in their house.

As for electricity, initially they pulled it from the street lamps in the main road. People told me that although it was not legal and they could be fined if they were caught by the state officers, it was their only option to bring electricity into their houses. Pulling the electricity from the street lamps was free, but they would have liked to have electricity legally in their houses and pay the electricity bill. They organised and visited the Mamak Municipality and TEDAŞ (Turkish Electricity Distribution Company),[4] which used to be the only legal authority in Turkey providing electric infrastructure, to ask for the electricity. Ali, who came to Ege Mahallesi in 1984 and has been the *muhtar* of Ege since 1996, told me that:

> We applied to TEDAŞ. In order to provide electricity, TEDAŞ needed to participate in an auction, however there was no auction for Ege at that time. They told us that *because of this, you need to wait for a long time. But, if you need it urgently, we could provide you the lamppost.* Then we began to install one or two lampposts monthly.

In the beginning, there was no sewerage infrastructure in Ege. People dug a deep pit and used that for sewage. They covered it with a piece of metal. Once a month, they asked the municipality to bring a vehicle and empty their sewage pits in their garden. My interviewees told me that the sewerage infrastructure facility was provided by the Mamak Municipality by the time the water pipes were installed. In fact, providing services for electricity, water and sewerage was the responsibility of the municipalities, but *gecekondu* people did not have time to question this and what they did was to do their best to get these services as soon as possible. It should be noted that not all *mahalleli* got water and electricity in their houses at the same time. People who had more resources or more people who could work at installing water pipes and electric cables to their houses got them earlier. But by the second half of the 1990s, all the houses were provided with water and electricity.

Çöplük in northern Ege threatened people's health. People in Ege told me that the smell of this rubbish area was unbearable. The local area was full of mosquitoes. They complained about it many times to the Mamak Municipality but they could not get any answer. One day, Ege people hired a van, loaded some rubbish onto it and unloaded it in front of the building of Mamak Municipality to show everyone and the people in charge how the rubbish was disturbing. Another day, Ege residents organised other people in nearby neighbourhoods. As Sıtkı told me, 'everybody came with a stick' and they went to Tekmezar, which was 40 minutes walking distance from Ege and was the last stop for the buses in the 1980s. They did not let the vehicle that carried rubbish to Ege district come to the *mahalle*. They were attacked by the police force. Sıtkı described this attack:

> Some of us were beaten with truncheons; some of us were dragged along the road by the police. But, we had no other option.

As a result, Ege people finally succeeded in persuading the municipality to take action in this area. *Çöplük* started to be covered by rubble in 1979 and by 1985, it was ultimately covered and a coal yard was built on the covered area (Özuğurlu 2005:46) (see Figure 5). When this area was completely covered, it was rapidly occupied by new settlers. This time, the new settlers were disturbed by the coal yard since it affected the air. They petitioned the legal authorities to remove it and organised protest meetings. The legal authorities reminded them that their *gecekondus* were not legal and tried to stop their protests.

Becoming *Mahalleli*

In the beginning, the first settlers of Ege were 'strangers' to one another. Due to chain migration, some first settlers had known one another before, since they were *hemşehri*s (relatives); however, this did not apply to all of them. They came from the different villages of Central Anatolia. There were Alevis and Sunnis, implying that there were people of different faiths. But here it is important to speak about whether they were perceived as 'unusual' or 'unknown' strangers by one another. Unusual strangers are 'often individuals who are clearly identifiable as members of particular ethnic, class, age and lifestyle groups' whereas 'being among people who are unknown but not unusual has little effect' (Fischer 1976: 84–5). At this point, the social and economic background of Ege people and their first experiences in the city are the key factors in understanding what type of strangers they were to one another. Firstly, the village culture and their living conditions in their villages in Central Anatolia where they were born were similar, so their lifestyles were similar before coming to Ege. They were all socialised into a village culture in which they used to be less dependent on cash, cooperated for common needs, helped one another with daily chores and developed close social ties with their neighbours and the people in their community. The common village background contributed to feelings of familiarity and the building of a sense of community among *gecekondu* residents (Pekdemir 1988). Furthermore, when they arrived in Ege, their urgent needs were the same. Having a roof over their heads was their ultimate aim but owning a *gecekondu* went beyond fulfilling this. A *gecekondu* of their own meant security and it was a sign of their permanence in the city and of their success in surviving in the city. Finding jobs, surviving with little money, protecting their houses from demolition teams and surviving in the absence of infrastructure facilities were among their immediate concerns. They all saved as much money as they could in order to develop their *gecekondus*, their major fear was getting their *gecekondus* destroyed by demolition teams from the municipality and their major aim was to own their *gecekondu* houses as soon as possible. Their similar sociocultural and economic background was combined with their needs and concerns in their urban life. This made their daily chores and lifestyles very similar. Although their faith was different and not all of them were bound by *hemşehri* relations, their similar concerns about the city, common necessities and similar lifestyles did not allow these differences to divide people. So, they were 'strangers' in the beginning but they were not perceived as 'unusual strangers' by one another, rather, they were just 'unknown strangers'. Their common situation, problems and struggles for common needs made them closer to one another. They told me that since they had nothing, their problems were the same, so they became like brothers and sisters.

This sense of community was the primary factor for their common activities. For example, dealing with Mr Fazlı, getting the infrastructure facilities and removing the rubbish area were all for the benefit of everyone. Moreover, individual struggle would not work in forcing the state to take action to provide infrastructure services, so they all needed collaboration and collective action. The need for collaboration reinforced the relationships among Ege people, resulting in mutual help and solidarity. In the developmentalist period, the Turkish welfare system did not focus on social assistance for the unemployed and employment was the main tool that saved people from poverty. The people who were excluded from formal employment could benefit from emotional and material aid, which were provided through the mobilisation of kinship, neighbour and *hemşehri* relations.

The social relationships between the first settlers, especially the women, were place-based. Since women stayed at home more than the men, they contacted their neighbours more often. Strong relations among neighbours provided relative freedom for women in relatively traditional and closed societies (Ayata and Ayata 1996, Chapter 6). Women among the first settlers stayed at home when their husbands went to work or to look for a job. Staying at home alone was not what they were used to when they were in their villages, where they were always working and producing together with other people outside their homes. So, in *gecekondu* areas, as soon as women had finished the basic housework and sent their children to school, they got together. If there was something to do, such as building/improving the *gecekondu*, carrying water, making tomato paste, *erişte* and washing carpets, they did it together. It was not only the work they shared with one another, they also shared their happiness and problems. Ayata and

Ayata's research on the housing, neighbour relationships and property in different districts of Ankara showed that, compared to other parts of the city, women in *gecekondu* areas talked more about the gendered division of labour and its problems (1996:89). This research argued that neighbourhood penetrated into the daily lives of *gecekondu* women, they socialised with their neighbours more closely and their relations diffused into many aspects of their lives. Women among the first settlers used to ask for things from each other such as potatoes, tomatoes, onions and so on. They even bought some home and kitchen appliances, e.g. vacuum cleaners and saucepans, together and shared them. Sharing and seeing each other very often made them sisters, they said. Kader was in her 60s and we spent much time together watching TV, drinking tea and chatting apart from our two-day long interview. She said 'we had nothing, but we had one another, so we were at least happy' and followed with:

> If I was sick, it was certain that other neighbours would come and do the housework, take care of the children. When I needed to go somewhere, like hospital, I would never worry about my children. I was sure that one of the neighbours would look after them. Even the children were looking after one another at that time. We were like sisters with the women and with their husbands as well we were like sisters and brothers. We were asking everything from one another. You know in those days there was no market here. You did not need to go to the city centre if you needed a potato, you could just ask your neighbour. We sometimes bought kitchen stuff together. You see, we had nothing; it was why we were together always. We were suffering from the same problems, so we were the only ones who could understand one another.

They became not only 'neighbours' but also *mahalleli*, which means people who live in same neighbourhood (*mahalle*). *Mahalleli* became the first people whom residents of Ege would ask for help. Moreover, *mahalleli* was the key word to refer to 'us'. For Ege people, *mahalleli* refers to the proximity of people in terms of culture and sociohistorical background and, moreover, to the common interests of people. Besides their adherence to their families, *hemşehris* and relatives, they became closely linked to the other people of Ege. When my interviewees talked about some other resident of Ege, they usually said *mahallenin çocuğu* (son/daughter of the neighbourhood) and it was clear that they connected themselves to the other people of Ege.

It could be asserted that the use of the term *mahallenin çocuğu* showed the people of Ege to be 'us'. They became 'us' through their collective needs and actions. For them, 'us' meant *garibanlar* (powerless people, dispossessed). Using 'us' when talking about a particular class, gender or nation refers to the priority given to what unites 'us' (Bauman 1990:45) and the use of 'us' by the first settlers of Ege refers firstly to their powerless, precarious position in the cities, which was given priority. Secondly, it can be suggested that their collective memory made them 'us'. As 'local communities, constructed through collective action and preserved through collective memory, are specific sources of identities' (Castells 1997:64), in the early years of migration, being a *gecekondu* person in the larger sense and being an Ege person in a narrow sense became a new identity for them. If we consider a group to be 'us', it is only possible to think of some other groups as 'them'. So, 'us' and 'them' are constructed through a clear antagonism between them (Bauman 1990:41). In this sense, for the first settlers of Ege, 'they' were the middle-class urbanites. The middle-class urbanites were strangers for Ege people, but they were not only 'unknown' strangers, they were also perceived as 'unusual' strangers, since Ege people considered urbanites' middle-class lifestyle to be fundamentally different from their own. For the majority of Ege people, especially for the early comers, the urbanites were more educated, cultivated, perceptive (*gözü açık*) and had enough resources to enjoy their lives as they were going out in the evening or they could have summer holidays. For most of the early settlers, the urbanites are alienated and morally inferior compared to the rural people as well as the *gecekondu* people. On the other hand, Gülden, who was not sent to school by her father although she desired to go, aspired to the way that urbanites speak and tried to learn from them. She told me that she aspired to be like the women who are employed, but on the other hand when she saw the urban women with clothes not covering their bodies; she told me that 'I do not want to be one of them.' So, *gecekondu* people define urbanites as the 'other', which has many pejorative meanings such as immorality and alienation, but this 'other' also has some features that *gecekondu* people would like to have to improve their lives.

Political Polarisation in the 1970s

The 1960s were years of rapid change. Considering the relatively higher numbers of jobs available in the formal labour market and decent working conditions, *gecekondu* people had social upward mobility during the 1960s and 1970s. So, these decades were hopeful years for the *gecekondu* youth of that time. There was an increasing student mass and an enlarging industrial proletariat (Zürcher 2004:254). Then, due to global economic instability and oil crisis, the late 1970s were marked by widespread social unrest, increasing politicisation of the urban poor, the political polarisation of the extreme right and socialist left and political violence.

The extreme right movement appeared as the *Ülkü Ocakları* in the 1970s; they were known as 'fascists' by the people of Ege and many other left-leaning communities. *Ülkü Ocakları* literally means Houses of Ideal and the activists of *Ülkü Ocakları* were usually called *Ülkücüler*, which can be translated as 'Idealists'; however, they are mostly known as Grey Wolves in the literature in English. They were an ultranationalist and neofascist[5] youth organisation and formed the grassroots organisation of the MHP (Nationalist Action Party). Many of the leaders and high-ranking politicians of the MHP came from *Ülkü Ocakları*. The security service and police force had ties with the MHP and this provided a free rein to *Ülkücüler* as the grassroots of the MHP (Bovenkerk and Yeşilgöz 2004:590). *Ülkü Ocakları* is inspired by a Turkish-Islamic synthesis. They focused on recruiting Sunni Muslims of the mixed regions by fanning their fear and hatred of the Alevis, thus provoking violent incidents (Bruinessen 1996:8). For *Ülkücüler*, Alevis were identified with communism at the political level and with irreligiosity and being out of Islam in terms of faith, so Alevis were both 'political and moral other' (Ertan 2012:205–6). Therefore, there was no room for Alevi people and this was why the *Ülkücüler* could not appear in Ege Mahallesi or in other *mahalles* with an Alevi majority during the 1970s.

Until the two waves of migration, the Alevi population used to live in the countryside, not in the city centres. Since they clustered in the same villages, they barely had any contact with Sunni people and there was no apparent violence or conflict between them. Considering the weak ties of villagers with politics and the central government, it could be suggested that there was no political discourse reflecting Alevi identity. When they arrived in the cities, they encountered Sunni people and the extreme right for the first time and they realised that there was a grassroots leftist movement whose discourse overlapped with Alevi identity.[6] Although socialist groups, which were known as 'revolutionaries' by the people of Ege, did not directly link their political discourse to Alevism, since they focused on the struggle against the extreme right and did not support Sunni Islamic dominance, Alevis easily became attached to the leftist ideologies. Moreover, Alevi people had a long tradition of opposing the Islamic features of the Turkish state from Ottoman times; therefore, Alevis were considered de facto leftist people by the public at large. The revolutionary left, regarding the Alevi rebellions of the past as proto-Communist movements, considered the Alevis to be natural allies. As Erman and Göker (2000:100) suggested:

> Although there were various orthodox Marxist groups with differing strategies, in general they tended to resort to the ahistorical, class-accentuated use of the cultural and historical content of Alevism in order to gain the populist support of the subaltern Alevis, especially of the poor peasants and the urban poor.

For the public at large, the place of birth or hometown of a person revealed their political ideology. For example, Deniz, who was an Alevi and used to be a revolutionary left-wing activist, told me, 'When people learnt that I was from Sivas, without knowing anything more about me they said ok then you were a leftist, you were a communist.' The political polarisation was apparent even in the physical appearance of the people. Besides their place of birth, faith and hometown, even the shape of a moustache could be a symbol of one's political ideology. Male *Ülkücüler* and their male sympathisers had Fu Manchu moustaches and left-wing males had walrus moustaches. For example, when Ferhat explained the relationship between *gecekondu* dwellers and demolition teams, he told me that:

> Your political side was important. If you were from the same side, it was fine. It was so easy to understand; even looking at one's moustache was enough to understand it.[7]

Ege as a Part of 'Little Moscow'

The political polarisation contributed to the basic features of chain migration which caused slum districts to become homogeneous in terms of ethnicity, place of origin and faith. People from the same ethnicity/religious/political ideology preferred to live together to protect themselves from the violence and this accelerated the clustering of likeminded people or people from the same sect or ethnicity. For example, Sefer, who came to Ankara in the 1968 and rented a *gecekondu* in İskitler neighbourhood, which was known as a right-wing *mahalle*. His son's name was Ulaş, which was the first name of Ulaş Bardakçı, a famous revolutionary of the 1960s and 1970s in Turkey. He told me that he could not call out his son's name publicly so he used another name. He had never been disturbed or exposed to any direct violence by his neighbours but he did not feel secure and this was why he moved from İskitler to a left-leaning *gecekondu* area.

Since the majority of people among the first-comers were Alevi, Ege was famous for being left-wing. Ege and neighbouring districts as far away as Tuzluçayır, which were highly populated by Alevis and Kurds at that time, were called 'little Moscow'. My interviewees told me that in the 1970s it was quite usual that in the entrance of each *gecekondu* neighbourhood, local young people used to ask strangers whether they were Alevi or Sunni, left-wing or right-wing in order to protect their neighbourhood from the 'fascists'. People were also asked where they were from. It was the basic question to understand the political ideology of a person at that time. They told me that, during the 1970s, activists or politicians from the MHP could not enter Ege district to talk to the people. Even when a member of the MHP's party car was passing through Ege silently to go to other *mahalle*s, all the local children and youths would stone it.

During the 1970s, the socialist groups were mostly organised by university students and these activists were the targets of state violence. In this sense the left-leaning *gecekondu* areas were a kind of shelter for activists from socialist groups (Pekdemir 2008:745). For example, Sırrı Süreyya, who is an MP now, was a university student and an activist with a socialist organisation in the 1970s. He started to live in a *gecekondu* area and be active in *gecekondu* areas, including Ege, since he was wanted by the police for political reasons. He said that when the police came to the neighbourhood they could not differentiate the revolutionaries from the local people since the revolutionaries used to live and appear like the *gecekondu* people and *gecekondu* people used to protect the revolutionaries. The second generation who lived in Ege during the 1970s were also partly affected by the leftist ideology and some of them became left-wing activists. In Ege, the socialists contributed to the prevention of rent-seeking activities in *gecekondu* areas and protection of the left-leaning *gecekondu* neighbourhoods from possible attacks by *Ülkücüler*. When Osman, who came from a right-wing family, talked about the socialists of the 1970s, he mentioned his appreciation of Nazım, who was a local person and became an activist with the socialist left as follows:

> Sister, you know the leftist people focused on brotherhood and solidarity, they also appreciated labour a lot. So, they had the tendency to share everything and to look after oppressed people. Let me say what would happen if our boys [*Ülkücüler*] took control [. . .] It would be very bloody; they would kill many of the inhabitants. I am so thankful to God that it was the revolutionaries who took control [. . .] Sister, I should say that if Nazım *Abi* wanted, he would be a millionaire now. He and his friends distributed all the plots to the landless people who came from the villages. He could have reserved all the plots for himself. You know, at that time they were powerful but he and other revolutionaries did not do it. You see that he got by with his pension and he only had a very small *gecekondu*. So, he deserved respect a lot.

The police and juridical services are available for the upper class but nonexistent for the majority of crime victims, who are usually poor and marginalised (Goldstein 2005:397). From the very beginning of their squatting, Ege residents said that the state ignored them in terms of service provision and crime prevention. In the absence of protection from the state, the 'revolutionaries' used to fill the gap left by state authorities in terms of crime prevention and contribute to sustaining the sense of community which enabled people to be more conscious about their community. Sırrı Süreyya used to be a revolutionary in Ege and in some other neighbouring *gecekondu* areas at the end of the 1970s. He mentioned the relationship between sense of community, revolutionaries and the absence of crime in those years as follows:

When we came to these neighbourhoods, the robberies started to disappear. First of all for us, gambling was a kind of crime against humanity. Prostitution was a crime that we would never allow. We were building new lifestyles in *gecekondu mahalles*. You know, we used to spend our time, eat and read together. All of a sudden, the local people found themselves in a new social structure. All the incentives behind crime are about the relationship between people and consumption. We tried to break down this relationship. The revolutionaries of that time were the university students who would be doctors, lawyers, governors in the foreseeable future. But the local people realised that these bright students lived with them, they had the same lifestyle. So they trusted them. I remember at that time we did not have personal wardrobes. You could wear the clothes of people who you lived with in *gecekondu* areas. So we were not so dependent on consumption and our relation with consumption was so different [. . .] So, local people did not even think about committing crime thanks to this new lifestyle.

Cevdet came to Ege in the 1970s when he was a high school student. At the time of the interview, he ran a local off-licence shop in Ege. His account of the socialist movement summarises the interrelatedness of the sense of community of *gecekondu* people and the influence of the socialist movement:

[. . .] our neighbourhood was strong, I mean in terms of leftist social movements. We used to stand guard at night. Well, we had to do this. And we had to participate in protest meetings. Otherwise, you would be excluded from the community. In those days, you would not think about whether to participate or not, you just participated, as I said, you had to do this. And, the friendships and human relationships of that time were much warmer and closer. People were disciplined before.

Nazım, who used to be among the local socialist activists in the 1970s in Ege told me the following:

Being a revolutionary is something different. Not everybody can be like them. Me, I cannot call myself a revolutionary. It requires a high level of consciousness and commitment. The revolutionaries consider ethical and moral issues more than anybody. They never used drugs or committed crimes in those times. In the 1970s, the revolutionaries were very active in Ege and they were supported by the community. They would never let any person sell or use drugs, get involved in gangs or prostitution and they would punish the criminals if it occurred.

'We stepped in the same mud': Transgressing the Boundaries of Political Polarisation

Being a part of 'little Moscow' does not mean that all the first-comers were leftist and Alevis. Moreover, it should be noted that not the all Sunni people were supporters of the right-wing parties. There were many people in Ege, as in other *gecekondu* areas, who were Sunni and left-wing. There were some people who were not supporters of the leftist movement and who were Alevi. So, despite common sense, faith did not perfectly overlap with political orientation. Ege people told me that this political polarisation used to automatically put them into camps and they had to prove that they were leftist in order not to be excluded by the *mahalleli*. If they were not left-wing, they had to remain silent in order to survive in Ege which was a part of 'little Moscow'.

First settlers who did not support left-wing parties complained about some of the income-generating activities of socialist groups. I was told that every night leftist people wearing masks over their faces visited the houses and asked for money. For the majority of Sunni people, it was the Alevis who collected the money and if they did not pay up, they could be killed. Most of the left-wing people did not agree with the fact that socialist activists were charging money, while some of them narrated this situation as a 'necessity' of that time and more educated leftist people (regardless of their faith) thought that it was one of the biggest mistakes of the revolutionaries at that time because they frightened many people and made these people hate them. Tuncay, who is a sociologist and came to Ege when he was a high school student, was a left-wing activist in the 1980s. He said:

> Revolutionaries [...] Who were they? They were innocent young people aged 16–17. They were told that 'the organisation needs

> money, go and collect money'. Of course the socialist movement had some mistakes.

This, combined with the clear-cut segregation between left-wing and right-wing *gecekondu* areas, meant that people could not enter *mahalle*s with a different political ideology. All of this resulted in the people of Ege considering the political polarisation of the pre-1980 period as a state of terror.

Due to Alevi support for the leftist movement, most of the people who lived in Ege district in the 1970s and early 1980s perceived this political polarisation as a division between Alevis and Sunnis rather than between the left and the right. This was clear from the way in which they explained it. When I asked them to talk about the pre-1980 era, they asked me, 'Do you mean Alevi-Sunni stuff?' They mostly referred to the conflict between the fascist movement and the revolutionary left movement as an 'Alevi-Sunni' fight. Kader is Sunni and she said that she always supported left-wing people. Her account of the political polarisation is a good example of the perception of the conflict as an Alevi-Sunni fight and her confusion about her political ideology:

> It was such chaos! They [*Alevis*] were in the majority in our district. We could not say anything; we were only keeping our silence. We were even afraid of turning on our lights when we woke up for *sahur*.[8] They [Alevis] knew that we were Sunni so they might kill us or harm us. We used to read the Qur'an secretly. But in due course, we also got powerful since many Sunni people moved to Ege [...] Me, I am leftist. I do not like the right-wing. I am a big admirer of Bülent Ecevit [*the leader of the CHP in 1972–80*].[9]

It is clear in Kader's narrative that when it comes to political polarisation, the boundaries between 'us' and 'them' are redefined. In this case, 'us' is defined through the faith background of the people of Ege. However, the redefinition of 'us' and 'them' in terms of being Alevi or Sunni disappears when it comes to the collective needs of the Ege community, and being a right-wing, Sunni person did not prevent them from acting collectively with the majority who were Alevi and leftist. For example, Zeynep, who is in her 60s, used to be a right-wing person and is still engaged with Sunni religious *cemaats*[10] (communities). She and her husband, İbrahim, were complaining about the Alevi and leftist people. İbrahim called Alevi people *gavur*[11] (non-Muslim) and thought that they could not have a close relationship with them. However, Zeynep claimed that she was one of the people who mobilised other Alevi and Sunni women to go to the municipality to protest and complain about the water problem during the 1970s. Her husband supported her and he told me that:

> I would have loved to go with them. Unfortunately, in those years I was working and I could not participate in their visit and protest. It was important to come together and solve the problem collectively; otherwise, you could not get anything.

The story of two next-door neighbours, Deniz's family and Semih's family, tells much about how the sense of community overcame the divisiveness of political polarisation and faith background. Semih declared himself to be 'the son of the right-wing' and he came from a Sunni and right-leaning family. He was a drug addict and told me that he had been engaged in a number of illegal activities such as beating men for money and hiring gangs to rape somebody's wife for revenge. Semih introduced me to Deniz and gave me insistent advice to talk to him for my study.

Deniz's family came to Ankara in 1977 from Sivas. They were a left-wing Alevi family. Deniz used to be an activist with an orthodox Marxist organisation, having joined at the age of 14 and had spent time in prison for political reasons. His parents and his three brothers supported him as well as his political activities and views. His brother Onur, who ran a café-pub in Kızılay, was a university student with his long hair and earring, told me that:

> There is nothing wrong with my brother. I am proud of him. I tried to understand other people [. . .] I mean our relatives and *hemşehris* who broke their relationship with us immediately after my brother Deniz went to prison. They were scared. They thought that contacting us might be dangerous for them.

Despite being a conservative Sunni and right-wing family, Semih's family did not break up with Deniz's family because of the political activities and imprisonment of Deniz. Deniz's other brother, Can, told me, *They know that we are Alevi and we know that they are Sunni*. During the interview with Deniz's family, all the family members mentioned Semih's illegal activities. However, they all said that they had a close relationship which was based on mutual trust between the two families. Their narratives were shaped by common memories, such as the day that their *gecekondu* house was destroyed by the demolition teams and Semih's family came to help rebuild, and how the children of the two families played together when they were young. Besides mentioning the mutual trust and collective memory, members of these two families emphasized that they could easily go to each others' houses, eat together and ask for help without any hesitation. Deniz's family said that they felt more comfortable in Semih's house than in their relatives' and *hemşehris'* houses.

Semih and Deniz's families emphasized the fact that they have been neighbours for 26 years. On this point, Can said that *Our problems have always been the same. The absence of proper roads is not only my problem, it is also their problem.* Deniz's words about Semih's family briefly summarised the sense of proximity and how collective memories and daily practices erased the differences of political ideology and faith:

> We have never had this kind of problem [*of different political ideologies and faiths*] [...] I mean, from the very beginning of our life in Ege. You know, these are Alevi, these are Sunni, and these are supporters of the MHP [...] I have many friends who vote for the MHP, we still keep in contact. We grow up together. We always go to the same schools. After all, they walked on this mud, so did we. [*Sonuçta şu var, bu çamuru onlar da çiğnedi, biz de*]. When our house was destroyed, this did not please them. Or, when their house was damaged, we were not delighted. At our funerals, we were in solidarity, helping each other.

In spite of their conflicting political ideologies and religious identities, the first settlers were in the category of 'us'. As Bauman (1990:93) suggests, they were not a '"specimen of a category", a case to which some universal rule may apply', but they were 'unique' cases for each other. Since their relationship was a personal one, it was their quality which determines their relationship with one another rather than their performance. This feeling of 'us' certainly affected the way in which Ege people behaved towards one another. In turn, their behaviour towards one another made them 'us'.

Relationship with Mainstream Politics

In the first decades of Ege, when the people were acting as a community, like the other *gecekondu* dwellers in Turkey, people in *gecekondu* areas could be analysed and addressed as a category. This was reflected in the political language, the laws about housing and urban policies during the 1960s and 1970s. Politicians talked about *gecekondus* and *gecekondulular* (people who live in *gecekondu* areas). But if *gecekondu* people had not acted as a community and worked for these provisions, Ege would not have been provided with water pipes and lampposts and the coal yard and *çöplük* would not have been removed. Moreover, thanks to the willingness of Ege community to work together, they developed these provisions and got the infrastructure to their houses.

Their struggle for the provision of services, even though it was a tool for populist policies, empowered Ege people. They believed that the provisions they got were their rights and their struggle was to get their rights. For example, when Ege people talked about the provision of water and electricity facilities they mentioned that *we, all together, succeeded at it*, *we worked, we struggled and we won*. It could be suggested that Ege people were so engaged with politics and their lives were so significantly affected by the changes in politics, that when they needed to remember the date of an event (such as getting their title deed, finding a job, giving birth etc.) they referred to the political party in power at the time or the political party of the mayor. For example, they used the following expressions: *It was during Demirel's rule that I moved to Ege, I got the job when the mayor was from the CHP* and so forth. When they talked about the improvements or the problems in their district, they mentioned the different attitudes of political parties and leaders. The possibilities of finding a job or becoming unemployed were also affected by the changes in political parties. When the CHP, which was a relatively left-wing party in Turkey, came to power and was largely supported by the Alevi population, many of the inhabitants of Ege District managed to find a job through their personal contacts. Moreover, Ege people told me that when the Mamak Mayor was from the CHP, their roads were improved. Research on Boğaziçi neighbourhood by Demirtaş (2009) confirmed this. Boğaziçi is within walking distance of Ege and the ethnic, social and economic backgrounds of its inhabitants are similar to those of Ege. She also found that, when social democrat mayors were in power in local politics, Alevi communities in Boğaziçi and in other low-income neighbourhoods were briefly put in an advantageous position (2009:197).

On the other hand, a separation between political commitment and commitment to their society was the rule in people's relationship with mainstream politics. Studying the electoral behaviour of *gecekondu* people in Turkey's three largest cities (İstanbul, Ankara and İzmir) in the 1960s and 1970s, Özler stated that 'urban squatters have allied with different political parties based not on a difference in ideology, but on their material interests' (2000:45). Ege people, like other *gecekondu* people, prioritised commitment to their community rather than commitment to their political ideology or faith background, especially in *muhtar* elections which would affect their lives directly. *Muhtars* have always played a key role in *gecekondu* areas, including Ege. They are the ones who contact the municipality and other administrative bodies. Besides, people who need to apply for welfare have to ask for documents proving their eligibility and these documents can only be obtained from *muhtars*. When NGOs or rich people would like to distribute goods such as meat, clothes, money and so on at the Eid festivals, they first contact *muhtars* and the *muhtars* select those most in need in their neighbourhood. So, people really need to have close contact with the *muhtars*. In the central areas of cities, where middle-class people live, *muhtars* only play a bureaucratic role. People go to the *muhtars'* office only to get documents, for example, birth certificates or written proof of place of residence in middle-class *mahalle*s. But since *gecekondu* dwellers had (and still have) closer contact with politicians, they expect more from their *muhtars* and the election of *muhtars* has always been crucial for them. My interviewees told me that they tried to elect people who were good at networking with politicians in higher positions and had the motivation to go to the municipality often and also those who might develop good relations with the municipality. For example, when the mayors of both Ankara and Mamak were from the CHP, Vesile Arı, who was an Alevi woman and CHP supporter, was very active in the collective actions of Ege people. She was elected as *muhtar* of Ege by the local people. Sıtkı, who was a first settler and still living in Ege, explained to me that he supported her not just because she was Alevi and left-wing like himself, but also since he thought that she could struggle for the district and be active due to her close contacts with Mamak council and the CHP. İbrahim, who used to be an activist in political Islamist parties, explained his reason for voting for a left-wing candidate in *muhtar* elections as follows:

> She supported the CHP and the CHP was the power in Ankara, so she could do many things for the district, we voted for her and she did not disappoint us, she helped in providing service to our districts through her close networks in the CHP.

Hatun's account of the development of Ege supported Sıtkı's as she told me that Vesile led and organised people in struggling for roads and water after she became *muhtar*. Hatun's son, Deniz, told me that:

> It was so obvious that in this neighbourhood nobody loved Vesile. But at least she was regularly visiting the council and said everything to the mayor without any hesitation. Sure, it was also related to the fact that she was linked to the CHP.

Conclusion

Ege people, like other rural migrants, did not come to Ankara with blank minds. They brought their skills, perspectives, lifestyles and the social relations which they gained in their villages, to their destination. Thanks to what they brought with them, they were able to survive in their new neighbourhood. They worked hard, were less dependent on money than the urbanites, skilled enough to solve their own problems and collaborated with one another. Since it was a chain migration, more people from the same original location, ethnicity and religion clustered in Ege. However, Ege was not an absolutely homogeneous district in terms of ethnicity, religion, original location and political view. This did not result in severe separation between them since their common problems and collective action overcame the religious, ethnic and hometown differences among them. This accelerated the trust between them and trust was an important factor in building a community in this new place.

Their common activities in ameliorating their neighbourhoods are interlinked with building social cohesion and a sense of community.

These activities strengthened their relationships and stood as the backbone of community building and their sense of community. As suggested by Soytemel's research, shared space can enable the urban poor to cultivate survival and coping mechanisms (2013:2). Also, this sense of community enabled them to act together. In this sense, it is hard to decide which the starting point in the creation of Ege was, whether it was the building of a community or whether common activities preceded the other. So, it could be suggested that building a community and building Ege physically through common activities emerged at the same time, supporting each other. If the people had not felt that they were part of the community, they would not have worked for the improvement of Ege; on the other hand, if they had not struggled for infrastructure facilities for their *mahalle*, they could not have become a community or developed a sense of community. Even so, it was a conditional cooperation, driven by the pursuit of material gain. This cooperation continued as long as the community in Ege shared the benefits. People in Ege sustained their community and cooperation until the late 1990s when the urban reformation projects started to be implemented and Ege people's interests became diversified.

CHAPTER 4

URBAN REFORMS IN EGE

Over decades, the urban ecology of Ankara, like that of Istanbul and Izmir, was transformed through the expansion of the settled area of the city as *gecekondus* were built in areas where least resistance was encountered (Keyder 2005:126). So, as Ankara expanded, Ege, like many other *gecekondu* neighbourhoods, ended up being close to the city centre. Since the beginning of the 1990s, the attitude of the government towards *gecekondu* areas and migrants has changed dramatically. They no longer considered the phenomenon of *gecekondus* as a tool for providing cheap houses for the urban poor and did not attempt to solve the problem of *gecekondus* through legalising and transforming them into apartments. The new idea was to solve the problem of *gecekondus* through project-based entrepreneurialism which was based on cooperation between the municipalities, central state authority and capitalists. There was no room for the *gecekondu* dwellers in this alliance, which focused on gentrification.

There were some migrants who came to *gecekondu* areas after the late 1980s. After 1985, late comers hoped that their *gecekondus* would be legalised, as had happened to previously built *gecekondus*. However, the last gecekondu amnesty only included the *gecekondus* built before 1985; therefore, the *gecekondu* houses built after 1985 were not legalised due to changes in government policy after the late 1980s. Because of this, in many of the *gecekondu* areas including Ege the population was heterogeneous in terms of ownership of their homes. Southern part and northern part of Ege had a different legal status in terms of urban plans. Southern Ege contained 1,230 *gecekondus*, 704 of which were authorized

(Eroğlu 2011:60). People who do not have title deeds or have only provisional title deeds in southern Ege are called 'occupiers'. Northern Ege covers 253 *gecekondus*, most of which were built after 1985, which means they were unauthorised and ineligible for redevelopment since the last The Gecekondu Amnesty only covered *gecekondus* built before 1985. Starting with the legalisation process of houses in Ege, this chapter will discuss how the legalisation of *gecekondus* and urban reforms affected people, solidarity and sense of community in Ege.

Legalisation of Ege District

Construction Law No. 2805 in 1983 and no. 2981 in 1984 legalised the *gecekondus* built before 2 June 1981 (Keleş 2010:521). In 1986, a change in these laws made by Law No. 3290 legalised the *gecekondus* and other illegal buildings which had been built before 10 November 1985. This was known as the last Gecekondu Amnesty. To administer these laws, Special Technical Offices (*Yeminli Özel Teknik Bürolar*) were introduced. These offices were in charge of receiving the required application documents from *gecekondu* owners, providing them with *Tapu Tahsis Belgesi* (provisional title deeds) and running the technical procedures. Giving these jobs to private bureaux in 1984 was compatible with the general political and economic atmosphere of the 1980s when the state started to shrink and attempted to privatise public services.

The main aim of the distributing of title deeds was to solve the problem of property before the implementation of improvement plans. After the amnesties passed, experts from the Special Technical Offices came and measured the size of plots to determine the share for each *gecekondu*. They also measured how much of the plot should be left for roads. According to the law, each person is assigned a maximum of 400 metre square of land. Law No. 3290 permitted the reconstruction of existing single-storey *gecekondus* on 400 metre square of land up to four-storey houses. The amnesties of the 1980s were followed by improvement plans to accelerate the amnesty. For Ankara, the improvement plan was defined in Law No. 2805 in 1983 and 22 improvement plan areas (Sat 2007:29) were designated. This could not be considered as proper planning since these improvement plans were limited to defining the property ownership and regulations for construction (Güzey 2009).

Mamak District started to be planned in 1987 and the planning was completed in 1995. In 1992, an improvement plan for Ege was prepared. This meant that Ege could be legally planned and developed and people could legally build houses and develop them. The acquisition of construction rights resulted in a significant rise in land prices in *gecekondu* areas and this increase was higher in neighbourhoods on the urban fringe (Sat 2007:33–4), such as Mamak District. Ege was declared to be an urban renewal project area but it was not developed immediately after the improvement plan was drawn up. However, inclusion in an improvement plan was a sign of the development of an area in the foreseeable future; therefore, the level of increase in land prices in Ege was remarkable.

The 1990s was a time when there were almost no spare plots to build a *gecekondu* in Ege due to the fact that: (1) the population of Ege was increasing, and (2) the improvement plans including Ege had been completed and all property ownership was legally documented. So, this was the era when Ege was completely settled. Regardless of their status in terms of owning legal title deeds *gecekondu* owners looked for other places to build *gecekondus* in order to have more security and to be able to provide houses for their children. In this respect, for Ege people, Yakupabdal, which is a village of Ankara within ten minutes driving distance of Ege, was suitable since this area was nearly at the farthest eastern edge of Ankara and there were almost no houses there and the plots were cheap. The plots in this area became more expensive as more people bought them. However, the plots in Yakupabdal are still cheaper than other places closer to the city centre since the area has not yet been opened to zoning or included in the improvement plans. This time, people were also provided with formal title deeds for their plots in Yakupabdal. More importantly, however, since this area has not yet been zoned, people are not legally allowed to build houses and they cannot get building permits. These houses should not be called *gecekondu* since they are built by people on their own plot; nevertheless they are called 'unregistered houses'. However, people from Ege called these new houses *gecekondu* since they undertake more or less the same process as when building *gecekondus*.

The houses of Ege people in Yakupabdal can be demolished by the municipality and this has happened to some of the Ege people who have built a *gecekondu* there. However, there has not been any urban reformation project for this area, which indirectly means that houses are not immediately demolished. But still, the people know that they run the risk of getting their *gecekondus* there demolished; however, they think that even so it is better than not having a spare *gecekondu*, which gives a feeling of greater security. People think that in due course they will be able to legalise their houses in Yakupabdal as was the case in Ege. For them, due to the frequent Gecekondu Amnesties and the many changes in the construction law since 1948, their construction might force the state to legalise their houses. It could be suggested that building a new house in Yakupabdal shows that *gecekondu* people consider their situation to be very fragile, so it can be a way of increasing their security. In this sense it could be suggested that changes in construction law, improvement plans and the unstable attitude of the government in terms of *gecekondus* has resulted in leaving *gecekondu* people alone in struggling against their insecure situation.

Increasing Value of Ege

Ege is linked to Çankaya, which is the most prestigious district of Ankara and where there are business and state institutions, including the presidential palace, by Çankaya-Mamak viaduct. This viaduct reduces transportation time to Çankaya to 10–15 minutes by car – there is no direct public transportation across the viaduct yet (see Figure 8). Since 2005, large shopping malls and business centres such as Metro Gross Market, Nata Vega and Ikea have been built close to Ege. Yılmaz (2011) claimed that these companies had obtained the land when it was cheap from the first owners, who were not informed about the plan that had been prepared for the area (p. 62). A 5000m^2 aquarium is located in Nata Vega shopping mall and it is a new city attraction. Moreover, shows and concerts by famous Turkish singers, some of which are free, in these shopping malls are attracting many people to the area.

Ege is also very close to the area of Doğukent Urban Regeneration Project and İmrahor Valley recreation area. Kentkur's report (2001), which was prepared by a private consultancy firm to provide information about Ege to Mamak Municipality in 2001, emphasized the fact that Ege can be a self-sufficient area in itself with close links to the city centre and integrated with the recreation area and forest land and that these features are unique to Ege (p. 5). These factors elevate the area's prestige.

Ege is 15km from the city centre and is located in a strategic position which has a transportation advantage. The width of Natoyolu Street – the main road through Ege – is 50m, which is suitable for two-way traffic. Southern Ege is located in a valley (see Figure 9) and this is important in terms of urban aesthetics. In the Ankara Master Plan 2023, Mamak District is indicated as being among the most disadvantaged districts of Ankara in terms of socioeconomic indicators. In this sense, it is expected that the development of Ege will contribute to the overall development of Mamak District. The city planners whom I interviewed emphasized the significance of Ege as follows:

> Ege is a very beautiful and special area. It looks towards Çankaya and it has an amazing view. So, it has potential to be developed. The Ege Urban Reformation Project aimed to develop here and Ege's development will also accelerate Mamak's development.

As Dündar (2001) suggests, all these developments have led to a revaluation of the area and left it under speculative pressure, resulting in a speeding up of its transformation (p. 399).

Ege Urban Transformation Project (EUTP)

Ali, the current *muhtar* of Ege, and some other residents told me that in 1997 Mamak Municipality began to prepare the first urban reformation project. At that time the mayor of Ankara was from the Welfare Party, which was a political-Islamist right-wing party and was succeeded by the AKP, the current political party in power. However, due to the conflict among the local municipality, city municipality and the *muhtar* of Ege, this plan could not be implemented until 2001 when both municipalities were governed by politicians of the AKP. This project, which was the first urban renewal project of Mamak Municipality, covered southern Ege, a 225 hectare area starting from Natoyolu Street and stretching to İğnelidere Forest area. The aim of the project was declared to be 'transforming *gecekondu* areas which developed in an unhealthy and irregular pattern into liveable urban areas' (Kentkur 2001:28).

Considering laws 2981 and 3290, EUTP could be perceived as a revised version of the improvement plans. Since Ege is becoming an increasingly prestigious area, the private sector regarded it as a profitable area; therefore TOKİ (Mass Housing Administration) did not need to undertake the project here and this area could be left to the private market through the hands of Mamak Municipality. Currently, in this project, the role of Mamak Municipality is restricted to preparing a plan showing the location of public areas such as green areas, kindergartens, schools, sports areas and describing the basic features of the buildings. The construction businessmen and the companies become the main actors in this transformation process. They plan the buildings according to the regulations determined by the municipality and contact the *gecekondu* residents who have legal title deeds in order to try to get an agreement. Ege people can choose the construction companies or the construction businessmen they want to deal with about their plots.

Currently, in EUTP, ten plots comprise a parcel and agreements with construction companies are based on parcels. In each parcel, one plot belongs to the municipality and it can sell it to third parties but the priority should be given to the people who have a plot in that parcel. Expropriation does not occur in Ege where people leave their parcels to private firms and own the new flats when they are finished. This is why the people of Ege did not exhibit an extensive negative reaction. The usual agreement between *gecekondu* owners with legal title deeds and the firms is as follows: a person gets one flat if (s)he has a 140 metre square plot in the parcel. If (s)he has more than this, (s)he can either have one flat and some extra money or have two flats and pay some money back to the construction businessmen/firms. People with title deeds are not legally forced to get an agreement but they told me that since everybody is getting an agreement, they have to do the same sometime; otherwise they may have many problems. The problem is that, according to Turkish law, if the other people who have plots in the same parcel go to court, the person who does not get an agreement will be found guilty.

Since the value of Ege district is increasing, luxury apartment blocks with large gardens, swimming pools and sports areas are appearing in the area step by step. This shows that this project is being undertaken to open Ege up to upper-class people. The price of these new flats is increasing day by day. Buying a flat in Ege became a tool for investing in the future (Yılmaz 2011:86). In the winter of 2012 a new flat in Ege cost between TL 180,000–270,000, which is more than double the price of a flat for middle-class people in other parts of Ankara, which are older areas close to the city centre. A *gecekondu* in good condition costs around TL 50,000 in Ege, at the time of my fieldwork. So, roughly speaking, in this calculation, it seems that *gecekondu* owners will make money through this agreement. Compared to the quality of houses in the city centre, the new blocks in Ege are much better. A house of the same quality in the city centre might be double the price when compared to the new houses in Ege. When the urban reformation project is accomplished there will be communal areas such as sports fields, parks for kids and these areas and the new houses will be under the supervision of private security. Since large shopping centres have been built in Ege very recently, white-collar people who work in these centres have already moved to Ege and due to these centres and those that will be built in the future, people expect that Ege will no longer be a suburb in (at most) five years. All of these factors are attractive to the middle class.

Strategies of Title Deed Holders

Only people with title deeds get a flat when they enter into an agreement with the construction firms. For the people with title deeds in southern Ege, getting flats in return for their *gecekondus* is a good deal and they feel well-off. But they would like to increase their benefits from this deal. This is not a communal benefit as was the case in getting title deeds and infrastructure facilities in the 1970s and 1980s; rather it is an individual benefit to be sought personally, not collectively. Because of this, they do not act collectively. At this point, their strategies to get the most out of the deals and minimise the cost of losing their *gecekondus* are determined by their individual resources and assets. The only thing that they cooperate in is to talk to among themselves about the construction firms and learn different strategies from each other. However, since the rules of the project are determined by the municipality, they cannot set their own rules or increase their bargaining power significantly through individual strategies.

If the householders do not need money urgently they normally wait until the construction firms find their plots necessary in order to increase householders' bargaining power. But this is not the case for most of the people. For example, Cemal, who was among the first inhabitants of Ege, is unemployed, has serious familial problems and is about to divorce. He tried to find a construction firm as soon as possible to transfer his rights on his parcel. The money he got from the construction firm was around half of the money he would have got if he had waited until his *gecekondu* house was to be replaced by a multistorey apartment block. After being paid by the construction firm, he went back to his home village where he thought he could survive with this money for many years.

When southern Ege people agree with a construction firm, they move out of their *gecekondus* and demolish them on their own in order to be able to sell the materials. They need to find a temporary place to live until their new houses are finished by the construction firms. Rather than asking the municipality to find them a temporary place or forcing the construction firms to do so, they depend on their household resources. Most Ege people are not capable of paying rent in Ankara. If they have a *gecekondu* in Yakupabdal, they move there. People who have kept their houses in their home villages temporarily return there. Some Ege people, mostly the single young men who live with their parents, take house loans from the banks and buy houses for themselves. If this is the case, the other family members move into these houses until their new homes are finished. So, Ege people's strategy for finding a temporary place to stay varies depending on the household's assets and resources. In general, renting a new house is their last option due to the unaffordable rents in Ankara.

In the case of Ankara, Harvey's argument might be applied. He suggests that the richest will not move if they do not choose to do so and this results in squeezing various intermediate groups between the social pressure emerging from below and 'immoveable political and economic forces above' (Harvey 2009:173). The populations of *gecekondu* areas are included in these intermediate groups and their choices are limited compared to those of the middle-class people who will move to *gecekondu* areas after the urban reformation projects are completed. Güzey's research on 31 urban reformation projects in Ankara shows that the level of displacement of the original population is high in prestigious areas, whereas the percentage of displacement falls to under 50 per cent in less prestigious areas (2009:31). Since Ege is becoming more prestigious, the expected displacement rate could be high. Moreover, despite their aspirations of living in luxury apartments, most of my interviewees are very worried about life in a flat. Their concerns, particularly about the cost of living in the new flats and turning them into more profitable investments, can show us that the majority of them will not be living in Ege after the project is completed.

Southern Ege people with title deeds are worried about how to afford the service costs of these luxury buildings. Moreover, most of them are provided with one tonne of coal each year and a food pack quarterly by the district governorate or municipality. Their heating is predominantly dependent on this coal and the food package significantly decreases their monthly expenses. If they move into new flats it is highly likely that they will not be entitled to this welfare since the ownership of a luxury flat will prevent them from proving that they are poor. The new buildings will be heated by gas that they will be obliged to pay for, indicating that the coal provided by the district governorate/municipality will not be useful anymore. There is a large dispute among Ege people in which some people who recently moved to flats heated by gas and are still receiving the coal sell it to other people in order to make money from it. This might be an option for people when they are in new flats. However, once the state authorities realise this deal, they cancel all the welfare received by these people. So, due to the unaffordable costs of their future flats and the loss of benefits, many Ege people with title deeds plan to sell them and buy more than one flat in less expensive parts of Ankara.

In this way they will be able provide a house for their sons/daughters. According to Turkish Civil Law, daughters and sons take an equal share from their parents' inheritance. Due to the patriarchal structure of the family, families are concerned with the housing problem of their sons more than their daughters. This is why the parents, particularly the fathers, solve the distribution of their property among their children during their lifetime. But this does not mean that no families in Ege are planning to provide a house for their daughters. Prioritising the housing problems of sons is only the general pattern and 'norm'. For example, Kemal considers his daughter's future and housing problems. He is a retired worker and among the first-comers to Ege. He has three children, his sons are married and Kemal lives with his daughter, mother and wife. Kemal told me that his daughter earns very little money and she contributes most of her earnings to the household expenditure. He has a $280m^2$ plot in Ege. He recently gave it to a construction business firm and he will be given two flats in return. He is planning to sell one of them to buy two other flats in other parts of the city and he will give one of these to his daughter.

Self-Perception and Concerns about Apartment Life

During our interviews and daily conversations, the people of Ege defined their social status as 'middle'. When they were asked what they meant by 'middle', they usually told me that they meant people who could survive with what they had. The usual idiom that they used was *kendi yağıyla kavrulan*, which means a person who can stand on his/her own feet. Richard Sennett (1998) mentions a similar account in terms of understanding the perceptions of class of American bakers. He said that class signified little to them and the bakers said they were middle class. At this point, Sennett suggests that considering the American obsession with individualism and the fact that in America class is interpreted as a personal quality, the bakers were responding in terms of how they assess themselves rather than how much money or status they had (1998:64–5). This was also the case for Ege people.

Although Ege people defined themselves as 'middle', they did not call themselves 'middle class'. They did not use the term 'class' in defining either their own position or that of people other than those living in *gecekondu* areas. This tendency of not using the notion of class in explaining social stratification is not specific to *gecekondu* people. As Mardin (2006) suggests, despite wide socioeconomic inequality, the social classes are weakly organised in Turkey and this is the main reason for the absence of class consciousness in the country. In general, it could be suggested that people in Turkey use other categorisations, such as poor-wealthy and urbanites-peasants. Besides being in the middle of the scale of poor and wealthy, especially the first and second-generation *gecekondu* people feel themselves to be peasants. However, the third generation indicated that they are urbanites although they mentioned the place where their parents were born as their place of origin.

The majority of Ege people did not think that they were poor. Taking into account the fact that the hunger line for a four-person household was TL 949 per month and the poverty line was TL 3,092 in Turkey in September 2012 (Türk-iş 2012), almost nobody in Ege is above the poverty line. Moreover, it could be suggested that the household income of the majority of families in Ege is around the minimum wage, which is

TL 715 at the time of the interviews. So, based on these statistics, the majority of Ege people live under the hunger line. The most remarkable fact was that even people without any assets or regular income did not feel themselves to be poor. For example, Kader lived alone in her brother's house and she paid the rent whenever she could. She was not too concerned about paying the rent because of this. Nevertheless, she did not have a regular income. The only cash she got was the *fitre* and *zekat* (charity in Islam) from well-off neighbours or other people. She received a tonne of coal and four packages of food which were distributed quarterly by the Mamak Municipality. Despite all of these, she said that she was 'middle'. The reason for this could be that Ege people, like many other rural migrants, compared their present with their past. For example, Lütfiye, whose economic situation was very similar to Kader's, told me that she could at least buy her medicine in Ankara and if she were in her home village she would not be able to do so. All Ege people with title deeds feel that they are well-off as a result of EUTP since they will soon have one or two luxury flats. But it is important to bear in mind that this gain does not change their position in the labour market or the class structure in Turkey. In this sense, this gain will unlikely contribute significantly to their social upward mobility.

The recent presence of middle-class people[1] and the new shopping malls are signs of development to Ege people. For them, this development is also for their benefit. When they compare the previous situation of their neighbourhood with the present one, they emphasize these shopping malls. On the other hand, they stress the fact that they are not able to shop in these malls because of the high prices; they told me that they went to them just to visit and look at the displays. Visiting these shopping malls and participating in the opening ceremonies of the new ones are a kind of leisure time activity for them. They are proud that the 5,000m^2 aquarium is close to their neighbourhood; however they mentioned the fact that hardly any of the people in Ege have seen it because the tickets are not affordable. It could be suggested that the hegemonic discourse of development for all is shaping Ege people's perspective on the recent changes in their neighbourhood. Furthermore, for them it is the first time in their lives that the spaces which reflect the middle-class lifestyle have come to their neighbourhood. For most of the people in Ege, EUTP is a kind of social service and an attempt at improving Ege; it is part of the development of their neighbourhood and

Figure 1 The *gecekondu* that I rented in Ege.

Figure 2 A breakfast prepared for me and my mother in a *gecekondu* in Ege.

Figure 3 A *gecekondu* house with a chimney made from a barrel and a storage area covered with banners.

Figure 4 A couple building a *gecekondu* in Ege in the 1970s. Image courtesy of Emine Öztürk's family photo archive.

Figure 5 A family photograph taken beside the coal yard at the beginning of the 1990s. Image courtesy of Emine Öztürk's family photo archive.

Figures 6 and 7 Gülay's *gecekondu*. First they built these two rooms and the corridor (above). The room to the left of the corridor is now a kitchen. Before, this corridor was used as a kitchen. In due course, they added the living room and the children's room, which are connected (below).

Figure 8 A view of Çankaya-Mamak Viaduct from Ege.

Figure 9 Ege is located in a valley. Image courtesy of Güven Aydoğan.

Figure 10 Former waste dump. Image courtesy of Güven Aydoğan.

Figure 11 Hacer's garden, which she uses as a cat shelter.

Figure 12 Ege during urban transformation.

should have been done before. Ege people with title deeds were quite content with this project and they said that it should have been started much earlier. For them, the primary reason why this project started as late as the 2000s is about politics, the delay is a result of the fact that Melih Gökçek, the mayor of Ankara for 15 years, was punishing Ege people because they would never vote for him.

The existence of middle-class people and middle-class consumption spaces, combined with the gain that will be obtained through EUTP, make Ege people feel they are getting closer to being 'middle class'. As the number of luxury apartments increases in Ege, people in *gecekondus* start to be more ambitious to live in apartments. They think that the ideal life is in the apartments whereas the *gecekondu* is old fashioned and destined to vanish. Sayer suggests that a characterisation of the social field which is based on the unequal distribution of goods and commodities, as well as biases in the valuation of use-values and the people associated with them, leads to 'overvaluing anything associated with the dominant' (2005:122). The idealisation of life in apartments goes hand in hand with undervaluing *gecekondu* life, which is assumed to belong to the subordinate. In a binary construction, the *gecekondu* belongs to the peasant, poor, uncultivated and backward whereas the apartment symbolises urban, wealthy, polite and progressive. The attitude of overvaluing apartment life was most obvious among teenagers and young women who were born in the city and 'modern-life' oriented, discontented *gecekondu* dwellers. For example, Türkan was born in Ege in 1974 and graduated from a girls' college in the centre of Ankara where all of her school mates were from middle-class families. Currently her husband's monthly income is quite a lot higher than the average household income in Ege. They could afford to move into a flat; however Turan, the husband, prefers to stay in their *gecekondu* until it is demolished to save more money for their future. Türkan would like to move into a flat, where she thinks life is more civilised. Their teenage daughter Selin told me that she abstained from making friends with other teenagers in Ege and made friends only with young people at her high school. She told me that she did not like living in a *gecekondu* at all. For her, apartment life was more modern, whereas a *gecekondu* was behind the times. This is why she used to refrain from inviting her school friends to her house until Türkan persuaded her to do so. On the other hand, Necip, Türkan's father, as a first-wave migrant, was emotionally attached to his *gecekondu* house in Ege and was quite upset that it would be destroyed in the near future.

Erman's research indicates that, among *gecekondu* dwellers, the main reason for the preference for apartment life is the higher standards (1997a:101). This was the case for Ege people. My interviewees, especially women, complained about the heating and cleaning of *gecekondus*. Most of the houses are heated by a stove and there are generally only two stoves in each house; one is in the living room and the other in the bathroom. The stove in the bathroom is lit when the family takes a shower. They do not have more stoves in order to reduce the consumption of coal and even try to light the stove in the living room only at specific times of the day. So, the house gets cold quickly and lighting the stove is tiring and time consuming. Women told me that, despite wiping and sweeping their homes frequently, it was barely possible to keep them as clean as they liked due to the poor construction of *gecekondus*. So, they would like to move to a flat to have a better heating system and to make household duties less burdensome. On the other hand, they talked about their friends who recently moved into flats from *gecekondus* and turn on their heaters as little as possible in order to pay less. So, while they are dreaming about a comfortable house with a good heating system, they are worried about their future heating bills and are quite sure that they will not be able to afford them. At this point, they will have the properties but they will never be able to enjoy their features. In brief, the objective difficulties of *gecekondu* life are coupled with undervaluing it as an inferior lifestyle. This results in alienation from *gecekondu* houses. One of my interviewees told me that:

> Now, the *gecekondus* are surrounded by apartments. People watch them through their windows and they dream of being there one day. People think that if they live in a flat, then they will be happy and have an ideal life.

They do not take care of or improve their *gecekondu* houses since they plan to move to the apartments soon and they have given up growing vegetables in their gardens. Gül, my landlady, has a place to grow things in front of our houses. She tells me that she used to grow many things there but she told me: *Nowadays, I do not want to do so. Because what we will do is not clear yet, you know, the urban reformation project.* Kader also used to grow many things in her garden, but not anymore. She told me, '*You see I have a suitable place to grow many things. But I do not know, I do not want to grow anything*.

As suggested by Sat, life in apartments brings sociocultural problems for *gecekondu* people who used to live in single-storey *gecekondu* houses with a garden (2007:35). As slum areas are viewed as urban villages (see Gans 1962, Chapter One), so *gecekondu* people consider the *gecekondu* settlements to be an extension of their village life. My landlady Gül did not want to spend the summer in her home village although her husband insisted on going there every summer. This was because she thought that life in the village was not so different from the life in Ege, where she at least had some friends. Fadime has been in Ege for 30 years and she told me that since the living conditions, daily practices and social relations in Ege were not so different from those in her home village, she was not surprised when she arrived in Ege.

Considering the fact that *gecekondus* correspond well to their lifestyles, it is not unexpected that Ege people are concerned with the difference between lifestyle in *gecekondus* and a life in flats. The most frequently mentioned point is the freedom provided by a *gecekondu* settlement, which is related to privacy: they can listen to loud music, beat their rugs in their gardens, go out and enjoy their garden anytime they like. Besides, they know their neighbours and the other inhabitants of Ege. This gives them a sense of localism which is based on mutual trust and familiarity. Taking into account the fact that the satisfaction with privacy and localism are key factors in a sense of community (Wilson and Baldassare 1996:38), it could be suggested that Ege people strongly belong to *gecekondu* life, which is the basis of their sense of community. In this sense, in addition to belonging to the peasants, the *gecekondu* symbolises warm community ties, intimate relations and solidarity between *gecekondu* dwellers, especially for those who were born in rural areas or are left-wing by orientation. In contrast, since they suppose that life in apartments brings in formal relations, it is frightening for them in terms of social relations and privacy.

For the majority of Ege people, life in a flat is like life in a jail, so if they move into a flat they think they will lose their freedom and privacy. The narratives about the restrictions of apartment life go hand in hand with the stories of 'uncultivated' people who have recently moved into flats from *gecekondus*. For Ege people, what makes these people 'uncultivated' is their unrestricted behaviour in the use of public areas, such as leaving their shoes in front of the door, shaking out carpets through the window and making noise. It is surprising because these are the things they used to do in their *gecekondus* and would like to keep doing in apartment life. Their narratives show that living in a flat requires being polite, which is assumed to be a sign of civilisation and progress. Hayriye and Şeker have been next-door neighbours for 30 years and, according to EUTP, they will be living in the same apartment block when the project is completed. They used to call each other by their nicknames. Şeker's nickname was 'bad apple' (*kurtlu*) and was given by Hayriye. One day they were talking and making jokes about their future lives in the new flats:

> Hayriye: When we are in the new flats I will shout 'bad apple' at you as I do here.
> Şeker: No, not anymore, I will kill you if you do so in the apartment. You are supposed to call me [she changes her voice here] 'Mrs Şeker' and I will reply you 'yes Mrs Hayriye'.

The residents of Ege were quite aware of the material and symbolic distance between themselves and the urban middle class, whom they consider as the 'other'. Ferhat, who was quite contented with his life in the *gecekondu* house that he had constructed in 1982, was concerned with prevailing formal neighbourly relations in apartments:

> I know, in apartments people call each other 'Mr', so they will call me 'Mr Ferhat'. I do not like this. What is Mr!!! And why? Do not call me Mr Ferhat, call me just Ferhat. These social settings are not my cup of tea [...] Look at my furniture, it is 30 years old. The construction firm told me that a doctor, an MP and a lawyer have already bought flats in our future apartment block. How can I invite them to my home? How can I speak to them and make friendships?

For Sayer, shame is related to the failing of a group or individuals to live according to values and commitments that others will value (2005:152). It could be suggested that Ege residents, like many other *gecekondu* people, are aware that they are different from the middle-class people in terms of consumption practices, cultural and educational background and social class. Their narratives showed that their way of life was not appreciated by the middle class. This feeling of difference is not value-free but creates a sense of shame and inferiority among them. This is related to the idea that posh is equated with people who are supposedly superior (Sayer 2005:122). From the very beginning of their migration, especially since they have begun to have frequent encounters with the middle class after the urban reforms of the second half of the 1990s and after, they have started to see themselves through the eyes of the middle class. With the EUTP, they are going to be living with middle-class people in the same neighbourhood and even in the same apartment block. So, although their position in the labour market and class structure of Turkey will not change as a result of EUTP, their consumption practices in terms of infrastructure and accommodation might change, as well as their immediate relationships with their neighbours, which play a great role in *gecekondu* people's lives. This increases their tendency to compare and multiplies tension, so elevating the level of shame that they feel. As is obvious from the narratives cited in this chapter, they compare their furniture, social attitude and vocabulary to those of the middle-class people who have moved into the new flats in Ege. In that comparison, it can be seen that Ege people do identify apartment life with middle-class qualities whereas they seem to be closer to *gecekondu* life. So, they feel that they will not be able to fulfil the middle-class criteria in terms of cultural and economic capital and class position and this is why they feel that they will be looked down upon by their future neighbours.

The narratives that were shaped by the feeling of shame were more popular among *gecekondu* dwellers that had aspirations of upward social mobility and modern life. Tarık, who had a very difficult time he became well-off, celebrates EUTP, which will gentrify the area and complains about the *gecekondu* people who replace their *gecekondu* houses with luxury apartments:

> These people do not know how to live in apartments. They are still *gecekondu* dwellers, what does it matter if they move to luxury houses, they are the same. Women sit in front of the luxury apartments as if they still live in *gecekondus*. But, you know, most of them are not able to afford these houses, so they will be moving to

> other areas and middle-class, educated, civilised people will come to Ege. They will be the people who will develop Ege.

Among left-wing oriented people, being different from the middle classes and living in *gecekondus* are sources of pride. For this group, rather than apartment life, it is *gecekondu* life which is to be valued. They are community oriented and emphasize social solidarity and privacy in terms of the space provided by the *gecekondu* settlements. They undervalue the middle-class life and the apartments which symbolise a middle-class way of life in terms of promoting individualism, atomisation and consumption. Besides, they try to enjoy the facilities provided by the lifestyle in *gecekondu* areas. Deniz is a left-wing activist in white-collar employment and his five-person household income is around TL 4,000, which is five times the minimum wage and quite a lot higher than the average household income in Ege. During the summertime, he and his two brothers use the backyard of their *gecekondu* as an open-air cinema. They play a movie and reflect it onto one of their exterior walls with a projector. They invite their neighbours and watch together. These three brothers would never like to move into an apartment. However, they told me that since their mother had health problems, it would be better for her if they move into an apartment with better heating conditions. Tuncay came to Ege when he was a teenager in 1986; he is a left-wing activist and sociologist. His wife Aynur is a left-wing activist and research assistant at a university. After living for several years in a *gecekondu* in Ege, they bought a new *gecekondu* in Yakupabdal and moved in there. They have trees and grow different types of fruit and vegetables in their garden. They think that this is a privilege provided by *gecekondu* life for them.

Despite the fact that some Ege people would like to replace their *gecekondus* with luxury houses or move to other areas, the common feeling among nearly all Ege people was that they are emotionally attached to their neighbourhood. Although they are not being forced to leave Ege, it seems that the majority of the original population will be displaced when the EUTP is completed. They think that they were in Ege when the living conditions were not as good as they are now and they suffered from the lack of urban services and infrastructure facilities; nevertheless when Ege is 'developed' currently, they have to leave. One of my interviewees, Serpil, who came to Ege district when she was 14 in 1993, told me that:

> It was us who had to put up with all the dirtiness of this district, but when it gets developed, it will be the rich people who will enjoy it! In a way, they do not let us enjoy the improved version of our own district!

Occupiers in Southern Ege

Usually one plot belongs to the municipality and there might be one or more occupiers in a plot. So, not all the plots of the occupiers are in the same parcel. If there is no occupier's plot in a parcel, usually there is not a problem in negotiation and the *gecekondus* on such parcels can be transformed into multistorey apartment blocks quickly. If there are plots belonging to occupiers in a parcel, the negotiation process gets complicated. Despite the fact that the occupiers do not have any legal right to claim on their *gecekondu* houses, their houses are not simply demolished by the municipality. The city planners of Mamak Municipality told me that:

> They do not have any right to claim. However, so as not to make them homeless the municipality will try to provide some plot for them, if there is any. The usual pattern should be to provide them with small plots in parcels to enable them to have a contract with business firms. These people might be paid something and get a flat in this way.

When there are occupiers in a parcel, business firms take them to court and need a legal decision to displace them. The legal procedure takes a long time. It has two results on which the strategies of occupiers are based. If the private firms decide to take them to court, the occupiers do not move out immediately. They wait until the court makes a decision and they think that in this way at least they can live in their *gecekondus* for longer and do not need to rent a house during the court process. If the court decides that the occupier should move out, the occupiers do not allow the private business firm to demolish their *gecekondus*. Occupiers demolish their own houses without causing too much damage to the materials since they sell these materials and make some money. Secondly, the construction firms do not want to waste time with long legal procedures since the value of Ege is increasing quickly and spending time means losing money for them. They might make a financial offer to occupiers to persuade them to leave their plots without applying legal procedures. Occupiers' major strategy is based on obtaining these offers from private construction firms. So, when the legal owners of the plots on their parcel get an agreement with a firm, the occupiers do not demolish their *gecekondus* and they wait for an offer from the firms.

Occupiers who think that they cannot gain as much as they expect out of a possible offer by construction firms look for other ways to gain a legal title deed for some plot in their parcel, regardless of the size of this plot. If their close relatives have title deeds for plots in their parcel or in other parcels, they buy a small part of the plot from them in order to gain more power in negotiations with private construction firms. Turan came to Ege where his married sister lived in 1989. He built a *gecekondu* on the same parcel and got married to Türkan, whose family lived in another *gecekondu* in the same parcel. Since their houses are not covered by the Gecekondu Amnesties of the 1980s, now they have no legal right to claim. Turan's sister and Türkan's parents recently agreed with a construction firm to transform their houses into multistorey apartment blocks. Turan told me that he bought 20 metre square plots from Türkan's father and explained this as follows:

> I know I can do nothing with such a small plot. But, I have a legal right on this parcel now. When the business firms come, they have to persuade me. Ok, they can take me to court, but it is time consuming for the private firms. So, what they will do is to offer me much more money than the price of a 20 metre square plot. Let me say I can ask TL 15,000–20,000 to pass on my rights on this parcel. And, I can add some more on it and buy the municipality's share of the parcel. In that way, I can have a flat in the apartment buildings that will be built on our parcel.

Occupiers strongly believe that ultimately their *gecekondus* are demolished without significant compensation. For this reason, they aim to gain as much as possible. Putting it in different words, the strategies of the occupiers in southern Ege are not aimed at claiming housing rights, rather they are based on getting the most out of their negotiations with construction firms. The occupiers use individual tactics rather than acting collectively. In this sense their struggles are very similar to those of people with legal title deeds in southern Ege. Moreover, there is no solidarity between them and southern Ege people with title deeds in terms of negotiations with private firms and housing rights. People with legal title deeds leave the solution of the problem to the private firms and do not intervene or take part in the process. This shows that the collaboration which existed among them during the period when they were getting the infrastructure to their neighbourhood has already dissolved.

Expropriation of Northern Ege and Ege-Mutlu Housing Cooperative (EMHC)

The former waste dump of Ankara was in northern Ege between 1964 and 1978. This is why northern Ege is still called *Çöplük* (Waste Dump). Now, it is an empty area and not used for any specific purpose (see Figure 10). The level of coal gas created by the condensed solid waste was measured in 1993 and the experts suggested that this accumulated waste was producing high levels of coal gas, which might explode. This would have affected the nearby houses violently so this area was declared unsuitable for human settlement. Therefore, construction was forbidden in northern Ege in 1993 and Ankara Municipality expropriated this area in 1994. This meant that the area became public land and the municipality had the authority to decide how to use it. It also meant that people could not legally claim any rights to this area. Since none of the people had title deeds, the municipality only paid them the cost of debris (*enkaz bedeli*).

The relationship between people of northern Ege and political parties, especially the social democrat central left parties, was based on clientelism, due to their left-leaning Alevi identity. The majority of people in northern Ege were Alevi by background, as was the mayor of Mamak in the 1990s (Eroğlu 2011:126). The mayor was from the SHP (Social Democratic People's Party) and this party, like other central left parties, was supported by Alevi people. He was under pressure from the people who were directly affected by the evacuation decision and he needed to take steps. He offered to initiate a housing cooperative in 1995 for northern Ege people. People were told that they could own their house by paying small amounts of money monthly. However, they did not know the type of houses and the payment conditions. Based on the *gecekondu* Prevention Law No. 775, the Ministry of Public Works and Settlement provided cheap land in the Tuzluçayır *Gecekondu* Prevention Area, which was within walking distance of Ege. The cooperative, Ege-Mutlu Yapı Kooperatifi (EMHC), was established in 1995 by the people and it was legally attached to the ministry. They elected board members for the cooperative and started to pay monthly instalments. After some months, they could no longer pay because the monthly instalments continuously increased. The building lasted for seven or eight years and the monthly payments increased 80 times in nominal value during that time (Eroğlu 2011:127). Most of the residents had to hand over their rights to third parties and get back what they had paid until they sold out. The cooperative should have been composed of only *çöplük* people; however, my interviewees told me that there were other people who became members, paid and got houses when they were finished. They told me that people who were close to the managers of the cooperative, who were among the *çöplük* people and close to the mayor participated in the cooperative. The number of cooperative members among northern Ege people had declined from 344 to 161 by the time the construction was completed (Eroğlu 2011:127). Northern Ege people who used to be cooperative members mentioned the sudden increase in the wealth of board members and their relatives and emphasized their fraudulent activities. Hacer narrated this process as follows:

> They told us that if you established a cooperative, you could own a house for the price of a packet of cigarettes monthly. Then, the people close to the head of the cooperative and some other people from Mamak Municipality joined the cooperative, so people of this neighbourhood who were the real sufferers could not benefit. A few people from the *çöplük* area whose incomes were higher than the rest, some employees of Mamak Municipality, enjoyed these houses. The head of the board had his wife, brother and mother as members of the cooperative and now he has at least three or four houses through the cooperative. I also joined at the beginning, then the monthly payments increased and I could not pay any more, so I quit. At that time they gave me some money back. Some of the people even could not get back what they had paid.

Eşref runs a small shop with his two brothers and came to northern Ege when he was three months old. His family were members of EMHC. They paid the monthly instalments for eight years and had a flat. He narrated their experience of the housing cooperative like this:

> Yes we have a flat now, you know, in the cooperative apartments. But ask me how we paid for it. You should see my brothers, mother and father how hard they worked to be able to pay the continuously increasing monthly instalments. The board of the cooperative [. . .] I know that the wife of the cooperative board head suddenly had golden bracelets from the elbow to the shoulder. How do you think that happened?

This housing cooperative, which was suggested as a compensation for northern Ege people's houses, was no different from other cooperatives that were initiated by other groups of people in other areas of Ankara. So, it was not possible to consider this offer as a compensation for the *gecekondus* of people in northern Ege. The residents think that their losses, caused by the expropriation of the *çöplük* area, were not compensated by the provision of cheap land for EMHC. All of them agreed that buying a house through this housing cooperative was not much different from buying a house in regular ways. So, the EMHC's aim of compensating them and providing them with cheap houses did not work for any of them.

Unlike the people in northern Ege, the city planners of Mamak Municipality thought that this was compensation and that people were being provided with accommodation which they could pay for easily but that they did not choose to do so. Ms. Sevcan, a city planner of Mamak Municipality told me that:

> You know our people, when they do not see that the danger is approaching, they ignore it and do not take any action. We have informed them several times since the 1990s that their houses will get demolished. They thought that since their houses had not been demolished yet, the municipality could not demolish the *gecekondus* anymore. They were offered houses which were built by their own cooperative, but they did not pay. They had to pay very little, but they did not. Only a handful of them did it.

In the report of Kentkur (2001:19–20), it was also mentioned that, since northern Ege people were provided with land from the Tuzluçayır *gecekondu* Prevention Region by the Ministry of Environment and Physical Planning, the problem of property ownership had been solved in the area. In short, in the case of a demolition, people of northern Ege would not be compensated.

The majority of people in northern Ege, regardless of whether they acquired a flat from the EMHC or not, did not demolish their *gecekondu* houses in the neighbourhood. The people who could pay the monthly instalments to the housing cooperative got their flats and some of them moved into these new homes and rented or sold their *gecekondu* houses in northern Ege. This created further problems since the new owners of these *gecekondu* houses were not compensated by the cooperative but in the municipality records even the houses that had been sold were indicated as having been compensated. In some cases the married son of the household moved into the new flat and the rest of the household stayed in their house in northern Ege. People who could not afford the cooperative did not move anywhere. In short, the housing cooperative did not result in the evacuation of northern Ege.

Attempts at Demolition and Alliance with the Left-Wing

Since this area was expropriated and the municipality had 'compensated' people for their houses on paper, it decided to evacuate the area and people were sent notification to move out in 1996. However, by that time even the houses built by the EMHC had not been finished yet. In 1999–2000 and 2005, the municipality decided to evacuate northern Ege. In all these three cases, the people did not leave their houses. This decision of the municipality became an inspiring moment for the reunification of northern Ege people and the leftist movement, which had enjoyed a close relationship with Ege until the early 1990s. When demolition teams came to northern Ege, left-wing people and organisations, along with hundreds of university students, came to struggle against the demolition teams alongside northern Ege people and they did not let the teams in. Hacer told me that, since hundreds of people were waiting at the entrance of northern Ege, the demolition teams could not run the risk of precipitating a violent fight between the police and the people. She said that, if they had entered, lots of people would have died since the people were so determined. The majority of houses in this area were not demolished due to the strong resistance of the people.

It could be suggested that the relationship between left-wing organisations and the *mahalleli* was consolidated by 2005, after ten years of collaboration. But this unification was different from the previous one because, before the 1990s, Ege people themselves were the left-wing activists and many left-wing activists lived in *gecekondu* areas. In those times, there was an organic relationship between the left-wing and *gecekondu* people and *gecekondu* areas were both primary living and activity areas for left-wing groups. So, the left did not support the struggle of *gecekondu* people from the outside. But this time Ege district, like many other *gecekondu* areas, was not the 'homeland' of the left-wing activists as used to be the case and the left-wing's activity was limited to supporting *gecekondu* people from the outside. For the left-wing activists who lived in Ege, this is because *gecekondu* areas are undervalued and considered as peripheral even by the leftist groups. The outsider position of left-wing groups and people created a relationship that *gecekondu* people considered to be temporary and based on personal interest. So, *gecekondu* people's attitude towards left-wing groups is based on pragmatism. Moreover, this was a new type of relationship in terms of left-wing discourse. Up to and including the early 1980s, it was the working relationship that attached the left-wing movement to *gecekondu* people. It was the 'working-class' feature of the *gecekondu* people through which the left-wing movement related to them and propagated. At this point, it can be claimed that, since the 1990s, the left-wing movement in Turkey stopped restricting itself only to the struggle against problems generated by working relations.

McAdam suggests that a feeling of injustice precedes social movements (1999:51). People who feel their position to be unjust get together through a reinterpretation of their position. In this sense, the people of northern Ege define the situation created by the urban reforms as unjust. This injustice has rebuilt a collective identity for them. Currently, the people of northern Ege are organised around the Housing Rights Offices that were initiated by Halkevleri which was a nationwide left-wing organisation. In this area, there are several representatives who were informally appointed by the local people. These representatives attend the general meetings of the Housing Rights Office, in which representatives of other *gecekondu* areas also participate. They inform the people in their neighbourhood about the decisions made in these general meetings. Moreover, representatives speak to the local governors, political parties and other political authorities. Sabahat is one of the representatives for northern Ege and she explained the features and the responsibilities of the representatives like this:

> I have been a representative for some years. It is not a formal election. Once people were talking about the general problems of our mahalle, they said, let Sabahat become representative and others confirmed it [. . .] When we gather to talk to someone, for example the mayor, district governor and so on, the representatives go inside the office of that person and talk to him/her and the rest wait outside [. . .] I attend the meetings of the Housing Rights Office and I inform people in my community.

Most of the people in northern Ege have a left-wing global perspective, which was partly generated by the Alevi tradition in Turkey. In this sense, they have a positive attitude towards the activists of Halkevleri. They generally appreciated Halkevi activists' efforts. Cezmi, who is left-wing by orientation and Alevi by religious background said:

> They are, I mean, young people from Halkevleri are like my sons and daughters. Whenever they visit our *mahalle* I accommodate them. I invite them for lunch. They work for my rights more than me, so why shouldn't I support them?

Just as the first settlers of Ege formed a strong solidarity and collectivity, now they need this kind of collectivity again in order to protect their rights. This is not only because their problems are the same but also the solution can only be achieved through collective action. So, their common problem forces them to act collectively. My interviewees in northern Ege insisted on their belief that if they did not act collectively they would not gain any rights and would have already been displaced. They believe that individual tactics – such as the ones used by the people in southern Ege – are not enough and they need to act collectively. The neighbourhood had a memory of the collaboration which contributed to getting the infrastructure and amelioration of their neighbourhood. This history was remembered again in the mid 1990s.

Northern Ege people were encouraged not to demolish their houses in spite of the demolition decision of Mamak Municipality because they believed that Mamak Municipality had not been able to demolish their houses on three occasions due to their collaboration, solidarity and determined struggle. At this point, first of all, Halkevleri gave them a feeling that they were not alone in their struggle. Secondly, it brought in organised methods through meetings and representatives, so providing a formal framework for solidarity. Besides Halkevleri, some of the northern Ege residents work like housing rights activists. Hacer is the most prominent of these. She has a close relationship with various intellectuals, local newspapers, university students and left-wing groups and she mobilised her networks to contribute to the collectivity of local people. She tries to persuade people not to demolish their houses and to struggle until they receive compensation. Since Hacer has been living in Ege for around 30 years, the *mahalleli* are familiar with her and trust her. So, she was able to organise the people. But with the Halkevleri and Housing Rights Offices, which Hacer also supports, they could have regular meetings and collaborate with other *gecekondu* people in different areas. Thirdly, Halkevleri provided information about their legal rights and the plans of Mamak Municipality. I interviewed Sabahat, who is from Çorum and has lived in Ege for 25 years and when I asked her about the evacuation decision of the municipality she explained it to me and then she suggested I talk to Candaş, who is an activist with Halkevleri. She told me that:

> He knows every detail much more than all of us. Talk to him if you want to learn more [...] You know, they work for us. Once, he even rented a minibus and took us to the protest meeting, he paid himself. We owe them too much.

In northern Ege, the leftist orientation of the people and the history of left-wing solidarity contributed to the close relationship between local people and Halkevleri. However, as Aynur suggested about the relationship between left-wing groups and *gecekondu* people, for northern Ege people this collaboration is a pragmatic one through which they can achieve their rights. Cezmi's wife, Sema, explained why she collaborated with Halkevleri, saying, *They are working for my rights*. But the left-wing people of southern Ege with formal title deeds did not collaborate with northern Ege people so much. Only a few people, who were emotionally attached to either the left-wing or to northern Ege, collaborated with them. Furthermore, occupiers in southern Ege were not struggling and in solidarity with northern Ege people. This was mainly because the type of ownership of their *gecekondus* and the municipality plans implemented in these two areas of Ege were different.

The last notification was sent to the people of northern Ege in the winter of 2012. The theme of the notification was the same as the previous ones and urgently instructed people to move out of their houses within 15 days. Since their houses had not been demolished during the previous three attempts by the municipality, they were more encouraged to stay. However, this time the municipality was determined to evacuate the area. The immediate motive was to open up the main roads, on which there were several *gecekondu* houses. Additionally, this latest move could be related to the fact that the EUTP was about to be completed and most of the *gecekondus* in southern Ege were about to be replaced by multistorey luxury apartment blocks. Ege is becoming more prestigious day by day and the existence of *gecekondus* in the northern part is disrupting the prestige of the neighbourhood. Fazilet, who moved to northern Ege seven years ago, pointed to the recently built apartments approximately 200 metres away from her house and told me that:

> The construction firm of these apartments complained about us to the municipality. The firm claimed that our houses, I mean, our *gecekondus* ruin the view from these apartments and this is why they could not find customers for them.

The city planners of Mamak Municipality told me that they had asked Hacettepe University to check the coal gas level of the former waste dump and now they were waiting for the results of the investigation. If it is not dangerous, the municipality will transform this area into a sport and leisure park. If it is still dangerous, the municipality will turn it into a green area and will wait until the danger recedes. It could be suggested that transforming this area into either a green area or a leisure park is an investment that is designed to contribute to the value of Ege and elevate the value of Mamak. In any case, the *gecekondus* around the former waste dump will be demolished.

Strategies of Mamak Municipality and Northern Ege People

Although people do not have legal titles, northern Ege dwellers told me that the municipality could not demolish their houses without getting the written permission of the residents. I was told that the municipality had some strategy to solve this problem. As it was explained to me, first of all, since the beginning of 2012, the municipality had started to send officers who told local people that if they demolished their own houses they would be able sell or reuse the materials, whereas if the municipality demolition teams came, they would damage the materials so they would not be able to reuse or sell them. My interviewees told me that the municipality had invited local people and talked to them one by one and tried to persuade them to sign a document on which it was stated that 'I hereby declare that I allow Mamak Municipality to demolish my house and I do not claim any right to my *gecekondu* house or my plot.' People added that the reason behind the municipality talking to them one by one was to prevent them from advising one another not to sign this document. Interviewees told me that they were promised a house or a plot if they signed. But, the next day when they visited the municipality and talked to the people there, this time they were told that they would not be given any house or plot. People who had signed this document talked with other people in northern Ege and decided that they had made a big mistake. Now they tried to apply legal procedures to cancel their signatures on the documents. I was told that about 15 houses had been demolished by their owners. Most of these were built on plots that would be roads according to the new plan. Since the demolition of these houses was inevitable, people did it themselves in order to save the materials used in their *gecekondu*. Inhabitants of northern Ege think that another reason to start the demolition of the houses with the roads was to empty the edges and squeeze the houses in the middle. Demolition of all the houses at once would create expansive negative reactions from the *mahalleli*, as was the case in previous demolition attempts. So they claim that in this way the municipality aimed to decrease the level of solidarity and resistance among *mahalleli*.

A considerable number of *gecekondus* in northern Ege were rented and the owners no longer lived in this area. For *mahalleli*, this diminished their bargaining power and level of solidarity. In their eyes, the people who rented their *gecekondus* to other people were well-off and, as Eşref told me, 'They would not dare to come and struggle for their houses since they would not care about a loss of TL 150 rental income'.

The tenants did not participate in the northern Ege people's struggles since they could simply move to another area and rent another house in the case of demolition. Northern Ege people who lived in their own houses tried to persuade the tenants not to pay their rent to force the landlords who no longer lived in the *mahalle* to struggle for their houses. Aynur talked about their aim to include the landlords who live out of Ege as follows:

> We should include tenants and the landlords who do not live in *Çöplük* in our struggle. Look at these landlords, they are good at making money by renting their houses in the *mahalle*; however, they think their tenants live here temporarily and they do not struggle for their houses and the *mahalle*. If the tenants do not pay the rent, the landlord could be forced to do something. So, we keep talking with the tenants and trying to persuade them not to pay their rents.

The Mamak Municipality did not send demolition teams until the end of July 2012. On 26 July 2012, the municipality demolition teams came to northern Ege with police reinforcements. This time the people tried again to prevent the teams from demolishing their houses. Locals were helped by the activists from Halkevleri; however, this time there were not as many people struggling against the police as before. Some people lay down in front of the demolition vehicle; some did not come out of their *gecekondus*. But the police used tear gas and high-pressure water hoses to terminate the resistance. People, among whom there were old ladies, disabled people and children, were injured. This conflict lasted 6.5 hours and finally ten *gecekondus* and two shops were demolished. Northern Ege people told me that, since the resistance was not as powerful as on previous occasions, the demolition teams were able to demolish some of the houses. On the other hand, the demolished houses and shops were on the main road and it was certain that they would be demolished at some point. So, this demolition was not unexpected for them.

A day after the demolitions, Ege people organised a protest meeting in front of the Mamak Municipality. They tried to persuade the municipality to provide them with houses built by TOKİ in different parts of Ankara. There was a rumour that the rest of the houses would be demolished after the Eid Festival, which was at the end of August 2012, but this did not happen. Housing rights activists plan to take this case to the European Court of Human Rights.

What do Northern Ege People Want?

Almost none of my interviewees in northern Ege demand to continue living in this area. But they certainly do not want to be homeless. They want to be provided with a house which they can afford. They told me that, until now, the municipality has attempted to demolish their houses three times and it has still not demolished all the houses in northern Ege. Since people had prevented demolitions before, they kept hoping to stop future demolitions. Most of them plan to struggle until they get compensation for their houses. They think that if they do not move out, the municipality cannot demolish the houses easily since they will resist and the municipality may provide them with houses.

Although they do not insist on living in the same area, some of them are emotionally attached to their houses or invested in them. Because of this, it is very hard for them to move out. For example, Hacer is one of the most colourful people in Ege. Despite her low income, she provides a shelter for over 60 cats (see Figure 11) – the number can vary due to births, new cats arriving and deaths – and for her it would be almost impossible to move all her cats to a new place. Cezmi, whose father bought his *gecekondu* in 1988, has worked a lot in his garden and has a variety of fruit trees there. He told me that:

> Yes of course I struggle for compensation for my house. But, look at my garden, how can I leave this garden that I have worked on for years?

Fazilet was a neighbour and a close friend of Hacer and Cezmi. She bought her *gecekondu* in northern Ege in 2005. She decorated the floor of the living room, rebuilt the interior walls of her garden and built a separate room next to her house to be used if her sons wanted to establish a small shop. She told me that she would struggle to prevent the municipality from demolishing her house without compensation; however, she was concerned about all her previous expenditure on her house and did not know how the municipality could compensate her for all of this.

Conclusion

As suggested by Soytemel (2013), the gentrification processes have negative impacts on the urban poor's collective capabilities and support mechanisms (p. 10). Since the mid 1990s, the struggles and strategies of Ege people have changed due to the different legal status of their *gecekondu* houses. People with legal title deeds in southern Ege feel that they are going to be well off when they are provided with flats in the new apartment blocks. Since the plots of people without title deeds in southern Ege are in different parcels, the common struggle does not work for them. Moreover, due to the fact that their positions are different from those of people in northern Ege, they have not collaborated with each other. People with formal title deeds in southern Ege will benefit from the urban reforms so they do not support the occupiers or northern Ege people. The case of Ege shows that solidarity and the motivation for collective action are based on mutual benefit and common interests and when the people's perceived individual interests are not compatible with the interests of the community, the solidarity dissolves.

CHAPTER 5

DISSOLVING OF THE COMMUNITY

Ege residents were able to successfully sustain their sense of community and they acted as a community until the early years of the 1990s. The urban reforms that affected people in Ege unevenly was one of the major factors that lead to dissolving of the sense of community in Ege. This chapter will start with the discussion of the coup d'état of 1980 and the rapid liberalisation that followed immediately after, which together eroded the opposition movements and reduced the level of community action. The dynamics of the breakdown of social cohesion in *gecekondu* areas through focusing on the case of Ege will be discussed. Important factors include: an increase in crime, the individualisation of society, increasing levels of neoliberal implementation and a weakening of the left-wing movement and a sense of community.

Changes in State Structure

Turkey witnessed a rapid liberalisation, which ironically emerged under the military government, which stepped down in 1983 after preparing a more restrictive constitution in 1982 and the coup d'état was followed by austerity measures and marked the end of policies aimed at diminishing the gap between social classes through employment opportunities. The Turkish state adopted an outward-looking market development strategy to open the country to globalisation and its role shifted from an arbitrator to a mediator between the global economy and the domestic economy (Keyder 1987, Kaya 2008:178).

As in many other countries, in Turkey rapid liberalisation and globalisation pushed a large proportion of the labour force into informal employment. Despite the fluctuations during 1984–85 and 1986–87, the ratio of the informal economy to the official economy significantly increased after 1980 (see Central Bank of The Turkish Republic 2000, p. 25 Figure 4 and p. 22 Figure 3). The ratio of the informal economy was 8.9 per cent in 1980 and increased to 11.7 per cent in 1984 and 15.7 per cent in 1989 (Central Bank of The Turkish Republic 2000: 21 Table 6). For the countries of the First World, Wacquant suggests that urban marginality is not a result of economic backwardness but of 'rising inequality in the context of overall economic advancement and prosperity' and it is a by-product of a double transformation in the sphere of work (1999:1641–2). In less developed countries like Turkey, proletarianisation and polarisation could be discerned as two major consequences of globalisation (Kaya 2008:163). The growing numbers of informal jobs had poor working conditions and led to the degradation and dispersion of basic employment; on the other hand, overqualified jobs shaped post-1980 employment patterns. Hence employment opportunities in formal manufacturing remained limited. As shown by much research, for the urban working class, employment no longer granted foolproof protection against the menace of poverty and marginality (Buğra and Sınmazdemir 2005:6).[1] Considering the increasing gap between jobs requiring high levels of skill and low-skilled manual jobs in terms of working conditions, employment appeared to be one of the sources of social inequality, urban marginality and poverty.

Social insurance, which was mainly based on formal employment and decent employment opportunities, could not be the main tool for *gecekondu* dwellers to improve their lives as they used to be before the 1980s. Protecting labour would be a cost to capital owners, so it was aimed to deal with the problems of *gecekondu* people through extra-market tools such as four reconstruction amnesties of the 1980s. Despite the increasing poverty after 1980, the transformation of *gecekondus* to important assets by the Gecekondu Amnesties of the 1980s and the occasional opportunities created by the flexible economy provided some early comer *gecekondu* dwellers with opportunities to improve their living standards and income. Their survival skills, hard work, use of family labour and their skills in independence about money contributed to this improvement. As suggested by Pınarcıoğlu and Işık's study on Sultanbeyli in İstanbul, the early comers 'enjoyed their privileged positions in the real estate market and benefitted from the labour market' (2008:1363). Small groups of individuals in Ege became quite affluent blue-collar employees, some became civil servants and owners of local shops and shops in the city centre. Most of them tried hard to move out of *gecekondu* neighbourhoods in order to improve their living conditions and new rural migrants or *gecekondu* dwellers from other neighbourhoods rented or bought their *gecekondus*. The weakening of territorially based communal bonds contributed to the strategies of distancing themselves from the identity of urban working class. Wacquant suggests the expression 'I am not one of them' for this kind of distancing and suggests that this weakening 'undermines local solidarities and confirms deprecatory perceptions of the neighbourhood' (2000:114). The newcomers could not benefit from the Gecekondu Amnesties, which meant that they did not have the legal title deeds for their homes. In this sense, they did not have the same assets as the early comers. The newcomers' opportunities to become employed in the formal sector with decent working conditions were very limited compared to those of the early comers. So, among the *gecekondu* dwellers, there has over the years developed a clearly marked differentiation of wealth and occupation. The heterogeneity among slum dwellers in terms of employment status and household income reflects the divisive effects of neoliberal policies on the lower classes. The early comers passed on their marginal positions to the newcomers, who were ready to accept working under inferior conditions and became the real marginalised segment of society.

Withdrawing the policies protecting labour had broader implications for the common political language and academic literature as well as the self-perception of the people. Class was not a unit of analysis and labour could no longer create identity and value (Sennett 1998:64–71). Indeed, the retreat from socialism was a world-wide trend which highlighted nonclass identities and inequalities (Kaya 2008:161, Wood 1998). At the end of the twentieth century, avoidance of labour became a common theme within the social sciences and class was increasingly perceived as an outmoded and redundant issue (Dinerstein and Neary 2001:25, Crompton 1993:14–6). This tendency directly influenced the *gecekondu* dwellers' self-perception and the way in which they were positioned in political discourse. For the policy makers, after the 1980s, the link between identity and the labour of *gecekondu* dwellers broke down. Boratav names the policies of the governments of the 1980s 'corrupted populism' (2004:152) and suggests that during these years governments apparently aimed at corroding the class positions and consciousness of the working class. *Gecekondulular* (slum people) were no longer addressed as the urban working class and *gecekondulular* referred to an identity which did not reflect the class position of the people or their status in production relations.

The suppression of the oppositional element resulted in a silent society in terms of political activism and collectivity. The suspension of all political parties and two socialist trade union confederations and the declaration of a state of emergency throughout the country exacerbated the situation. Society in general had a constant fear of talking about politics and coming together to raise their demands. On the other hand, it terminated political polarisation. Therefore, people of different political ideologies and faith backgrounds could live in the same neighbourhood and this contributed to the increasing diversity of slum areas in terms of faith and political ideology.

Ege people who were brought up during the period of political polarisation in slums before 1980 told me that they started to feel more comfortable in terms of political violence and polarisation. Even people who said that they would never vote for right-wing parties and that they have always been close to the centre-left said that they celebrated the military government, which put an end to the 'anarchy'. People in Ege did not need to prove that they were left-wing and right-wing people did not need to disguise their political orientation. For this reason, it was mostly the Sunni people who lived in Ege during those years who celebrated the termination of political polarisation. This resulted in greater feelings of comfort for Ege people. However, feeling comfortable in terms of political polarisation and abstaining from collective action gradually engendered a kind of ignorance about political issues, social movements and, most importantly, local problems. People seemed to be content that the political polarisation and the violence had ended but they were also quite aware of the fact that it was due to this political polarisation that they had been able to easily come together and claim their rights in an organised way. In my interviews and my daily conversations, the coexistence of narratives celebrating the termination of political polarisation and complaints about the ignorance of people in terms of political issues and local problems shows the interrelatedness of these two situations. When Ege people talked about the consciousness of people in their neighbourhood and compared the past and the present, they mostly said that nowadays nobody was interested in what was happening. Cevdet's narrative on the political polarisation and collective action has been mentioned previously and he continued to talk about the depoliticisation of *gecekondu* people like this:

> Now, community ties have weakened. Listen to what is being talked about in coffee houses [. . .] Everybody is complaining about the current political and economic situation. But, nobody likes to do anything together. For example, some years ago, I think it was around 1995, we blocked this main road as a protest. The coffee house in Ege and another which is just five minutes walking distance from Ege were extremely crowded. Look, we were protesting and blocking the way and lots of people were sitting in the coffee house and playing cards. Come on, this was for all of us, not just for my benefit. We were doing it to ask for service provision from the state. No one came from the coffee houses to join us. And finally, a female friend went into one of the coffee houses and said 'shame on you!' and in spite of this no one came to participate with us. You see [. . .] If this was the 1970s or early 1980s all the guys would have gone out and participated. It's because the people are comfortable now. But, now, look at the society; no one cares about the community anymore!

Ferhat gave the example of the protest meetings of the 1970s:

> You should have seen the May Day meetings. Everyone from the *gecekondus* participated. Thousands of people I mean. But now look at the current situation. Even in the 1990s, in commemoration of Uğur Mumcu[2] and of the Sivas Massacre[3], many people participated. But this year only 50–100 from all Mamak came to the commemoration of the Sivas Massacre. I don't understand [. . .] Are people getting sillier?

While Sırrı Süreyya, who used to be a revolutionary in *gecekondu* areas, including Ege and is now an MP, said that today's socialist movement fails to get strong support from *gecekondu* areas because the people no longer embrace *gecekondu* identity:

> In those times, people claimed that they were *gecekondulu* (slum people). Slum people used to be proud of who they were. But now, you can never find a slum person who accepts and is happy with being *gecekondulu*. They might even disguise that they live in a *gecekondu* neighbourhood.

Rapid liberalisation has reshaped cultural patterns and lifestyles and sharply marked the class differences through working conditions and consumption patterns in Turkey. Being a worker was devalued and leading a modest life was no longer seen as a merit in the post-1980 era. The rich became the ideal citizen; Turgut Özal, prime minister during the years of rapid liberalisation, publicly said, 'I love the rich'. Gaining money, regardless of the means, was encouraged politically after 1980. For example, due to the significant decrease in real incomes, the deteriorating situation of employees in the civil service was one of the hot debates during the 1980s and Mr Özal said, 'My civil servants will find their way' (*Benim memurum işini bilir*).[4] This expression was an encouraging message for civil servants to engage in bribery. It could be suggested that this message was addressed to a larger audience, reminding people of the income-generating opportunities of liberalisation and advising citizens to maximise their profits through creating their own opportunities. So, earning money by hard work was no longer a merit; rather, being an intelligent person who found ways of gaining money without working was the ideal.

In contrast to the pre-1980 period, now it was 'nasty' not to consume and show off. Once it was only a small group of privileged people who consumed, then consumption hit the mass market and included the middle class (Ayhan Tarhan 2006:124). But this new mass consumption was based on highlighting status and class differences rather than disguising them. In this sense, as Aydın suggests 'highly educated professionals of the upper middle class in big cities have taken advantage of global economic policies and improved their living conditions' (2009:299). This liberalisation promised big dreams for the lower classes through individualistic success stories such as the examples of arabesque singers, football players and pop art figures coming from lower class or rural families or having a *gecekondu* background and ending up being very rich and popular. These success stories were combined with Özal's political promise to 'create one millionaire in each district'.

Although the self-regulating market system precluded state intervention to resolve social and economic problems, the need to respond to increasing levels of poverty after 1980 did not remain unrecognised. Poverty became a subject of heated debate during the 1980s in Turkey. These discussions were similar to the poverty discussions of the sixteenth century in Europe (Buğra 2007:33–4). Social inequalities were not discussed in terms of the decreasing power of the working class and the loss of its instruments and struggle to gain resources. The problem was reduced to an abstract notion of poverty. Özal's government, which was the liberal government founded immediately after the coup d'état of 1980 and resembled Margaret Thatcher's government, established The Social Assistance and Solidarity Foundations (SASFs) in 1986 with Law No. 3294 for poverty alleviation. However, the budget of the SASFs was used for other aims and it was not used widely for poverty alleviation during the 1980s.

Social Assistance

The Islamist political movements were quite aware of the urban marginalisation of the late 1980s and 1990s. Although the Islamist Welfare Party (RP) was a fringe party, it became a major partner in the coalition government during the 1990s. Between 1991 and 1998 the Welfare Party took seats in the Turkish Parliament and was in government in an alliance with the True Path Party in 1996–97. 'Just Order' was the slogan of Necmettin Erbakan during the 1990s. It was suggested as an alternative to secular and West-oriented development strategies, which aimed at integration with the global market and were inspired by the corrupted moral values of capitalism (Özcan and Turunç 2011:69, Aydın 2005:198). Therefore, the electoral base of this party consisted of the poor and the disadvantaged and those who were excluded from the benefits of growth in the age of globalisation (Öniş 1997:745–8, Ayata 1996:52–5). Hale and Özbudun suggests that the rapid rise of the RP was associated with the weakening of the nation state and especially of the welfare state and erosion of social rights (2010:13). The RP was inspired by the Islamic tradition of charity, lay stress on social assistance and channelled the budget of the SASFs into poverty alleviation. The SASFs' resources were allocated by the local governorates (*kaymakamlık*), which were appointed by the central government. This is why *gecekondu* people call this welfare '*kaymakamlık yardımı*' (governorate assistance). In addition, the councils that were governed by mayors from the Welfare Party mobilised their resources, such as networks among businessmen, to allocate social assistance for local people.

In 1992, the Green Card Scheme was introduced as a noncontributory programme to provide poor and uninsured people with access to health institutions; it was meant to be a social assistance mechanism. Until this scheme was implemented, the healthcare system had provided free health services exclusively to the population employed in the formal job market. The allocation of a Green Card is based on means testing and this scheme failed to provide broad coverage to all those in need. Applicants have to prove that they are poor and Green Card holders have to renew the card annually. In spite of the fact that it is quite limited in terms of benefits and only covers expenses for in-patient care provided by hospitals of the Ministry of Health and university hospitals upon referral (Ağartan 2012:461), for a significant number of *gecekondu* dwellers the Green Card appears to be the only available channel for accessing the healthcare system. Although fitting into the scheme's poverty criteria is sufficient to be eligible for a Green Card, local officials have power over the decision making process (Yoltar 2009). This scheme has been used arbitrarily and as a political tool, for example, the number of allocated Green Cards might change at election time.[5] So, the deprived population's access to healthcare depends on the decisions of those in political authority. By 2011, the number of beneficiaries had reached 9.1 million (12.7 per cent of the total population) (World Bank 2013:8). However, this scheme fails to provide broad health coverage to all those in poverty in the sense that 36–37 per cent of the population is not covered by health insurance and almost half of the rural population remains outside health insurance coverage (World Bank 2005:72). This indicates that a significant proportion of the population, who live in a society that has already fallen apart, also suffer from the lack of a protective state. Therefore, for numerous people, neither the state nor their community is a shelter against poverty any more.

The Turkish Armed Forces (TSK), as well as the secular political elite and secular section of the population, were not comfortable with this rise of political Islam. For the Turkish military, which declares itself to be the defender of the secular character of the Turkish Republic, the accession of the RP into government was a threat. On 28 February 1997, the TSK initiated a meeting of the National Security Council and took a series of decisions concerning the rising power of political Islam in Turkey. The RP was driven out of the party coalition and its credibility was undermined. In 1998, it was banned for violating the principle of secularism in the constitution. The Virtue Party (FP) was then established by former MPs of the RP. However, the Constitutional Court also banned the FP for violating the secular articles of the constitution after a long process of trials in 2001. This led to a turning point for the Islamist movement and resulted in a division between the advocates of National Outlook and the younger generation in the Islamist movement. The former established the Felicity Party (SP) and the latter the Justice and Development Party (AKP) in 2001. The AKP, in contrast to former Islamist political parties, portrayed itself as a pro-western party, presupposing harmony between Islamic civilisation and the West and emphasized incorporation into the global system both on a domestic and an international level. In the general election of 2002, the AKP won a landslide victory and over two-thirds of the seats in parliament. So, for the first time in Turkish history, an Islamic-leaning political party, the AKP, came to power without any alliance with other political parties. Despite the higher economic growth, under the AKP's rule, privatisation and employers' flexibility over labour use increased while the once-secure jobs decreased and more people became employed in precarious jobs (Bağımsız Sosyal Bilimciler 2006:16–25, Kurul 2012:92–3).[6]

Social Assistance as a Tool of Inclusion

Since the social insurance system is based on formal employment, the population covered by this system has shrunk due to the decrease in formal and secure job opportunities. Combined with the decreasing protection from society, this has resulted in exacerbating the precarious situation of the population at the urban periphery. In order to compensate for this, the AKP stressed the role of charity in relieving the burden of social spending on the public budget. So, despite the fact that the AKP was in agreement with the basic tenets of modern capitalist development and globalisation, it followed the same path as the Welfare Party in terms of social policy. It stressed the social assistance allocated by the councils that it administered. Defining itself as conservative democrat, the AKP kept social assistance outside the realm of social rights, disregarded collective labour rights and undertook a mechanism which only indirectly relieved those who suffered under the market system (Çelik 2010:74–5). According to Buğra, the AKP's philanthropy is characterised by 'the mutually reinforcing role of Islam and neoliberalism, which together provide a uniquely strong support to the traditional tendency to undermine the responsibility of political authority in combating poverty' (2007:46). *gecekondu* dwellers, as urban marginals, are a major target group of this philanthropic social assistance.

In Turkey, the social assistance system, which includes financial aid and aid in kind, is based on means-testing for the population excluded from regular employment and minimum living standards. It provides very limited protection to those who are excluded from the formal employment and in this sense it is similar to southern European welfare models (Buğra and Keyder 2006:212). In order to be eligible, people have to collect the required documents, apply to the council or the governorate and prove that they are poor enough to receive the welfare. Ownership of a car or the formal employment of a family member can be an obstacle to receiving the welfare.

The majority of my interviewees had received social assistance from the Council and through Mamak governorate (*kaymakamlık*). If they provided evidence of entitlement to the welfare, they were given one tonne of coal each year and a food package quarterly by the council. SASFs distribute the coal and some cash for students in poor families through Mamak governorate. *Muhtars* play a key role in this assistance since they have the authority to provide the proof of poverty (*fakirlik kağıdı*) that certifies a person is poor. In this sense, they have the authority to determine who the deserving poor are (Soytemel 2013:7). Moreover, since they have the most in-depth and up-to-date knowledge of their neighbourhoods, they could collaborate with local municipalities, local party branches and provide information to other organisations to arrange the distribution of the assistance provided by these organisations (Soytemel 2013:7). The food package consists of cheese, oil, olives, sugar, flour, tea, pasta, rice and tomato paste. People complain about the low quality of these foods; however, they say that 'at least we do not need to pay for them'. The coal is such poor quality that in the winter time, from the smell of the smoke one can guess that people are using it.[7] The amount of the distributed coal is not sufficient for a year, but most people are careful with it and get by without paying for more. It is the women's responsibility to manage to get by with the insufficient amount of coal they receive. For example, women only light the stove when their husbands and kids are at home. So they heat the living room in the early morning, since their children and husbands are at home before going to school and work; they do not heat the house again until their children and husbands come back.

Many scholars have suggested that there is a close link between the perception of welfare and trust in government (Edlund 1999, Taylor-Gooby 2011:463). In political science literature that focuses on legitimacy and welfare, welfare policies are considered to be one of the major tools by which confidence in governments is promoted (Gilley 2006:48–50). Taylor-Gooby's research shows that people who adopt a pro-welfare attitude have more confidence in governments (2010:465). The findings of my research show that the relationship between welfare opinions and trust in government and other state institutions should be interpreted the other way around. This means that trust in the government and formal institutions might directly affect people's attitudes to welfare policies. In Ege, almost none of the interviewees thought that the social assistance was distributed fairly. Corruption is an appropriate term to describe the economic dimension of state-society relations during the post-1980 period in Turkey (Buğra and Keyder 2006:212) and for Ege people this is the main reason for the ineffective distribution of welfare. In other words, it can be said that Ege people's mistrust of state institutions influenced their opinions of welfare. Petersen et al. suggest that citizens' welfare opinions are also shaped by their political values (2010:25). In this sense, Ege people's mistrust of the council, which is run by the AKP, the Islamist right-wing party, is reinforced by their negative attitudes since most Ege people are Alevi by faith background and have sympathies towards the central left. Kemal, who is Alevi and a supporter of the CHP, the centre-left and the largest oppositional party in the government, said that the AKP could cancel social assistance for beneficiaries who did not support it.

> I have never received any assistance from the council. I applied for myself but I was not eligible since I have a retirement pension.

> I respect this. But I applied for my daughter who gets by from working in the rubbish and collecting usable things. Look, she was not considered eligible. Now I am helping her, I am paying for her food [. . .] But Mashallah Melih Gökçek [the Mayor of Ankara] distributed it to everybody! He got his salary from the state but distributed the state's budget [. . .] To be honest, I was organising people of the CHP before the elections and organised a meeting in one of the neighbour's houses. But then he moved to Sincan since he was threatened by Melih Gökçek's guardians. He cancelled the meeting and moved to Sincan since he was afraid that his social assistance would be cancelled. Do you see?

On the other hand, Ege people who are closer to the AKP do not talk about corruption in the distribution of welfare by the council. These people accused the *muhtar*, who is a left-wing person, of privileging his *hemşehri*s and supporters when providing *fakirlik kağıdı* (proof of poverty) to be submitted to the governorate to receive social assistance from SASF. İbrahim, who used to be an activist in previous Islamist parties and now supports the AKP, says that:

> I applied for social assistance once, but I was not eligible, then I did not apply again [. . .] Yes, social assistance is good, if the distribution is fair. Look there are people who have a car, a house and a regular income whereas a real sufferer does not receive [. . .] This is all about the *muhtar*. The *muhtar* knows who is truly poor and who is not. He should show the truly poor. But he does not do this, because he privileges people who are closer to him.

Ege people who are, or used to be, activists for the socialist left or define their political view as socialist do not blame individual or institutional actors such as the council, the AKP, the *muhtar* or the governorate. In general they have a wider perspective and blame the whole capitalist system in which welfare policies are used to tame the grassroots people. This is reflected in the account of Tuncay, who is a socialist activist.

> Capitalism is an irrational system. It is consuming, vulgar and costly. This results in inequality and impoverishment. The problem is here that, people survive in a way. They are given coal,

> food [. . .] If they cannot receive it they gather food from rubbish in the streets. They survive, yes, but is it a decent life?

Although there can be intermediary positions and people who do not fit into this categorisation, it could roughly be claimed that Ege people's perceptions of welfare are significantly influenced by their attitudes towards the AKP and the government.

Most people in Ege thought that people who were close to the AKP, the party in power, would have more access to the available welfare. Moreover, the AKP is infamous for getting the votes of *gecekondu* people through the allocation of welfare. However, there were poor people who opposed the AKP and were receiving welfare. Even so, there were welfare recipients who were against the AKP but thought that only AKP supporters received it. Associating the receipt of welfare with indirect support for the AKP contributed to the segregation of Ege people.

The issue of desert in welfare policies has attracted a considerable amount of interest from scholars. Petersen et al.'s research shows that the desert of welfare recipients is one of the determining elements in shaping people's perceptions of welfare (2010:26–7). In Turkey, 'the discourse around social assistance is predicated on the notion of the "deserving poor" and "undeserving poor"' (Soytemel 2013:7). In this sense, most Ege people said that social assistance was needed but it should have been allocated to the needy that really deserved it. For Ege people, it was not the needy but the rich who got welfare from the council and governorate, so the welfare recipients did not deserve the available social assistance. So, the confusing organisation of social assistance creates new tensions among the *gecekondu* communities. They suggested that the council and the governorate should have a stricter controlling mechanism for means testing and should abstain from distributing it to people who had a regular income. Şeker, who received social assistance once from the council and once from the SASF, told me that:

> They should identify the disabled, the elderly and ones lacking any income and pay them rather than allocating food. [*Paused and hesitated to say*] To be honest [. . .] the rich receive the welfare now, right? It requires strict control and investigation. It is not the **deserving people, but the people who have strong networks who receive the welfare.**[*my emphasis*]

Welfare applicants may request reinvestigation in the case of rejection and raise complaints about fraud or about recipients whom they believe do not deserve the social assistance. In Ege, the accounts about deserts went hand in hand with stories of complaints made to the council and governorate to cancel someone's welfare. In the case of complaints, according to my research as well as the research done by Murakami, the officials respond promptly and investigate complaints through their database or unannounced home visits (2011:23). These kinds of complaints were known as 'spying' among Ege people. Considering the fact that welfare recipients do not have any control over social assistance, 'spying' can be considered as the only way that welfare recipients can intervene, at least in the distribution process (Murakami 2011:23). Despite the constant fear of spying, many welfare recipients share the food sent by the council or governorate with their neighbours, relatives and friends in their neighbourhood. In this sense, the allocation of food and coal started a new moral economy among the *gecekondu* dwellers. So, their relationship is not an easy or uniform one in the case of the distribution of welfare. It could be suggested that the ambiguity of the state's policy on *gecekondus* and welfare such as social assistance, which were mostly implemented through paternalist relations, urged both solidarity and envy, this led to spying among *gecekondu* dwellers.

Fraser (1987) mentions that, in many countries, female welfare recipients outnumber males and suggests that 'even a minimal and inadequate "safety net" increases leverage of women who are economically dependent on individual men' (1987:103–4). While this is the case for many women in Ege, it is considered a threat by the men, who usually spend their time in the coffee house in Ege and tend to be involved in illegal activities. They are mostly against social assistance because they say welfare support empowers women and that female welfare recipients do not depend on men any more. For them, this results in women challenging them and not respecting men's authority. Osman, the owner of the coffee house in Ege told me:

> I am against welfare support. Do you know what happens to women? They say 'I receive my food, coal and pocket money for my children, so why shall I be bothered with my husband? I can find a man anywhere.' You see, they do not bother to live with men any more. It will increase the divorce rate.

My research indicates that women and men experience social assistance differently. Most of the time, unemployed men are shy about applying for the available welfare support because of their masculine honour. Men pass this duty to the women and women go through the necessary paperwork to enable their families to benefit (Buğra and Keyder 2006:221–2). While this might show the empowered situation of women in terms of their visibility in the public sphere, it can also be suggested that, since seeking welfare is related to a family's low income, for male members of the household it is a kind of proof of their failure to fulfil their role as breadwinner. Although most of the men do not apply for this support, they silently accept it when they receive it. In some cases, men in precarious and informal work are opposed to applying for welfare support. In these cases, the women in the family applied secretly. Gülay, whose husband's business went bankrupt, told me that:

> My husband was unemployed. He was against receiving welfare. But I collected all the required documents and applied. When the coal was distributed he understood. Indeed, he became happy but he did not say anything.

Some of the men ask their wives to cancel the welfare when they improve their economic situation or find better jobs. Murat is a 19-year-old Ege settler. He has two brothers. Except for the younger brother, who was attending primary school at the time of the interview, all the members of his family were employed. He and his brother frequently change jobs and work for the minimum wage. His mother works part-time and gains around two-thirds of the minimum wage. The main income is his father's salary. When his father was unemployed for a year, his mother applied for welfare support from the council and they received it. When his father found a more secure job, he asked his wife to cancel the welfare support in order not to violate the rights of other deprived people. In this sense, receiving and applying for welfare support has a moral dimension for Ege people. Many people in Ege mentioned that truly poor people did not directly express or reveal that they were poor. The most significant feature of the truly poor for Ege people is that if a person is truly poor (s)he feels ashamed and this prevents him/her from applying for social assistance. My interviewees told me that this was another reason why, rather than poor people, the rich received the social assistance. My findings coincide with Murakami's research (2011), which investigates the attitudes of applicants and future applicants of a *gecekondu* district as well as of the officials in welfare distributing institutions in İstanbul.

Obtaining welfare depended on individual action, such as collecting the required documents and undertaking the application process. This reduced the motivation for collective action and solidarity and changed the way that *gecekondu* dwellers regard their activity in getting resources. These welfare policies are called *sosyal yardım* (social assistance) by the state institutions as well as the slum dwellers. It could be suggested that the government does not present welfare policies as one of the required jobs of a social state, whereas the Turkish Republic is constitutionally described as a social state. In the same vein, *gecekondu* people do not regard receiving welfare as a citizenship right, but as a favour from the government. But when it comes to welfare distribution they do not use 'we' as the real object, they say *the council distributes* or *thanks to the governorate, I have got my coal for this winter.* So, this welfare distribution does not empower them as political subjects, on the contrary it makes them subordinated and less powerful. Ege people regarded welfare either as a favour or as a tactic of the AKP to win the votes of *gecekondu* people. So, they do not see themselves as the real recipients of the welfare.

Despair and Crime

Limited opportunities for the working class have increased the competition among them in terms of employment opportunities. Low-skilled jobs, which mainly have poor working conditions, long working hours and poor wages, are the only attainable jobs for many people in *gecekondu* areas like Ege. For some male *gecekondu* youth, these jobs are frustrating, boring, routine and do not promise the social upward mobility that provides them with the opportunity to obtain urbanites' living standards. Even for low-skilled jobs, there is intense competition. Young men with few skills requiring employment told me that to be employed they found a *tanıdık* (acquaintance) to obtain a reference. When Semih, who was born in Ankara, does not have a regular job and spends most of his time in the local coffee house, talked about unemployment and the new job opportunities generated by the recent shopping malls around the neighbourhood, he stated that:

> You know, now there is IKEA, very close to here. I went there for a job interview. They asked me to work six days a week, working eight hours a day. The work was carrying furniture. I would be paid only 800 liras (GBP 270) per month! I did not take the job. We were accused of being lazy. Come on, offer me a desk job where I can earn 1,500 liras monthly, then let's see who is lazy!

Furthermore, the children of migrants, the *gecekondu* generation, grew up in urban areas and they witnessed the different lifestyles of upper-class and *gecekondu* people and suffered from the widening disparities between the social classes. The interviewees among the second and third generations told me that their accents and clothes would disclose their *gecekondu* identity and this could lead to them being excluded. Hayat came to Ege when she was three years old and now she is 29 and has two kids who go to the primary school in Ege. She told me that her family was quite poor when she was a child. She described her youth in the 1990s:

> I was working as a sales assistant in a patisserie in Tandoğan [*a district in the city centre of Ankara*]. The customers were different from me. I mean [...] their outfits, the way they speak [...] I aspired to be like them. I was insisting that my parents buy me new clothes. They sometimes even did not buy new clothes in Eids.[8] But now I do not blame my parents. They came from the village, so they did not know this kind of thing.

Ege men who had temporary jobs and usually hung around the local coffee house told me that their appearance or accent might be obstacles to finding jobs in the city centre. On the one hand they appeal to urban middle-class life and on the other hand they expressed anger against the men with urban style. For example, during one of our daily conversations with the men in the local coffee house, they mentioned the men who wore earrings and had long hair in Kızılay (the city centre). One of the men in the coffee house said that he looked for an argument with those kinds of men to beat them up and the other men agreed with him. They were different from their parents in the sense that they see becoming middle class as the only way to be a respectable member of society. So, despite harbouring hatred against the exclusionist capitalist system in which they are structurally disadvantaged, the younger *gecekondu* generation aspire to obtain the living standards of the urban upper class and are willing to be a part of this system.

Research shows that gangs appear and the rate of crime increases when people are frustrated by the realisation that they are not likely to find jobs which can enable them to rise above their parents' socioeconomic level and they are suffering from significant social inequality (Portes and Rumbaut 2001:50, Carmichael and Ward 2001:115, Jennings et al. 2012:205–7, Ochsen 2010:55–8). Illegal activities, including organising around local gangs, offer an exciting income-generating facility which is a substitute for legal economic activities. A group of men in Ege who hung around the local coffee house was called the 'Beautification Association'; they excluded women and behaved like a gang. According to Law No. 5253, the locals can launch associations and the coffee house in Ege is the club of the Metehan[9] Beautification Association. Moreover, according to the same law, article 20, the police require a written judicial decision to enter these associations. It is common knowledge that in Turkey some of the coffee houses for gambling are established in the name of beautification associations in order to suffer less control and pay less tax. Not surprisingly, the one in Ege was extensively used for gambling and smoking marijuana, which are illegal in Turkey. The usual visitors to this coffee house were mainly men who were either born in Ege or had lived in Ege for most of their lives.

Despite the desire to gain money, not all the gangs accumulate profit and disperse it to their members and usually their economic activities are focused mainly on paying entertainment bills (Joyeaux 1960, cited in Sanchez-Jankowski 2003:205); therefore, illegal activities do not usually enable them to attain the desired socioeconomic level. Men in the local coffee house mentioned that some of them used to acquire a large amount of money in a night but then spent it in a week. So their income could not be considered a means of upward mobility. However, being part of a gang is a means of achieving power for oppressed *gecekondu* youth. The owner of the coffee shop told me that he used to be part of a larger gang outside of Ege and described his life as 'we used to live so fast, we've slowed down now'. He said that now he was the older brother (*abi*) of male youth in Ege. He mentioned his 'fast days' and what it meant to be an older brother for the young males of Ege as follows:

> We woke up late in the afternoon. In the evenings, we used to wear our suits and attack. We used to visit all the casinos and nightclubs in Ankara and collect our money. Of course there was nothing left from it. First, we were crowded; we had to pay for the young team members' food, clothes and pocket money. And we used to smoke joints and take cocaine, which was extremely expensive. Now I've slowed down. If I like, now, I can get all these *young men* to sell drugs [*he asked a teenager boy in the coffee house to confirm this with him*]. I am their older brother, they can't reject me. However, I would never do it. I do not want them to suffer like me. I always prevent drop outs from school. I recommend them to study. But they took me and the others as their role model and most of them quit school at an early age.

Sanchez-Jankowski states that member of gangs do not commit themselves to full-time work, which would monopolise their time and energy, so that they can be primarily involved in the gang and its leisure activities (2003:205). Instead, they get temporary or part-time jobs in order to afford the entertainment since the gangs cannot focus on profit accumulation. Yonucu's research suggests that the club culture among *gecekondu* youth is a sign of their desire to be a part of society and a way to narrow the gap between themselves and the urban youth through consumption (2008:65). Moreover, the local coffee houses were usually the only available entertainment for many *gecekondu* men. Based on the life stories of men in the local coffee house in Ege, I can suggest that, after a point, membership of the gang or the 'male club' in Ege became the primary activity that shaped their lifestyle and other activities seem to be secondary. Gülden, Semih's wife, always complained about her husband, who did not have a regular job and smoked marijuana. For her, it seemed that, if he were not so committed to the local coffee house and if he stopped going there, he could quit smoking and find a regular job. Rahmi, one of the men in Ege who usually went to the coffee shop, won some million liras in a national lottery in 2002. For him, this was the point that his life deteriorated irreversibly because he spent all his money on drugs, nightclubs and gambling with his friends, the majority of whom lived in Ege. The money ran out quickly, but he still continued to be a part of the gang, smoking joints and gambling. For him, the money from the lottery deepened his relationship with the gang and now it became a lifestyle for him.

Due to the high rate of unemployment, young men are readily available in the coffee house and this can lead to a small dispute turning into an event of violence (Erman and Eken 2004:63). Despite the fact that during my stay I did not witness or hear about any case of violence, the availability of men in the coffee house created a kind of tension in Ege. Women, especially young and single women, hesitated to walk past the coffee shop. Parents tried to prevent their teenage sons from spending time around the coffee house in order to prevent them from interacting with its regular visitors and the gang which gets together on the nearby corners.

Ege people know that there have been illegal activities in their neighbourhood since the 1990s when the sense of community started to dissolve and the collective struggle nearly stopped. The second and third generation who were born in Ege or those who came to Ege at an early age, could not sustain the sense of community as their parents did. When they became adults, their parents had already solved the basic problems of their neighbourhood through collective action. So, the second and third generation in Ege did not need collectivism and solidarity. This was the main reason for the lack of a sense of community among them. For example, despite living in Ege for many years, the younger generations of the families who built the *gecekondu* houses together may not know each other very well or meet frequently. Moreover, with the introduction of numerous private GSM companies, affordable pay-as-you-go rates in small denominations and private broadband companies in the 2000s, cellular phones and the internet were widely used among the *gecekondu* youth. Teenagers in Ege told me that surfing the internet, facebooking and computer games were their main leisure activities. Therefore, Ege youth tend to communicate with one another and their family members less, instead they tend to spend their time on the internet and mobile phones. For the majority of Ege people, the mass consumption of telecommunication and internet technologies was one of the prominent reasons why Ege youth had lost their sense of community.

In addition, Ege residents mentioned that they were not familiar with their new neighbours who had been displaced from other *gecekondu* neighbourhoods as a result of urban transformation projects in Ankara.

The change in the composition of the population has sharply affected the sense of community in *gecekondu* areas since people become less familiar with their neighbours. The first settlers of Ege do not develop close relationships with the newcomers but tend to minimise their dealings with them and retreat into their own small community. Döndü has lived in Ege for 30 years. She agreed to allow a construction firm to transform her house and she was about to move to another part of Ankara at the time of our meeting. She told me that:

> Some of the old neighbours died, some of them moved to other districts. The people of Ege changed. Now, we are a bunch of old neighbours [. . .] Yeah, of course new people are coming. But new people cannot replace the old neighbours. You know, they don't approach you, even if you approach them, and how can you connect with people who you've only recently met?

Auyero's (2000) research on Argentina's slums indicates that slum people complain about the increasing rate of crime and drug usage in their neighbourhood and the main difference between the present and past of slum areas (particularly during the 1970s) is the much lower level of political mobilisation (pp. 108–9). In this sense, the case of Ege, as in many other Turkish *gecekondu* areas, is similar to the slums in Argentina, which was hit by a coup d'état followed by a neoliberal restructuring process in 1976. It could be suggested of slum areas that used to be politically mobilised, that the increase in illegal activities and crime is related to the lower levels of political mobilisation. So, the vacuum left by the absence of a strong left-wing and the sense of community was not filled by the state authorities. People told me that they suffered from a kind of absence of the state authorities in their districts. They told me many stories about how the police disregarded cases of theft. Hacer narrated a theft story like this:

> The police do not care about us. My gate was stolen. I called the police, it was midnight. They came very late and asked me whether I had a witness or not. At midnight, how could I have a witness? They did not even record my application. You see?

For Ege people, the state not only turns a blind eye to crimes and illegal activities in the area but also supports them covertly. This is why they see no point in denouncing drug users and sellers and gamblers since they suppose that the police are in league with them. The men who were involved with the gang and the regular visitors to the coffee house mentioned that they did not hesitate to talk openly about what they were engaged with since the police already knew what they were doing. The facts that the local police station was only 500 metres away from the coffee house and that I witnessed regular police visits there prove this account. Moreover, these men told me that if the police did not let them gamble or smoke, they would not be able to do so. According to an ex-drug dealer, the state made money out of drug dealing as he said:

> When the police caught drug dealers, they took the drugs from them and gave them to me and when I sold them we shared the money.

The socialist people of Ege suggested an additional explanation for the inaction of the state in terms of crimes. It seemed to them that the state considered the inability to consume might create frustration, which might lead to uprisings in slum areas. Therefore, they claimed that disregarding the illegal activities in these areas was a state tactic. They told me that this is why the Turkish government not only clamped down on the left movement after the coup d'état in 1980 but had also tried to keep potential dissidents busy with other activities since the 1980s. Tuncay, who is a left-wing Ege resident, claimed that the Turkish state even promoted alcohol consumption in *gecekondu* areas.

> Did you know that the area of highest alcohol consumption in Ankara is Mamak? You know, Mamak is composed of *gecekondu* areas, most of which used to be liberated areas of the socialist movement. Now, the parks are full of young men drinking beer in the evening. The state supports this on purpose. In the 1990s, there were beers and if you found the lucky cover you won an extra beer. Most of these were in local shops in the slum areas. I do not believe that it was just a coincidence.

It could be suggested that neoliberal policies created economic insecurity, which was accompanied by a physical insecurity (Goldstein 2005:397). At this point, Erman and Eken suggest that the 'unregulated territories' of *gecekondu* areas, which exist outside of state regulations and functions, are appearing on the urban periphery (2004:67). People told me that drug dealers hang around the local primary school and this is why they tried to accompany their children when they went to school. The parents of teenagers, especially female teenagers, said that they did not want to raise their children here because of their fear of crime. Since they no longer found their neighbourhood safe, the residents of Ege did not want to go out at night or let their children play in the neighbourhood in the late evening as they used to do some years ago.

Conclusion

The rapid liberalisation of Turkey followed the suppression of oppositional elements, which used to be the main instruments for *gecekondu* people to obtain available sources. Their strategy to obtain these sources shifted to an individual-based one. This was compatible with the promotion of individualism in the post-1980 era and people were far less inclined to engage in collective struggle after the violent suppression of oppositional movements. Moreover, austerity measures implemented after 1980 resulted in significant segregation among the lower classes in terms of wealth and occupation. These sharply decreased the level of solidarity in Ege, as in many other *gecekondu* communities. The vacuum left by the absence of a sense of community and left-wing activism was not filled by the state authorities, which led to the feeling of insecurity increasing in *gecekondu* areas. Starting in the 1980s, the economic issues in urban areas were reduced by politicians to a mere problem of 'poverty'; the government initiated social assistance programmes, which were effectively used by the Islamist local governments and politicians in the 1990s and 2000s. These social assistance programmes initiated a moral economy in which beneficiaries shared the welfare. On the other hand, they created another tension around who was deserving of social assistance and a divisive mechanism in which entitlement to welfare is assumed to indicate support for the political party in power.

CHAPTER 6

A SOCIETY IN TRANSITION

Urbanisation has been considered to be one of the pillars of transition from a traditional society to a modern one (Schnaiberg 1970:419, Martinelli 2005: Chapter 2). But in light of the lack of sustainable social housing policy, the appearance of *gecekondu* areas lacking infrastructure facilities, the enlarging informal economy and migrants' dependence on hemşehrilik and kin networks rather than being individual members of the urban community, the urbanisation story of Turkey has been defined as haphazard and unplanned by urban planners, politicians and scholars alike. In this sense, the contribution of urbanisation to modernity in Turkey has been a contentious issue. Therefore a great deal of early research is dedicated to understanding the extent to which *gecekondu* dwellers transform into modern individuals (see Yasa 1966, Hunter 1964, Clinard 1966, Schnaiberg 1971, Levine 1973). However, in the early studies on *gecekondus* in Turkey, modernity was equated with an urban middle-class lifestyle and the adoption of consumption practices, so the early researchers tended to examine *gecekondu* dwellers' habits of reading newspapers, going to the cinema and theatre, brushing their teeth and so on. In the context of modernity and urbanisation, more recent studies examine *gecekondu* people's relationship with the state and politics, the *hemşehrilik* bond and the effect of apartment life in changing the lifestyles and values of *gecekondu* people after the urban transformation projects. It could be suggested that the available contemporary literature problematises the extent to which *gecekondu* dwellers turned into modern individuals who are bound by citizenship ties and can survive independently of their *hemşehri* and kin networks.

In terms of modernism, this research does not consider *gecekondu* dwellers' potential for adopting an urban middle-class lifestyle in terms of consumption practices as the early research did, but rather, along the same lines as recent research on *gecekondus*, it seeks to unpack the process by which the *gecekondu* dwellers develop aspirations to be a part of the larger urban economy with less dependence on *hemşehri*, kin and family networks. Throughout my research, increasing educational opportunities and changes in women's employment patterns seem to be the major dynamics through which the younger *gecekondu* generation has become familiar with the wider urban economy and urban middle-class people.

Education as a Tool of Alienation and Social Upward Mobility

The founders of the Turkish Republic were striving, by means of educational reforms, to be 'fostering the secular and nationalist values' (Özdalga 1999:419) and they saw education 'as the source of modern citizenship' (Pak 2004:325). However, in 1963, 40 years after the establishment of the modern Turkish Republic, there was still no school in one third of villages according to reports of the Turkish Great Assembly. In 2012, only 18,683 villages out of approximately 35,000 have a primary school and 6,613 have a secondary school (Ministry of National Education 2012:38). So, in spite of the great emphasis on universal education, there are still villages lacking even a primary school. For further education, kids in villages have to go to towns or enrol at the regional boarding schools. Additionally, children have economic value in rural areas. Sending children to further education or even to a primary school in the villages means losing valuable family labour in rural areas. Considering the patriarchal structure of the villages and the economic value of female children, particularly in terms of household chores, girls were more disadvantaged in terms of educational attainment. Fadime, who came to Ege at the end of the 1970s, told me that since there was no primary school in her village she was not able to go, even though her brothers were sent to the primary school in the neighbouring village. Hacer told me that she aspired to go to school but her stepmother did not allow her to continue after her second year because she wanted her to take care of her younger siblings. In brief, due to patriarchal values, the significance of child labour and an absence of schools, the first-generation migrants had not had the opportunity to go to school regularly. Among my interviewees, the highest educational level of the first-generation migrants in both the first and second wave was primary school.

There are greater educational opportunities in urban than in rural areas. Moreover, Ankara is more advantageous than many other urban areas in terms of educational institutions since it is the capital of the modern Turkish Republic. The availability of educational institutions contributed to the schooling of the children of rural migrants, especially at primary school. However, there were serious barriers for the migrants in squatter settlements to attaining further education. Tansel's study, based on the data collected by a household survey around the country by the State Institute of Statistics of Turkey, indicated that, although living in a squatter settlement did not influence the probability of primary schooling compared to the schooling of urbanites, it had a significant negative effect on the probability of middle schooling (2002:466). For example, there were no high schools until the early 2000s in Ege and all the kids had to go to high schools in districts closer to the city centre.

A regular household income is a determining factor in the schooling of migrants' children as well as of other children (Tansel 2002:467, McIntosh and Munk 2009:115). For households lacking a regular income or with a low regular income, the opportunity cost of children's schooling, which is associated with the children's labour and their delayed entry into the labour market, is high. In addition, the cost of schooling, such as clothes, books and transportation, weighs heavier for the first-generation migrant families. Economic value and the cost of schooling were the major reasons for drop outs from schools for the first generation migrants' children, particularly in the initial years after their migration. This is because, in the first years after their migration, most of the households lacked regular incomes and children's labour was inevitable. In this sense the families traded off the immediate costs of sending their children to school against the future benefits. Burhan, who had a shoe repair shop in Ege, arrived there in 1976 when he was a nine-year-old boy. He finished primary school in Ankara but could not attend middle school:

> [*dropping out of school*] [. . .] was not my preference, the life forced me to do it. I mean poverty. At that time, if you found a loaf of bread, you were missing the soup. We used to carry other people's

> coal only for a bucket of coal [. . .] Studying was not a priority as it is now. I did every kind of work when I was a kid. I worked as a street seller, construction worker, I carried bricks [. . .] My brother was like me, he was working with a shoe repairer when he was a kid. In due time, we improved our economic situation.

Considering the fact that regular income directly influenced the children's schooling and rural migrants could improve their economic situation over time, as in Burhan's account, birth order also played a major role in the schooling opportunities of the first-generation migrants' children. Younger children of the first-generation migrant families had more opportunities to go to school. This was because by the time the younger children got to school age, the family had improved their economic situation with the help of the older children. The gender of siblings was the other prominent factor that influenced the school attainment of the children of the first-generation migrants and girls were obviously more disadvantaged. But the daughters of the first generation had greater opportunities, at least in terms of primary schooling, than their mothers, who grew up in their villages, thanks to the availability of local primary schools in the city.

In spite of the serious barriers for the children of the first generation in terms of educational opportunities compared to their counterparts with urban-born parents, some of them obtained university degrees, found white-collar jobs, moved to other parts of Ankara and started to live in apartments like urbanites.[1] They were mostly the children of the first-generation migrants who had better job opportunities. So, these were mostly the children who had not had to work during school time. Gül and Mahmut, my landlady and landlord, had two sons and a daughter. All of them were university graduates, had white-collar jobs and lived in the urban centres. The parents told me that they never let their children participate in paid employment and Mahmut used to work at two different jobs while the children studied. The educated children of the first generation did not have the same lifestyle as their parents. Gül and Mahmut go to their home village every year but the children do not accompany them. Once their younger son, who was a teacher, came with them to their home village and wanted to help in the construction of a village house. Gül told me that she felt very sorry for her son since he was not used to working outside at manual jobs like his parents, therefore he was terribly affected by the sun and could not carry on helping them.

Importance of Role Models

Research shows that *gecekondu* youth are still disadvantaged in terms of further educational attainment (Tansel 2002:467) compared to the urban middle classes. Dropping out of school is not uncommon in Ege. For many Ege people this is due to the social environment of *gecekondu* areas. Hakan, who was a 30-year-old third-generation migrant and a teacher in the local primary school, conceptualised this as due to 'the lack of role models':

> The level of education in Ege is increasing but it is still low. You know, the kids here do not have true role models. All they see is the groups of young males smoking at the corners. So the kids copy them, what do you expect? In our time, we did not have role models. We did not know many people who attended university and got a job. At that time, we did not even know what a university was [...] Yes, I got a university degree, but it came about by chance. When I was a teenager, all we did was hang around; you know what young men do [...] In my last year at high school one of my best friends was studying for the university entrance exam because he had an older brother who was a university student. Whenever I visited him, I studied with him and I got the chance to go to university and become a teacher.

The narratives of other members of the third generation seem to support Hakan's suggestion about the significance of role models on the educational aspirations of *gecekondu* youth and parents. My interviews and informal talks with the older generations show that, despite their hopes and support for the further education of their children, due to the lack of role models, they seemed to believe that it was not likely that their children would be able to get as good an education as the urbanites and rich people. For example, Nazım, who was a second-generation migrant and had only been able to finish primary school, told me that his youngest son is good at his studies and he can get a high mark in the university entrance exam, but he told me that he was worried about the cost. In one of our informal talks, he asked me *Do you know how much ODTÜ costs for a year?* ODTÜ (Middle Eastern Technical University) is one of the top universities in Turkey and I explained to him that since it is a state university they do not need to pay any tuition fees. He was surprised and asked me again *So, if my son gets a high mark, can he go to ODTÜ for free?* The people around us were also surprised when I confirmed this to him. It seems that none of the local teenagers had applied to ODTÜ and since it is a very prestigious university, the older *gecekondu* generations thought that it must charge so much money that it would not be possible for *gecekondu* youth to go. This conversation with Nazım and the reactions of the people around us showed me that *gecekondu* people still feel excluded from the better educational opportunities.

The story of Ebru shows the importance of role models in terms of motivation for further education. Ebru is a high school student and her brother is a sergeant. Her brother strongly supports her to continue on to further education. Her parents have advised her to become educated like him. She told me that her parents encouraged her by advising her not to worry and saying that she could go to a university and have a white-collar job like her brother.

Intergenerational Conflict

Education not only provides jobs and social mobility but also a new social setting. It is the prominent sphere where the children of migrants interact with the urbanites. So, education makes the second and particularly the third-generation *gecekondu* youth familiar with the urban middle class and their lifestyle. As a result of this dense interaction, the children of migrants adopt the values of their urban counterparts. In this sense, education contributes to alienation between generations in migrant families (Qin 2006:172–6, Nesteruk et al. 2009:437–8). This frightened some parents among the first generation, especially in terms of their daughters' interactions with the urbanites. The first generation were concerned about honour and traditional values and they feared that by interacting with different people at school, their daughters would become urbanites and would be corrupted by urban values. Serpil came to Ankara in 1993 with her parents and sisters some years after her two brothers arrived to work. At that time, she was a primary school student and determined to continue on to middle school. She told me that, in spite of her insistence, her father Orhan did not let her go since he said that she was an outgoing and impressionable person (*gözü açık*). Ijaz and Abbas' study suggests, for first-generation South Asian Muslim migrants in the UK, that concern about their honour determined their preferences about their daughters' schools (2010:319–22). Just as these migrants preferred girls' schools because of considerations of honour, so it was the case for first-generation parents in Ege. Türkan came to Ege when she was two years old in the 1970s. After middle school, she insisted on continuing her education, but her father did not give permission. Türkan told me, *I was natty* [süslüydüm] *and my father said I will not send you to high school.* Then, her mother asked for help from his friend's wife and his friend persuaded Türkan's father. He allowed her to go to a girls only school. She said that at that time the most convenient was the girls' vocational school in the city centre, in spite of the distance. Her life changed completely after her registration at this school in the city centre in the 1980s and she talked about her high school years as follows:

> First I asked myself how did I jump in among these people, how would I mix with them? There were not many rural students there. All were from Çankaya, Yıldız; I mean most of them from families with high incomes. While I did not have money for lunch and had to bring my lunch from home, they used to buy whatever they liked from the school canteen. After a while I made very good friendships and I still meet some of my high school friends [. . .] I realised that I had not known anything before I went to this school in Sıhhiye.[2] I met different people there. I learnt how to speak, how to behave in social relations. I developed myself. Now I would like to move out of this neighbourhood because of this.

Türkan continued her story by describing how much emphasis she put on the education of her son and daughter. Like Türkan, many other second-generation migrants, especially women, regard education as the primary instrument of social mobility and securing white-collar jobs for their children. For them, education not only brings enhanced future earnings but also provides a decent life for their children and prevents them from having a life similar to theirs. Interviewees among the second generation told me that they invested all their time and limited savings for the education of their children. Women schedule their time according to their children's school time and activities. They spend a considerable amount of their time in the local primary school and undertake voluntary jobs in schools, accompany their children to school to keep an eye on their school environment and protect them from possible dangers and they frequently visit their children's teachers. Women who were prevented from having any schooling in particular care about their children's education. For the second generation, the education provided by the state schools is not satisfying; therefore, despite their low income they send their children to additional private courses and register them for extracurricular activities such as sports and music classes. Serpil has an eight-year-old son and they get by on the minimum wage[3] of her husband. She told me that:

> I would like my child to do a sport at least. Swimming courses were 100 liras per month. It was expensive. I registered him for a taekwondo class for 60 liras per month. It's still expensive but at least we don't pay for the transportation, we go on foot.

The *gecekondu* generation, who are third-generation migrants and beyond, have more opportunities to attain higher levels of education than their parents. This is also the case for international migrant generations (Kristen and Granato 2007:44, Aydemir et al. 2008:8). My research findings suggest that, for the *gecekondu* generation, the birth order and gender of children is less significant in schooling and obtaining further educational opportunities than the schooling of the first and second generations. Since the second generation had a more stable economic situation than the first generation, the effect of birth order on the third generation's schooling was less pronounced. This was why third-generation men and especially women had greater educational opportunities than their parents and grandparents. While the second generation of the first wave and the second-wave migrants generally have only a primary school education and rarely have high school qualifications, most of their children were able to study for university degrees. So the educational attainment of *gecekondu* dwellers increases gradually throughout the generations. Based on their further education attainment, the third generation expects that they will be more successful in getting white-collar jobs and having social mobility than their parents.

It seemed that the second generation in Ege agreed that there was no reason why women should not acquire education. Moreover, for some Ege people, women needed education more than men. Their common reason for this was to provide women with a safety net through education against domestic violence, economic difficulties, sexual harassment and discrimination against women in many aspects of the social distribution of resources. They mostly stated that a man could do a variety of jobs, such as construction worker, porter, carrier and the like while a woman could not. Moreover, the main male breadwinners said that they did not want their daughters/sisters to be dependent on their husbands and wanted them to be able to challenge their husbands in the case of domestic violence. Yiğit was born in Ege in 1979 and had worked since he was a teenager; he was the main breadwinner for his household, which was composed of his mother, divorced sister and her daughter. At this point, he said that:

> My niece is everything to me. She is academically successful; she currently goes to the high school and will be taking the university entrance exam in two years. I told her that I am ready to pay all her educational expenses. She should have a university education and a decent job. I do not want her to depend on her husband. She should stand on her own feet.

The third generation *gecekondu* youth expected that their lifestyles would be very different from those of their parents when they grew up. This expectation is based on the higher level of education they achieved and their better chances of obtaining white-collar and well-paid jobs. While none of the mothers of the participants in the focus group were in paid employment, the male participants claimed that they would probably marry women in paid employment; the female participants Ebru and Gönül stated that they would be highly likely to have white-collar jobs. At this point Gönül said that:

> For our parents, working is only for money. But it is understandable. It is because their level of education is quite low. Most of them graduated from primary school. But people with only primary school degrees are not employed in prestigious jobs, so they work for little money. Their main concern is survival. But our working conditions will be very different.

The third generation claimed that their family relationships would be different in terms of equality between spouses and consumption practices. During the focus group interview, Cihan, who grew up in Ege and attended the local high school, gave an example of going to the cinema. He said that, while his parents had never been to a cinema, he would certainly go frequently with his future wife. As Gönül followed by defining *gecekondu* families as families ruled by one person, other interviewees among the third generation suggested that they would have a more democratic family. Ercan, who was a high school student, told me that:

> There will be a gap between my marriage and that of my parents. For example, my mother does not have so much autonomy, but my future wife will be able to do whatever she likes.

The latest generation suggested that, due to their different life expectations, there is an intergenerational conflict between them and their parents. In this conflict, they found their parents to be 'backward' people who tried to impose the values and norms of their own time on the young generation. They usually expressed this as, 'it is not like their time anymore' and 'the times have changed'. These issues arose when the immorality or disrespect in the narratives of the first and second generation are perceived as freedom by the third generation. Bünyamin, who attended the local high school, told me that when his female classmates came to his house his father told him off and asked him whether these girls did not have parents to control them. It was obvious that the female third-generation migrants suffered more from the morality critics of older generations in their neighbourhood. The third generation tend to explain this as being due to the backwardness of their neighbourhood. In this sense, they did not consider Ege people to be modern or cultured like the inhabitants of the metropolitan districts of Ankara. Therefore, it was obvious that they were comparing their parents and grandparents with the urbanites. For them, the values of the older generation were not consistent with those of the urbanites, but they expect that the gap between the older generation and the urbanites will disappear in due time. This is why they defined their social setting as 'a society that tries hard to be modern'. During a focus interview conducted with a group of third-generation high school students in Ege, they stated that:

> My father is modern on many issues. However, when he saw me walking with a male friend his facial expression changed. I say he is my friend, but nothing changes. He does not understand this issue. But this is about the way that he grew up. He grew up in such a social setting. (Ebru)
>
> Our clothing style was weird to them. My father never let me wear skinny leg jeans. (Özcan)
>
> They project their perspective onto us, they expect us to have the same life perspective. You know, this results in limitating us. (Gönül)

While the third-generation youth mentioned that their neighbourhood was not like Çankaya,[4] which was considered a modern and progressive neighbourhood where people could behave freely, they stated that their urban counterparts were also different from them. In explaining this, they mentioned different consumption patterns. For them, the life of urban youth was based on the consumption of famous brand products and their behaviour was artificial. For *gecekondu* youth, urban youth seemed to be artificial since the urbanite youth had different hair, clothing and speaking styles to attract attention and they looked down on other people. For them, despite their material resources and consumption capacities, the *gecekondu* youth have warmer relationships, which could not be traded off for brand new mobile phones and fancy sports shoes. However, they mentioned that *gecekondu* youth copied urban youth. Bünyamin said:

> It is said that 'if you wear a nice pair of shoes, go to Kızılay [*city centre*], then all the girls will want to date you.' So many poor young people style their hair. They do it to attract attention.

On the other hand, these parents try to give whatever they can to their children, in order to provide a better life for them. Since their children have much more than the older generations could imagine, these parents expect their children to be satisfied. Therefore, for the older generations the main reason for the intergenerational conflict emerged out of dissatisfaction and the disrespectful behaviour of the younger generations. Elif, who came to Ege in 1975 and used to work as a domestic servant, said: *there was not enough food, so we could not eat much.*

My kids look down on what I cook now. Hayat, who mentioned her encounter with urbanites and their aspirations in the previous chapter, continued her life story by talking about the relationship between herself and her children. This time, she compared her life to her children's lives as follows:

> Chicken [. . .] when our mother cooked chicken I had an argument with my siblings about who would eat the biggest portion. But, look now, when I cook chicken the children sniff at the food. When our parents bought us a pair of trousers we would not know how to thank them, but my kids do not thank us! Now, I do not buy clothes for myself but I buy them for my daughter because I do not want her to emulate anything. But she is not aware of this. Once she told me that, 'my dad has enough money and you can buy things for me,' so she does not understand that we do our best to provide her with anything she likes. I do not want her to suffer as I suffered in my childhood. On the other hand, I would like my kids to be aware of the poverty and severity of life. But no, they are not like this.

The complaints of the first and second generation involved issues of morality and respect. For them, the younger generation did not know how to respect society, their families or the elderly. However, for the first and second generation this was not a problem specific to *gecekondu* youth. All youth in Turkey is like this and the *gecekondu* youth copy them. The examples they commonly gave are about the more comfortable attitudes of young people such as smoking in front of the elderly, wearing fashionable clothes and the loose relations between young women and men. They usually emphasized that the boys and girls could not walk hand in hand in Ege and date one another. Osman told me that, in the 1980s, it was not possible for a woman to wear a mini skirt or that he could not smoke in front of older men as a young boy and young people could not openly have boyfriends/girlfriends. On the other hand, the third generation migrants did their best to empathise with their parents.

The expressions they used, such as: 'it was different in their time', 'they grew up in the village' and so on, show that the third generation accepts the fact that their parents and grandparents grew up in a different social setting than theirs. For this reason, they do not expect their parents to change and become similar to the urbanites quickly.

When a female high school student, Ebru, told me that her father did not feel comfortable with the idea of her having male friends, she added that, because her father was born and grew up in a village and in a traditional closed community, she could not expect more from him. Moreover, it seems that, in contrast to what the older generations suggest, *gecekondu* youth appreciate that their parents suffered due to a lack of economic resources and that they worked hard to provide their children with more resources. During my interviews with the teenagers of Ege, they expressed their appreciation of their parents thus:

> Gönül: My grandparents did not let my father go to school, although he would have liked to. They told him 'go and take care of the animals'. This is why he could not study. But he never asked me to work; on the contrary, he always supported me to study. So, I have to study.
>
> Ebru: Look, I always try to learn from my parents. They did not have the chance to go to school and this is why they do their best to enable me to study. They provide me with every opportunity; I have to study so as not to embarrass them.
>
> Cihan: My parents, too. I mean they are so regretful and angry with their own parents [...] You know because their parents prevented them from studying. At that time, I mean, they were in villages where people did not know about the value of education. Now they [my parents] do whatever they can to make us able to study.

Furthermore, despite their greater opportunities for education, the students among the third generation still need to find jobs during holidays and weekends. Temporary jobs during school summer holidays, such as sales assistant, pollster, leaflet distributing, waiter/waitressing for boys and girls and helping fathers at their workplace, such as in construction and restaurants and the like, for boys, are not uncommon among the third generation. In a focus group interview conducted with high school students in Ege, the participants stated that they either gave the money that they earned during the summer holidays to their mothers as a contribution to the household budget or kept it to meet their educational needs, such as for books, private courses and computers. In fact, this showed that the *gecekondu* generations understand that their parents give their children everything within their capacity and the *gecekondu* generation try to help by contributing to the family budget rather than spending their income on entertainment or clothes and so on.

In brief, while the parents among the first and second-generation migrants in Ege compare their children with their own childhoods, the children compare their parents with the parents of their urbanite friends. It could be suggested that the intergenerational difference in terms of expectations and consumption patterns has increased in the relationship between the second and third generation compared to the one between the first and second generation. This was mostly caused by the increasing use of technological facilities with the introduction of the internet in Turkey in 1994 and the greater opportunities for education among the third generation compared to their parents. The narratives of third-generation migrant youth show that they are caught between urban values and their parents' values. For them, acquiring urban values means modernity which will bring freedom, but these values are also associated with artificiality and alienation from warm human relationships.

Despite their hopes of obtaining white-collar jobs and having better living conditions than their parents, the third-generation youth in high school is worried and concerned about the increasing unemployment of university graduates. This has been a hot subject of discussion in Turkey, especially during the economic crisis of 2001 and 2008–12. Moreover, the jobs that used to be considered secure, such as teachers and state officers became less secure jobs[5] for which university graduates have to take a highly competitive exam (KPSS – the Selection Examination for Professional Posts in Public Organisations).[6] The unemployment rate for university graduates in the age group 20–4 was 32.2 per cent in 2010 (Tansel 2012:103). Considering the 'waitresses with engineering degrees' and 'thousands of unemployed university graduates', they told me that they were not so hopeful about the future. In fact, it could be suggested that further education promises fewer opportunities for social upward mobility for the third generation than it did for previous generations.

There has been a public primary school in Ege District since 1987. In the Turkish education system, the curriculum for the state schools is prepared by the Ministry of National Education and the same curriculum is applied to all state schools. Moreover, the allocation of teachers to the schools is not based on their professional qualifications.

However, many second-generation *gecekondu* dwellers with relatively higher regular incomes and more aspirations to raise their children as urbanites prefer the state schools in the city centre for their kids in Ege. They told me that the state schools in the city centre provide better education. On the other hand, it is quite obvious from their narratives that they are not considering the level of educational quality, so much as the social status of the people whose children attend these schools. They would like to prevent their children from making friends with other *gecekondu* children; rather they try to mix them with the children of urbanites. Aladdin was one of these people and he explained the reason for his preference of a primary school in the city centre for his seven-year-old son as follows:

> I do not want to look down on anyone, but you know the children of this neighbourhood, you know their levels [. . .] They swear, use slang language. I try to provide my son with the best of everything. I do not want him to be like one of them, I do not want to raise him in *varoş* culture [. . .] When you send your child to a school in the city centre, you should be prepared. For example, the child sees other parents who give a lift to their children by BMW. They use pencils from famous brands. So, you are not supposed to buy your kid low-quality pencils and the like.

In Ege, the children who are sent to schools in other districts gradually lose their connection to their neighbourhood. Basically, they do not have any friends in their district, so during the school holidays and in their leisure time they only stay at home. Since they socialise with the urbanites from the very beginning of their education, they become alienated from their social environment, parents, *gecekondu* life and their neighbourhood. For example, Türkan's daughter Selin, an 18-year-old high school student who was born in Ege district, told me that she did not want to live in a *gecekondu* and she hesitated to invite her friends to her house. She explained that the main reason for her detachment from her neighbourhood was that she did not have any friends in Ege because she had been going to schools in the city centre since kindergarten and socialised only with the middle-class urban kids. Considering the narratives of Türkan and Selin, it could be suggested that the alienating effect of education has increased among the third generation compared to the second generation. On the other hand, the third-generation migrant youth who have been socialising mostly with people in their own neighbourhood and attend the local schools are more comfortable in their social settings. They do not have aspirations to live in multistorey apartment blocks where they suppose there is no warm relationship between neighbours and young people. However, during our interviews when I asked the *gecekondu* youth about the kind of houses in which they would live in the future, they told me that they would be living in apartment blocks not in *gecekondus*. They explained to me that this is not because they prefer it, but because in the future there will not be any *gecekondus*. For them, in spite of the warm human relations in *gecekondu* areas, *gecekondus* are not an appropriate type of house for our time and are destined to vanish. At this point, *gecekondu* youth suggested that, although the neighbourhood relations were finished, the urban transformation projects are necessary and good for the whole country. Selim is a high school student who works during weekends and school holidays at a local grocery shop, where I shopped almost every day. Since he is academically successful he believes that he will be able to have a white-collar job and will have a better life than his parents. He told me:

> I will live in apartment blocks in the future. I mean, if I can find a decent job. If not, I will stay here [. . .] Apartment blocks, I know it isn't good for neighbourhood relations but the number of *gecekondus* is decreasing and there will not be any in the future.

In brief, the results of this research suggest that the teenagers who do not spend their time with other local teenagers and whose families are slightly better off than most of the local people not only want to live in apartment blocks, they also have aspirations to live there. On the other hand, the *gecekondu* youth who have a large group of friends locally and need to work think that since the apartment blocks fulfil the necessities of our time, they will have to live there. So, depending on their family income, future aspirations and the type of school they go to, the *gecekondu* youth have different views on urban transformation projects and the integration of *gecekondu* areas into city life. However, in general, the *gecekondu* youth is influenced by the idea that apartment blocks are the contemporary form of accommodation and are a sign of development and also that urban transformation projects are good for everybody, including *gecekondu* dwellers themselves. For them, the appearance of new high-rise buildings shows that their neighbourhood is in the process of urbanisation and modernisation.

Women's Paid Employment

The first-wave migrant women were rarely in paid employment. This was due to their unfamiliarity with urban areas, lack of required skills, their responsibility for the household chores and childcare and the lack of male family members' permission. Due to the lack of infrastructure in *gecekondu* areas during the initial years after the migration, the women spent a great deal of time on household chores and this prevented them from going out of their homes and neighbourhood (Wedel 2001:25). In Ege, for the first-generation women in paid employment, available jobs were limited to manual jobs in the service sector such as cleaning staff in companies and state offices. Domestic service (*gündelikçilik*) was one of the common jobs in informal employment for migrant women. In domestic service work, slum women worked in middle-class and upper middle-class houses on a daily basis without any social security. This job was mostly found through networks of other female relatives who were in paid employment, neighbours and *hemşehri*s. Although they earn more on average than in other informal jobs, this type of work is perceived as the most inferior job among the slum women since it is considered to be cleaning 'the other's dirt'.[7] It could be suggested that their main motivation for doing this kind of exhausting work was to gain money for the household. They considered their work temporary and a contribution to the family budget (Şenyapılı 1981:195) and quit as soon as the family overcame its economic difficulties. Considering the exhausting nature of the available jobs and the lack of opportunities to obtain social upward mobility, the women did not expect anything but money out of these jobs. For them, quitting the work meant 'being comfortable' (*rahata ermek*). As Çınar (1994:374) suggests about migrant women in İstanbul, many first-generation migrant women in Ege were proud of the fact that their husbands did not let them work outside. In the same vein, they seemed to be proud of their sons who asked them to stop working after they started to earn a regular income.

Duration of stay has a positive impact on women's school attainment and participation in paid employment (Schnaiberg 1971:89–94). Most of the male first-generation migrants changed their attitude towards the paid employment of women. For example, while Mahmut did not allow Gül to work in a factory in spite of her insistence, he let his daughter to go to university and get a job. He told me that he was ashamed now that he had not let Gül work. But at that time it was not easy for him since he wanted to avoid possible gossip. He continued:

> You know, at that time it was shameful *(o zamanlar ayıptı)* for a woman to work outside. I considered what our *hemşehris*, relatives and *mahalleli* would think about it. I did not want them to gossip that Mahmut got his wife to work. But times have changed. Now I am so proud of my daughter that she is standing on her own feet.

In spite of better opportunities for education, familiarity with urban areas and the fact that attitudes towards women's working outside have changed in a positive direction, not many women were in paid employment. For the second-generation migrants, paid employment depended on the number and age of their children, the available assistance from the other females around them in terms of childcare, the immediate needs of the family, their skills and the permission of the male members of the household (see Chapter 3). For them, employment meant more than gaining money and was a tool for 'standing on one's own feet', 'avoiding dependency on a husband' and 'gaining relative autonomy and freedom'. The women in paid employment preferred to keep their money for themselves and have secret kitties. Like Eroğlu who studied the women in 17 *gecekondu* neighbourhoods of Ankara (including Ege), my research suggests that women spend their income on household needs and mostly on their children (2011:224). Türkan said that when her children asked for something she avoided seeking permission and money from her husband since he would probably delay it. It was also to prevent disputes among the family members.

According to the results of this research both paid employment and educational opportunities dramatically increased for the women among the third generation compared to their mothers and grandmothers. In terms of jobs and educational opportunities, the difference between the second and third-generation migrant women was much bigger than the difference between the first and the second generations. Nearly all of the interviewees among the second generation agreed that girls should acquire education and should work. This change in attitude towards women's employment and education affects the first-generation migrants. For example, Orhan, who was strongly opposed to his daughter, Serpil, getting further education and working outside the home, supports his youngest, 19-year-old, daughter-in-law's decision to work outside.

My research suggests that the attitudes of women among the third generation towards women's working are different from those of the first and second-generation female migrants. For women in this category, working is a must for a woman and it should not require male permission. Significantly different from the women of the first generation, the third generation do not regard employment only as an instrument for income generation. For them, a woman should not depend on her husband and in this sense their concerns about working are similar to those of the second-generation women. The main point upon which their attitudes differ from the women of the second generation is that they have aspirations for their careers. Additionally, they feel responsibility for their families since most of their families have invested a considerable amount of their savings in their daughters' education. Ebru was a 17-year-old third-generation woman in Ege. Her parents strongly supported her education and her older brother, who was a sergeant and lived separately from his parents, paid for additional courses (*dershane*) for her. She said that:

> My grandfather did not let my father study although he desperately wanted to go to school. For the people of that time, money was more important. This is why he strongly supports my education. I appreciate this. We should take lessons from our parents and develop ourselves. My father made an effort for my education, so I must not embarrass him.

Younger third-generation migrant women search for university departments and vocational schools suitable for them. They ask their teachers to help them in choosing high schools and universities. If their parents have enough income, they attend private *dershane*s (additional prep institutions for exams). Some of them attend the complementary courses provided by NGOs or work in small jobs during the summer school holiday to save money to pay for *dershane*. Young women among the third generation prefer the university departments that they believe will provide them with secure jobs such as education, nursing, dentistry and so on. Additionally, they aspire to the occupations that are intimately linked to gender stereotypes. Their preferences for departments are quite different from those of their male counterparts, who mostly aspired to go to the engineering faculties. Young females in deprived families seek the shortest ways by which they can obtain a profession. Arzu's family have major problems, her mother has serious physical and psychological problems, they had to move frequently because of her father's job before he passed away several years ago and finally they do not have a regular income. At the time of our interview, she was a middle school student and would take the high school exam in two years. Her account revealed that all her life had been shaped by uncertainties. She told me: *I don't want to be homeless when my mother dies* and she went on:

> I would like to go to vocational school. It could be a vocational health school. I could be a nurse [. . .] To be honest, I don't fancy being a nurse, I don't like seeing blood and injures. But [. . .] let's suppose that I go to Anatolian High School,[8] what happens if I fail the university entrance exam? But if I go to a vocational school, at least I acquire a job immediately after finishing the school.

Women's Strategies for Accumulating Money

It is noteworthy that it is not only women in paid employment who are able to accumulate savings and keep secret kitties. *Gecekondu* women have various techniques to obtain money for their concealed savings. They could save the money from household shopping, by cutting back on personal expenditure and inflating claimed household expenditure (Eroğlu 2009:63). Moreover, *kabul gün*s have been a technique for women to save money or gold coins. *Kabul gün*s are reception days for women on fixed or known days of the week or month for entertainment where they eat various foods prepared by a hostess in the privacy of their houses. But it is common at these *kabul gün*s to present the hostess with gold coins or a predetermined amount of money. *Gecekondu* women tend to accumulate this money for large household expenditures.

In households with relatively high income and less male control, women's concealed savings can reach a considerable size and they usually buy gold to protect the money from inflation, which is a common way of saving for women in Turkey. Deniz's five-person household's income is around seven times the minimum wage, which is considerably higher than the average household income in Ege. His family is more liberal compared to many other families in terms of a relatively less gendered division of labour at home and a lack of strict male authority. For example, Deniz and his two brothers spend some of their time in the house working, their female friends can visit them and Hatun, their mother, does not ask permission to go out of the house. Deniz told me that whenever they had an unexpected expenditure Hatun came up with some *çeyrek altın*s (quarter golden coins). When I asked how she could manage to accumulate *çeyrek altın*s, she responded as follows:

> I save from my pocket money mostly [. . .] even from bread. For example, a loaf of bread left over from yesterday, so today I do not need to buy any. I keep the bread money for my savings. When I had accumulated enough I bought gold.

Gecekondu women keep secret kitties even in the case of a tight household income and strict male supervision. Gülden is a 30-year-old woman who has a nine-year-old son and a drug-addicted husband. She lives in a *gecekondu* which is separated by a wall from her in-law's house. Her husband, Semih, has temporary jobs and was unemployed at the time of the interview. He strictly controls her and does not let her to go out of the neighbourhood and she needs his permission to visit her neighbours. They do not pay the rent, their bills are paid by Semih's parents and they receive welfare from the council. She is rarely given cash by her husband or in-laws. So for her it is nearly impossible to keep concealed savings. She tries to accumulate food stock in order to channel her husband's money to reduce his spending on entertainment and to secure enough food for the household. She stated that:

> Let's say there are two bottles of vegetable oil in the kitchen. I conceal them and ask my husband to buy one. He is not spending his money for the household, you know him. It is not just for this. What if I do not have enough food one day? Whom can I ask? I cannot depend on him.

For the women who are firmly controlled by their husbands, keeping secret kitties is not always possible even if they work. Several years ago,

Gülden looked after her husband's friend's baby for a while. The parents of the baby paid her directly; they knew that her husband would spend the money on his entertainment rather than giving it to Gülden. She did not keep the money at home and asked her next-door neighbour to keep it safe for her in order to prevent her husband from finding the money and spending it on his entertainment. But after some time he started to ask his friend to pay him directly.

Women's Strategies to be Employed

The first and second-generation migrant women, who were not allowed to work outside by their husbands or fathers, did not give up and found various strategies. As Dedeoğlu (2008:113–5) argues, all migrant women are aware of the patriarchal pressure on themselves and that the gender ideology limits their resources. However, rather than challenging patriarchy directly, the migrant women try to find the best survival strategy with the scarce available resources provided within the patriarchal community structure and neoliberal economic system. When their husbands and fathers prevent them from engaging in income-generating activity, they do not challenge patriarchal authority directly and they seem to agree with the male authority. However, they do not give up and, as Kandiyoti (1988) would suggest, they bargain with patriarchy. The common strategy they use is to consult a person whom they think their fathers/husbands would trust. As stated in the previous pages, Serpil's father did not allow her to continue her education, so she decided to acquire a job. Her father did not let her do so. She did not say anything to him at that time but later she secretly asked for help from her aunt. The aunt persuaded Orhan and found her a job in a hairdresser's shop. She worked in this shop for four months and started to learn the required skills to be a hairdresser; however, her improvement and working life were undermined by her father's concerns about honour. One day she returned home with some flower-shaped beads in her hair, which were quite popular among the girls in the 1990s and that day Orhan beat her up and said: 'this girl is deviant'. He did not allow Serpil to work again in order to protect her from corruption. It can be said that, in the case of strict supervision by the father, marriage is the main strategy used by single women. Via marriage, the women are transformed into individuals in the community whereas single girls are invisible and are subject to the decisions of their family, mostly of male family members. Dedeoğlu's study also shows that after marriage women consider themselves individuals who have their own decision making power and they become freer to declare their ideas to their families (2008:116–20). On the other hand, with marriage, the women become surrounded by the authority of their husbands and in-laws. Consequently, it can be said that marriage is a double-edged strategy for women. To follow Serpil's story: She got married several months after her father prevented her from working outside. A week after her marriage, her husband found a secretarial job for her in the city centre. But this time her father-in-law was offended and quarrelled with her. However, she did not leave her job until she had her first baby.

Patriarchal social formations not only give men the authority to permit women to work, but also give them a say in the type of work the women do. While this increases male control over women, it also opens up another bargaining space for women who would like to work outside. Women who are prevented by their fathers/husbands from economic activity try to find a job that their husbands/fathers may consider suitable. For example, Turan did not let his wife Türkan work outside their home since he thought his income was more than enough for the survival of the family. Türkan did not insist on her request; however, she spoke to Turan's nephew who had a white-collar job and lived in a central district of Ankara and asked if she could work as a domestic servant in his house. The nephew agreed to this idea and Türkan started to work in his house part-time. Turan conceptualised this as *Türkan is helping my nephew* and he allowed her to work there since it was a safe area for him. In this bargain, men's power over women's income-generating activity and public visibility is not directly challenged; on the contrary, it is reaffirmed by the women. However, despite confirming male authority over their labour, women find a way to work outside and have more autonomy.

Under the sway of neoliberalism, *gecekondu* households had to find survival strategies to struggle against their increasing poverty. This pushed some women into paid employment (see Chapter 3). This could be interpreted as the primary reason for the increasing rates of participation in paid employment for the second and third-generation women compared to their first-generation counterparts. Considering the market conditions, their lack of education or the appropriate skills and language, the duties of a traditional housewife, the lack of public childcare facilities, discrimination against women in the labour market and the patriarchal social formation, home-based working is preferable for *gecekondu* women. Ege women who are under extreme male supervision in particular prefer this kind of work. Following Gülden's story, despite being unemployed, her husband, Semih, does not allow her to be occupied with any income-generating activity. For him, this is an assault since it challenges his masculinity. During our interview, Semih told me that:

> I would never let my wife work. Look, she doesn't need anything, she doesn't need to worry about the rent or the bills and she has enough food to cook. So what? Whether I am unemployed or not, this is none of her business. She should be just busy with cooking, cleaning and caring for our son.

He only let her to take care of his friend's baby because he knew this person and he interpreted this job as helping rather than working. After Gülden's child got sick, she had to quit this job. Like many other Ege women, she did not ask again. For Gülden, as for many other women, home-based working is a preferable option since it is an income-generating activity for which they either don't need to get consent or they can do without consent. She started to do craftwork for sale. Although this is a common leisure activity for women, Gülden told me that when Semih was at home she abstained from doing it since he might realise. When he went abroad to work a year ago, she was able to earn 300 liras (nearly half of the minimum wage) monthly from her craftwork.

Conclusion

Urbanisation, as one of the main pillars of modernisation, changes the values of rural migrants and provides the *gecekondu* youth and women with more chances of paid employment and further education. Becoming familiar with urban values has a significant impact on the attitudes of *gecekondu* youth and women, as well as those of the older generations, towards female education and employment, the role of education, the function of the moral economy and urban transformation projects. However, urbanisation has failed to provide the same chances as the urban middle class have to the younger generation and women in *gecekondu* areas in terms of employment in white-collar jobs and further education facilities.

CONCLUSION

Rural to urban mass migration was a response to changes in development policies in Turkey during the 1950s and 1980s. In most cases, male members of rural families migrated to the city first and the women followed them. Rural women supported their husbands in moving to the city at the expense of losing the community support in their villages since they considered migration to be a release from the strict control of in-laws and tough daily chores and to bring more opportunities for their kids. Due to the absence of social housing and affordable accommodation, migrants occupied land that mostly belonged to the state and built their houses on it. Since it was a chain migration, more and more people came from the rural areas and *gecekondu* communities emerged. My participants' life stories showed that when the available lands in central *gecekondu* neighbourhoods filled up, newcomers as well as second-generation *gecekondu* dwellers found new areas to build new *gecekondu* neighbourhoods such as Ege. This resulted in cities surrounded by *gecekondu* neighbourhoods.

Although most of the *gecekondu* women did not participate in paid employment at the very beginning, they built their *gecekondus* with the men, carried water and improved their *gecekondus.* Their skills of production at home were indispensable for the survival of the family because they enabled them to depend less on cash. The *gecekondu* dwellers, despite their diversity in terms of faith and place of origin, worked collectively to ameliorate conditions in their neighbourhood and obtain title deeds to secure their existence in the cities. This work shows clearly how inadequate the term 'slum dwellers' is to describe the dynamism and extraordinary talents that have emerged and developed in this area as a result of the long process of internal migration.

From the perspective of the state and capitalists, they were the new working class, who solved their own accommodation problems without placing a burden on the shoulders of the state or the market. Since the interests of *gecekondu* dwellers, capitalists and the state were compatible with one another, a series of Gecekondu Amnesties were passed between 1948 and 1986. But this was not a smooth or easy process of legalising *gecekondus*. During this time period, sometimes *gecekondus* were destroyed, sometimes the demolition teams turned a blind eye and sometimes the *gecekondu* neighbourhoods were provided with infrastructure facilities even before the legalisation of their *gecekondus*. Because of the ambiguity of this process, title deeds distribution became the prominent instrument in winning the votes of *gecekondu* dwellers. On the other hand, the *gecekondu* dwellers were not passive in their relations with politicians and they succeeded in legalising their houses and gaining access to infrastructure facilities thanks to bargains with politicians and their collective struggle. Moreover, the people whose *gecekondus* were demolished never gave up on rebuilding them since they did not have any other option and they hoped that there would be further amnesties that would legalise their *gecekondus*.

Gecekondu communities emerged as a response to changes in development policies and grew out of the necessity for collective action during the 1950s. The *gecekondu* dwellers were quite aware of the fact that if their numbers increased and they struggled together they would win the power to remain in the city and improve their living conditions. Although they had different faith backgrounds and places of origin, their new situation in the city was similar in terms of their immediate needs for jobs, housing and infrastructure and they shared a feeling of exclusion from participating in city life. As mentioned by my participants, these commonalities enabled them to overcome other differences and to act together for their neighbourhood and all these factors resulted in the development of *gecekondu* communities. Moreover, the relatively powerful left-wing embraced the *gecekondu* people and helped them to improve their living conditions and this contributed to the building of *gecekondu* communities during the 1960s and 1970s.

The coup d'état in 1980 marked a turning point for *gecekondu* communities as well as the rest of Turkey. It suppressed all the oppositional elements, therefore the leftist movement disappeared in *gecekondu* neighbourhoods and people became afraid to come together and act collectively. Moreover, due to the structural adjustment policies introduced immediately after the coup d'état, the gap between the social classes increased and the state gave up its previous role of referee among them. This brought in more insecure jobs, less state protection, the individualisation of society and the promotion of consumption. The need for cheap labour attracted more people from rural areas and the number of *gecekondu* dwellers increased. In their struggle against increasing poverty, *gecekondu* women started to look for jobs. The newcomers took up the jobs that no one else wanted; some of them became employees of the early comers and some of them bought/rented *gecekondus* from the early comers. Since the last Gecekondu Amnesty only legalised the *gecekondus* built before 1986, most of the newcomers did not obtain legal title deeds for their homes. So, *gecekondu* dwellers diversified in terms of the kind of job they held and ownership of their *gecekondus*; therefore migrants' position was not the same as before. This contributed to a decreasing level of solidarity among *gecekondu* dwellers.

The increasing level of poverty caused by the structural adjustment policies did not remain untouched. Following the coup d'état in 1980, the government introduced Social Assistance and Solidarity Foundations (SASFs) in 1986 with Law No. 3294 for poverty alleviation; however, the budget was not used effectively. The Welfare Party, a political Islamist party, used this fund, mobilised its resources and massively distributed food and coal throughout the municipalities during the 1990s. AKP, the political party in government and successor to the Welfare Party, enlarged the scope of this welfare during the 2000s. My fieldwork showed me that, for *gecekondu* dwellers, receiving this welfare directly denoted the recipients' political views. So, welfare distribution created a new separation dynamic for the *gecekondu* dwellers.

Capitalism created a new dynamic in Turkish cities, as well as in many other parts of the world, as a new instrument for generating income and marketing the cities was on the agenda of the AKP during the 2000s. In terms of urban planning, the 2000s were marked by urban transformation policies, which mostly aimed at gentrifying the *gecekondu* areas. In the face of these projects, which were based on formal ownership of squatter houses, the *gecekondu* dwellers' interests were not all the same.

The early comers, who had formal title deeds, were compensated when their *gecekondus* were destroyed and they became well-off. On the other hand, the newcomers' *gecekondus* were demolished without any concrete compensation since they did not have formal title deeds. At this point, the latecomers returned to their solidarity practices, struggled collectively for their housing rights and collaborated with the socialist movement. My findings clearly show that the *gecekondu* dwellers with formal title deeds did not contribute to the struggle of the dispossessed *gecekondu* dwellers. This division demonstrates the dissolution of the sense of community. Moreover, drawing on my interview data, I can say that most of the formal title deed holders will not be able to live in the future luxury apartments due to the monthly service cost and most of them were planning to sell these apartments in order to buy more than one house in a less prestigious area of Ankara to provide their children with houses. In brief, neither the dispossessed nor the beneficiaries will be able to enjoy the improvements in their neighbourhoods, even though they were the ones who overcame all the difficulties and turned Ege into a liveable neighbourhood.

Besides gender and the time of migration, generational differences created diversity among the *gecekondu* dwellers, especially in terms of educational attainment, job opportunities and dependence on family, kinship and neighbourhood networks. Although the level of education of the *gecekondu* generation is still not as high as that of urbanites, they have had more opportunities than their parents and grandparents. Many of them had the opportunity to continue into higher education. Education is the prominent space where the *gecekondu* youth get familiar with urbanities. Finding the kinship, family and neighbourhood networks to be constraints, they feel far more a part of the urban economy. So, the younger generation wishes to make space – physical, emotional and intellectual – between themselves and the older generation.Their expectations about their future jobs and lives increased and the younger generation in my fieldwork told me that their lives and marriages would be very different from those of their parents in terms of cultural practices, such as going to the cinema frequently and giving an equal say to each family member.

Although the younger generation in Ege told me that they had more chance of finding white-collar jobs than the previous generation, given the high levels of unemployment among university graduates they seemed to be worried. This is mostly why *gecekondu* youth preferred the vocational schools, which gave them access to the labour force sooner than university and the professions that they perceived to be secure, such as doctor, teacher, nurse and so on. The younger female generation told me that, although their parents had control over them in terms of having male friends and what they wore, they encouraged them to study. Since previous generations of women did not receive this support, the female *gecekondu* generation went much further than their mothers and grandmothers and there was a much larger education gap than that between male youth and the previous male generations. While the older generations were largely convinced that women should have equal opportunities in education with men, the younger females told me that they would like to work not only to generate income but also so that they could be independent of men.

The self-perceptions of *gecekondu* people were redefined at each step by their encounters with urbanites. Initially, their primary reference for defining their identity was place of origin. This was mostly because they used to depend on their kin, relative and *hemşehri* relationships to find *gecekondus* and jobs. During the developmentalist period of the 1960s and 1970s, *gecekondu* dwellers were silently welcomed by the welfare state since the political system was based on the inclusion of all classes. Moreover, the relatively powerful socialist movement appreciated them and wanted to be in solidarity with them since they were defined as *halk* (people) and working class by the socialist movement. Many *gecekondu* dwellers, especially the Alevis, were inspired by the socialist discourse and combined their rural background with the identity of worker. Since their primary concern was having a roof over their heads, they were mostly engaged with the problems around ownership of a *gecekondu* and improving their neighbourhood. In this sense, the building of *gecekondu* identity involved solidarity among the *gecekondu* dwellers and being *mahalleli* became another dynamic that defined their identity. What all these features of their identity had in common was that they were not urban people. Due to the gains that early comers made out of the urban transformation projects and their relatively better jobs in city centres, they started to feel closer to the middle class. But they still related many conflicting narratives which show that they still feel the difference between the urban middle class and themselves, especially in terms of consumption practices and level of income. The *gecekondu* dwellers who did not benefit from the urban transformation projects also told me that they felt closer to the middle class and had improved their situation. This was mostly because they compared their current situation with their past and therefore felt well-off. They also felt this improvement because of the investments in cities such as the construction of new roads, bridges, shopping malls and so on, even though their level of income did not allow them to enjoy most of these facilities.

In brief, my study in Ege shows that the emergence and development of *gecekondu* communities was a response to the changes in development policies and was generated by the survival strategies of the *gecekondu* dwellers. *Gecekondu* people had no option other than acting collectively and building up communities in order to survive and improve their lives. This work also shows that the sense of community in *gecekondu* areas had gradually started to dissolve by the second half of the 1980s when the gap between social classes widened and the whole of society became more individualised. This was also a time when the differences between first and second-comers in terms of occupation and the ownership of their homes became more obvious. This process of falling apart was accelerated by the welfare policies implemented during the 1990s. The urban transformation projects had the largest effect on this process since the differences between people crystallised as large numbers of the first settlers started to move out and middle-class people started to move into the gentrified *gecekondu* neighbourhoods. Moreover, while the older generations are anchored in kinship and neighbourhood networks, the younger generation do not have close ties with their parents' hometown, *hemşehris* or the local people with whom their parents worked in solidarity in their attempts to become integrated into city life and this breaks the very ties that were the basis of older generation *gecekondu* people's existence. Based on my research, I can suggest that the *gecekondu* areas are undergoing a huge transition period in which the people not only lose their houses and neighbourhoods but also their community. *Gecekondu* people, who are the urban poor, and the problems associated with *gecekondu* areas such as poverty, insecurity, unemployment, low levels of education and so on are dispersing to other areas of the cities. So, as the *gecekondu* areas gradually disappear, these problems do not disappear with them. As the sense of community dissolves, *gecekondu* dwellers turn into the urban poor with very limited social protection available to them from the established networks of community and the family.

This study sheds new light on the experiences of rural migrants and it is argued that, although they are heavily dependent on the moral economy of kin and neighbourhood solidarity upon their arrival, they abandon these ties once they become successful and feel ashamed of them and constrained by them. Therefore, the process of migration depends on the moral economy but also destroys it. In this sense, this study offers a new perspective to students of migration and development. Urban planners, particularly in developing countries with rapid rural to urban migration and urbanisation, should consider this work since it highlights the necessity for these planners to consider the lived experience of slum dwellers in particular, who need different forms, facilities and accommodation. Without such consideration, it would be extremely difficult for planners to continue.

While the majority of early studies on *gecekondus* focused on the processes of migration and the physical establishment of *gecekondus* (see Yasa 1966, Karpat 1976, Kıray 1970, Öğretmen 1957), contemporary studies highlight issues such as the moral economy, poverty, solidarity networks, welfare distribution and urban transformation in *gecekondu* areas (see Erdoğan and Bora 2007, Buğra 2007, Güzey 2009, Erman 2001, Özyeğin 2001, Eroğlu 2011, Çınar 1993, Dedeoğlu 2008, Özyeğin 2002, Çelik 2010, Murakami 2011). Since my research is based on the life story of a *gecekondu* neighbourhood from its establishment to integration, it can reflect on both the community's physical establishment and the other issues that contemporary studies focus on. As my findings related to the physical establishment of Ege are consistent with previous works in terms of the fact that *gecekondus* were built step by step and local people helped one another, it also suggests that once the *gecekondu* people obtained the necessary skills and knowledge about *gecekondu* building, they used them to establish other *gecekondus* later and they always remained hopeful about future Gecekondu Amnesties. The case of Ege, where people built more *gecekondus* in Yakupabdal, shows that *gecekondu* people, regardless of the legal ownership of their *gecekondus*, feel that their position is insecure and use the skills and knowledge that they gained during the initial years of *gecekondu* establishment to find spare plots and build houses.

Despite the emphasis on the potential for crime in *gecekondu* areas by the media and in mainstream political discourse (Keleş 2010: 483), research considering crime and *gecekondus* does not dominate. In addition to the few contemporary studies on crime and *gecekondus*, which suggest that the crime is related to exclusion and is a way of becoming accepted and being a part of city life (Erman and Eken 2004: 67, Yonucu 2008: 65), my research findings indicate a strong relationship between the increasing insecurity in *gecekondu* areas and the decreasing social solidarity and disappearance of social movements.

An early piece of research on *gecekondus* conducted by Kemal Karpat in three *gecekondu* districts in İstanbul showed that *gecekondu* people's religious and social identities and attachments are represented by their activities. These revolved around the community and religion, which was considered to be a part of the village communal culture (1976: Chapter 5). Drawing on his findings, he clearly stated his expectation that the idea of community would continue in some form despite some possible changes (Karpat 1976:128). His research was conducted long before the emergence of religious communities and Islamist parties who rely on the idea of community and succeed in addressing the *gecekondu* dwellers, but it did give insights that help us to understand the potential for *gecekondu* people to be recruited by religious communities and the Islamist movement which highlight the idea of community and become the current instruments for social cohesion and making more space for *gecekondu* people.

The political Islamist movement, which started in the 1980s, became empowered during the 1990s and in spite of the factions and diversity among the organisations in the movement, the AKP, which is a political Islamist party, came to power with an overall majority in 2002. The Welfare Party in the 1990s and the AKP in the 2000s mobilised their resources through local government, councils and their business networks and reached out to *gecekondu* people, who are mostly excluded by or at the margins of the existing market economy. The rise of the Islamist movement in the 1990s had a large impact on the studies of *gecekondus* in Turkey and the discussions about civil society, welfare, local communities and religious communities attracted the attention of many scholars (see White 2002, Işık and Pınarcıoğlu 2002, Çelik 2010, Buğra 2007, Erder 1996, Eroğlu 2010). Jenny White's work on Ümraniye, a *gecekondu* district of İstanbul, focused on the Islamist activists' methods of approaching *gecekondu* people and attempted to explain their success in recruiting them. Her study suggests that the Islamic movement's organisation and its messages were based on the local culture (2002:31), it channelled its available resources towards the daily necessities of *gecekondu* people and the Welfare Party benefitted from the practice of *imece* and moral economy among *gecekondu* dwellers in translating complex political ideas into a 'culturally embedded, personally transmitted message' (p. 210). So, the Islamists realised the importance of community – which was mentioned by Karpa (1976) – interpersonal dependence and mutuality for the survival of *gecekondu* people and were able to carry both their resources and their messages to the *gecekondu* communities. Işık and Pınarcıoğlu's (2002) work on Sultanbeyli, another *gecekondu* neighbourhood in İstanbul, took a step forward and discussed the transformation of social relations in *gecekondu* areas through the new channels opened up by the rise of the Islamic movement. Their work suggested that, in a social setting where the line between formal and informal, legal and illegal, was often blurred, the networks provided by the religious communities turned into a new instrument for the *gecekondu* dwellers to improve their welfare and transfer their poor conditions to newcomers (2002: 334–6). They concluded that urban areas in Turkey are not composed of anonymised citizens but consist of the sum of groups which are densely organised through community relations (p. 335).

The Islamic mobilisation is more about linking everyday practices, cultural values and social relations to new forms of public life and political practice rather than about religion itself (White 2002:271). However, its message was based on Sunni Islamic rhetoric. Due to the historical oppression of the Alevi population in Anatolia as early as Ottoman times, Alevi *gecekondu* dwellers could not be addressed by the message of the Islamic movement. In contrast, they could be easily addressed by the organisations inspired by Kemalist ideology since the majority of Alevis are attached to this ideology because of its promise of secularism. However, the secularist groups could not fit their secular, modern and Kemalist lifestyle ideas to local normative values (White 2002:258) and failed to reach *gecekondu* people or to provide them with new instruments for upward mobility. At this point, while the contemporary academic interest in *gecekondus* focused on *gecekondu* areas whose population was largely Sunni, who could be approached by religious communities and Islamic parties, my work focuses on a *gecekondu* neighbourhood where the majority of the population is Alevi. My research could be considered as complementary to the current works on *gecekondus* in the sense that it illustrates the survival strategies of a *gecekondu* community which is lacking in new instruments and channels for upward mobility. The Islamic mobilisation could be a new sphere for creating civil society, social cohesion, mutual support and a sense of community, as shown by the other contemporary works; however, it could also turn into a practice of exclusion for those *gecekondu* communities whose identity is not compatible with the lifestyle offered by the Islamist mobilisation, as suggested by my work. Moreover, my work illustrates that the solidarity practices and welfare distribution by the Islamic movement, regardless of whether it is handed out through formal or informal channels, could have a divisive role among *gecekondu* dwellers, as the receiving of welfare from the religious communities or the municipalities ruled by the AKP could be seen as a sign of political commitment on the part of the receiver. So, the Islamist mobilisation can rebuild social cohesion in mostly Sunni *gecekondu* neighbourhoods but, on the other hand, on a larger scale, it destroys the solidarity practices among *gecekondu* dwellers. Therefore, without considering the experiences of *gecekondu* communities that could not access the resources provided by the Islamic parties and the religious communities, which were the most successful movements in reaching the urban poor, neither the *gecekondu* dwelling experience nor the role of the Islamic movement in building civil society and social cohesion and distributing welfare can be grasped properly. In this sense, the role of the Islamic movement in providing new channels and relations for upward mobility should be considered in a broader framework which also includes the communities that cannot benefit from these new channels and solidarity practices and as a result become more marginalised.

ABBREVIATIONS

AKP	Justice and Development Party (*Adalet ve Kalkınma Partisi*)
ASKİ	Ankara Water and Sewer Administration (*Ankara Su ve Kanalizasyon İdaresi*)
CHP	Republican People's Party (*Cumhuriyet Halk Partisi*)
EUTP	Ege Urban Transformation Project (*Ege Kentsel Dönüşüm Projesi*)
FP	Virtue Party (*Fazilet Partisi*)
ISI	Import Substitution Policy
KPSS	The Selection Examination for Professional Posts in Public Organisations (*Kamu Personeli Seçme Sınavı*)
MHP	Nationalist Action Party (*Milliyetçi Hareket Partisi*)
RP	Welfare Party (*Refah Partisi*)
SAP	Structural Adjustment Policy
SASF	Social Assistance and Solidarity Foundations (*Sosyal Yardımlaşma ve Dayanışma Fonu*)
SHP	Social Democratic People's Party (*Sosyal Demokrat Halk Partisi*)
SP	Felicity Party (*Saadet Partisi*)
TBMM	Turkish Great Assembly (*Türkiye Büyük Millet Meclisi*)
TEDAŞ	Turkish Electricity Distribution Company (*Türkiye Elektrik Dağıtım Anonim Şirketi*)
TOKİ	Mass Housing Authority (*Toplu Konut İdaresi*)
TSK	Turkish Armed Forces (*Türk Silahlı Kuvvetleri*)

GLOSSARY

Abi	Older brother
Abla	Older sister
Alevi	Follower of Alevism which, in the context of Turkey, refers to Islamic heterodoxy
Amca	Paternal uncle
Amele Mahallesi	Workers' district
Ardiye	Literally meaning storage; *gecekondu* people bought the materials required for *gecekondu* construction there
Baraka	Shanty house
Bekar Odaları	Bachelor rooms
Bey	Sir/Mr
Cem	The central Alevi communal worship service which is performed in houses called *Cemevi*s
Çankaya	A district in Ankara home to mostly affluent people
Çöplük	Waste dump
Dolmuş	Shared taxi
Erişte	Noodles, a special kind of pasta mostly made by women at home
Fakirlik Kağıdı	Proof of poverty
Gariban	Dispossessed
Gecekondu	It literally means 'built overnight' and refers to squatter houses and areas in Turkey
Gecekondulu	Slum dweller

Gündelikçi	Domestic worker
Hanım	Miss/Mrs/Ms/Lady
Hemşehri	Fellow countryman
Hemşehri Dernekleri	Fellow countryman association
Hemşehrilik	A social link between migrants from the same place of origin
İhtiyar Heyeti	The Council of Elders; a body consisted of locally elected persons to assist *muhtar* in administering *mahalle*s/villages
İmece	A shared work process in which the work of each member is completed in order
Kabul Günü	Reception days for women on fixed or known days of the week or month for entertainment, where they eat various foods prepared by a hostess in the privacy of their houses
Kaymakam	District governor
Kaymakamlık	District governorate
Kızılay	A central neighbourhood in Ankara known for its trading and shopping centres.
Mahalle	Neighbourhood
Mahalleli	People living in the same neighbourhood
Mamak	The district in Ankara in which Ege is located
Muhtar	Elected governor of a neighbourhood or village
Salma	Village tax
Sunni	A follower of Sunni belief which, in the context of Turkey, refers to Islamic orthodoxy
Tanıdık	Acquaintance
Tapu Tahsis Belgesi	Provisional title deeds
Teyze	Maternal aunt
Tuzluçayır	A former *gecekondu* neighbourhood in Mamak
Ülkü Ocakları	Literally meaning Ideal Houses, a grassroots organisation of the MHP (Nationalist Action Party)
Yeminli Özel Teknik Bürolar	Special technical offices which apply Gecekondu Amnesties
Varoş	Slum area (with a strong implication of insecurity)

NOTES

Preface

1. For her article, see Şentürk, D. (2012).

Introduction

1. See UN Human Settlements Programme (2003) Chapter 3 and Davis, M. (2007), Chapter 2.

Chapter 2 Internal Migration and *Gecekondu* Communities in Turkey

1. The *dolmuş* is important in understanding the *gecekondus* of Turkey. Due to the lack of public transportation provided by local authorities, individuals in *gecekondu* areas initiated *dolmuş* transportation. So, while this satisfied the need for accessibility of *gecekondu* areas in the 1960s, this transportation business has become widespread in the long-term and is usually controlled by migrants in large cities. For further information, see: Tekeli and Okyay 1977, Dolmuşun Öyküsü, Çevre ve Mimarlık Bilimleri Yayınları, Ankara.
2. For a case study examining the legally defined role of *muhtars* in villages, their functions and historical changes in this role, see R.B. Scott (1968).
3. Hattatoğlu insists on the fact that home-based production was done by women, so calling this activity 'household strategies to struggle with poverty' or household labour might conceal the fact that it is women's labour that is spent on these activities (2007:19).

Chapter 3 Building a *Gecekondu* Neighbourhood, Community and Identity

1. Among the Alevi Kurds, there has always existed a dilemma about whether their loyalty should be to their ethnic or religious community (Çelik 2003). The Kurdishness of Alevi-Kurdish people in Ege was a bit ambiguous since they did not declare that they were Kurdish, what they said was 'we have Kurdish ancestry'. They did not know how to speak Kurdish and they emphasized the Alevi features of their identity rather than their Kurdishness.
2. The most well-known violence against Alevis is the Maraş Massacre of 1978 (see Sinclair-Webb 2007). The prime perpetrators of this massacre were the Grey Wolves, the grassroots fascist organisation of the ultranationalist MHP (Nationalist Action Party). It was an attack on leftists by the right-wing, on Kurds by Turks and especially on Alevis by Sunnis (McDowall 2005). Official numbers suggested that 109 people, most of whom were Alevis, were killed and 500 shops and homes were destroyed. The other prominent violent attack was the Sivas Massacre. This happened on 2 July 1993 and resulted in the deaths of 37 people, most of whom were Alevi intellectuals. On this day, the writers, intellectuals and musicians were in Otel Madımak in Sivas to commemorate Alevi poet Pir Sultan Abdal, who was a major figure in Alevi culture. After the traditional Friday prayers (*Cuma namazı*), militant Muslim fundamentalists set fire to the hotel. Every 2 July, thousands of people, especially Alevis, gather to commemorate the arson of the Madımak Hotel in Sivas.
3. A *mahalle* is the smallest unit of the Turkish urban and rural administrative system. A district is made up of seven *mahalle*s.
4. Turkish Electric Authority (TEK) was established in 1970 and in 1993 it was divided into two public companies TEAŞ (Turkish Electricity and Transmission Company) and TEDAŞ. So, although the name of the institution was TEK when Ege people asked for electricity in the 1980s, since people today mention the current name, TEDAŞ, I use this name.
5. Grey Wolves never defined themselves as 'fascists' or 'neofascist'.
6. For a historical discussion on the relation between Alevis and the socialist movement and central left, see Küçük, M. (2008).
7. Currently, a new type of greeting among male nationalists has emerged: They shake each other's hands, lean forward and touch their temples mutually from the right and the left.
8. Fasting during Ramadan is common among Sunni people and *sahur* is the meal eaten by fasting people just after dawn during Ramadan.
9. Early in his career he donned a symbolic working man's cap and was rarely seen in public without it. He also shunned luxury cars and big apartments and was untainted by accusations of corruption that plagued many of his political colleagues (Turgut 2006). His nickname was *Karaoğlan* (Black Boy). It could be asserted that this nickname revealed that the people thought Mr Ecevit was one of them. During the 1970s, the famous slogan was '*Umudumuz Karaoğlan!*'

(Black Boy is our hope!), which demonstrated that the working class and the grassroots leftist activists trusted him.

10. In its general meaning, *cemaat* refers to community in Turkish and in its narrow meaning it is a group of people who belong to the same religious group. Here *cemaat* is used in its narrow meaning of a religious community.
11. Literally, *gavur* means non-Muslim. In modern Turkish, *gavur* has a pejorative meaning and refers to Christian people (mostly western Christians) in an offensive way. In its general sense, the word can be used to describe a heartless, mean and unjust person. In Ege district, it was the first time in my life that I heard a person use this notion to describe an Alevi person. It was only İbrahim who used this word. Other Sunni people did not use it to describe Alevis.

Chapter 4 Urban Reforms in Ege

1. For the pilot field research of this study, I visited Harman neighbourhood. Multistorey TOKI (Mass Housing Authority) apartments were recently built in Harman and these buildings attracted middle-class people. The local people claimed that public transportation used to be unavailable on the hilly parts of Harman. They said that thanks to TOKİ buildings and the new people, the Council has provided them with public transportation. In this sense, the appearance of middle-class people in *gecekondu* areas which are under transformation has accelerated the improvement of urban services. The local people seemed to be welcoming the new middle-class people. Like Ege people, for Harman people, the residents of their neighbourhood would gain from attracting middle-class people. In one of my visits to the muhtar's office in Harman, a young female in a suit and with make-up dropped in for a written proof of residence. It was the first time that the muhtar had seen this woman. Soon after learning that she was a lawyer and lived in the TOKİ buildings, the muhtar told me '*this kind of people are what we need. We need people who were brought up in this district and have become successful like her.*'

Chapter 5 Dissolving of the Community

1. In spite of approaches which suggest that employment is a struggle against poverty, approximately 30 per cent of all workers in the world live with their families below the US$2 a day poverty line (ILO 2012: 41). This has been the case for Turkey since 1980. In Turkey, the proportion of employed poor in the population over 15 was 15.37 per cent in 2009 (TUIK, Results of 2009 Poverty Study)
2. Uğur Mumcu was a prominent Kemalist intellectual and investigative journalist. He was assassinated by a bomb placed in his car outside his home in 1993 and his murder has not yet been solved.

3. For more information about the Sivas Massacre, see Chapter 3, n. 2.
4. The hidden meaning is that if civil servants cannot survive on their low incomes, they are smart enough to accept bribes.
5. According to data from the Ministry of Health, the number of Green Card holders was 14,541,791 before the general elections of 2007. This dramatically decreased to 9,230,604 after the general elections (Çelik 2010:75).
6. For a critical discussion on AKP's labour market policies, see Bozkur and Yalman (no date). See also Yeldan (2005) for a detailed analysis of privatisation in Turkey.
7. Gülistan Aydoğdu, who lives in Ege, mentions the smoke from the coal in her short article on social assistance and the urban transformation project in Ege. See, Aydoğdu (2012).
8. Buying new clothes during Eids, especially for the unmarried children of the family, is a common habit in Turkey.
9. Metehan is another name for Ege district.

Chapter 6 A Society in Transition

1. Since these people do not live in Ege anymore, I interviewed their parents.
2. Sıhhiye is one of the central and oldest districts of Ankara.
3. The minimum wage at the time of the interview was 715 liras a month (GBP 250).
4. Çankaya is one of the metropolitan districts of Ankara. It is a fashionable business and cultural centre as well as the centre of government.
5. According the Turkish Statistical Institution, for the age group 15–34, only 65.3 per cent of graduates from the education department were employed in 2009 (TUIK 2009).
6. For a detailed account of the unemployment of university graduates in Turkey see Bora, A. et al. (2012).
7. For a detailed analysis of domestic service in Turkey see Özyeğin, G. (2001).
8. Anatolian High Schools were prestigious state schools that were established as an alternative to expensive private schools teaching in foreign languages in Turkey.

BIBLIOGRAPHY

Abadan, N. (1963). *Social Change and Turkish Women*, Ankara: Ankara University Press.

Acker, J., Barry, K. and Esseveld, J. (1983). Objectivity and truth: Problems in doing feminist research, *Women's Studies International Forum*, 6 (4), 423–35.

Afshar, H. and Dennis C. (1992). *Women, Recession and Adjustment in the Third World: Some Introductory Remarks in Women and Adjustment Policies in the Third World*, London: The Macmillan Press.

Ağartan, T. (2012). Marketization and universalism: Crafting the right balance in the Turkish Heath Care System, *Current Sociology*, 60 (4), 456–71.

Akbulut, M.R. and Başlık, S. (2011). Transformation of Perception of the Gecekondu Phenomenon, *METU Journal of the Faculty of Architecture*, 28 (2), 1–44.

Alpar, İ. and Yener S. (1991). *Gecekondu Araştırması*, Ankara: Devlet Planlama Teşkilatı.

Altıntaş, B. (2003). *Mendile, Simite, Boyaya, Çöpe ... Ankara Sokaklarında Çalışan Çocuklar* [Children working in Streets], İstanbul: İletişim Yayınları.

Altuğ, S., Filiztekin, A. and Pamuk, Ş. (2008). Sources of long-term economic growth for Turkey, 1880–2005, *European Review of Economic History*, 12 (3), 393–430.

Amis, P. (1987). Migration, urban poverty and the housing market: the Nairobi case, in J. Eades (ed.), *Migrant, Workers and the Social Order*, London and New York: Tavistock Publications, pp. 249–68.

Aslan, Ş. (2008). Yasalar ve Kamu Yönetiminin Politikaları Üzerinden Türkiye'de Gecekondu Sorunu, *Yönetim Bilimleri Dergisi*, 6 (1), 155–66.

——— (2009). Kentsel Mekanda Yeralma Biçimlerinden Tasfiye Edilme Projelerine Kadar Gecekonduya İlişkin Değişen Söylemin Toplumsal Anlamı, M. Akdağ and F. Atar (eds), *6.Ulusal Sosyoloji Kongresi Bildiri Kitabı*, pp. 952–63.

——— (2010). *1 Mayıs Mahallesi: 1980 Öncesi Toplumsal Mücadeleler ve Kent* [1 May Neighbourhood: Social Movements and City before 1980], İstanbul: İletişim Yayınları.

Ataay, F. (2001). Türkiye Kapitalizminin Mekansal Dönüşümü, *Praksis*, Spring 2, 53–96.

Auyero, J. (2000). The hyper shanty-town: Neo-liberal violence (s) in the Argentine Slum, *Ethnography*, 1 (1), 93–116.

Ayata, S. (1996). Patronage, Party and State: The Politicization of Islam in Turkey, *Middle East Journal*, 50 (1), 40–56.

Ayata S. and Güneş-Ayata A. (1996). *Konut, Komşuluk ve Kent Kültürü* [House, Neighbourhood and City Culture], Ankara: T.C. Başbakanlık Toplu Konut İdaresi Başkanlığı.

Aydemir, A., Chen, W.H. and Corak, M. (2008). Intergenerational Education Mobility among the Children of Canadian Migrants, Discussion Paper Series, IZA DP No. 3759 Institute for the Study of Labor [Online]. Available at: http://papers.ssrn.com/sol3/papers.cfm?abstract_id=1286697 [Accessed 10 October 2012].

Aydın, K. (2009). Social Stratification of Culture and leisure in Turkey, *Cultural Trends*, 18 (4), 295–311.

Aydın, Z. (2005). *The Political Economy of Turkey*, London: Pluto Press.

——— (2010). Neoliberal Transformation of Turkish Agriculture, *Journal of Agrarian Change*, 10 (2), 149–87.

Bağımsız Sosyal Bilimciler [Independent Social Scientists] (2006). IMF Gozetiminde 10 Uzun Yıl: 1998–2008 [10 Long Years under the Supervision of the IMF: 1998–2008] [Online]. Available at: http://www.emo.org.tr/ekler/22ed7eafe03b631_ek.pdf?tipi=36&turu=X&sube=0 [Accessed 23 May 2011].

Bailey, K. (1994). *Methods of Social Research*, New York: Free Press.

Bali, R.N. (2009). *Tarz-ı Hayat'tan Life Style'a: Yeni Seçkinler, Yeni Mekanlar, Yeni Yaşamlar* [New Elites, New Spaces and New Lives], 8th edition İstanbul: İletişim Yayınları.

Bartu, A. and Kolluoglu, B. (2008). Emerging spaces of neoliberalism: a gated town and a public housing project in Istanbul, *New Perspectives on Turkey*, 39, 5–46.

Başlevent Cem and Dayıoğlu M. (2005). The Effect of Squatter Housing on Income Distribution in Turkey, *Urban Studies*, 42 (1), 31–45.

Bauman, Z. (1990). *Thinking Sociologically*, Cambridge, Massachusetts: Basil Blackwell.

Bayraktar, U.S. (2007). Turkish Municipalities: Reconsidering Local Democracy Beyond Administrative Autonomy, *European Journal of Turkish Studies* [Online]. Available at: http://ejts.revues.org/1103 [Accessed 22 August 2013].

Bell, C. and Newby, H. (1971). *Community Studies*, London: George Allen and Unwin Ltd.

Bergan, R. (2009). Women home-based workers organizing for economic rights: case studies from Bulgaria and Turkey, *Gender and Development*, 17 (2), 219–29.

Biernacki P. and Waldorf D. (1981). Snowball Sampling: Problems and Techniques of Chain Referral Sampling, *Sociological Methods & Research*, 10 (2), 141–63.

Birbili, M. (2000). 'Translating from one language to another', *Social Research Update* 31 [Online]. Available at: http://sru.soc.surrey.ac.uk/SRU31.html [Accessed 8 July 2013].

Bora, A. (2007). Kadınlar ve Hane: 'Olmayanın Nesini İdare Edeceksin?', in N. Erdoğan and T. Bora (eds), *Yoksulluk Halleri Türkiye'de Kent Yoksulluğunun Toplumsal Görünümleri* [Social Reflections of Urban Poverty in Turkey], İstanbul: İletişim Yayınları.

Bora, A., Bora, T., Erdoğan, N., Üstün, İ. (2012). *Boşuna mı Okuduk? Türkiye'de Beyaz Yakalı İşsizliği* [White Collar Unemployment in Turkey], İstanbul: İletişim Yayınları.

Boratav, K. (1981). *Tarımsal Yapılar ve Kapitalizm* [Agricultural Structures and Capitalism], Ankara: Ankara Üniversitesi Basım Evi.

——— (2004). *Türkiye İktisat Tarihi 1908–2002* [History of Turkish Economy 1908–2002], Ankara: İmge Yayınları.

——— (2005). *1980'li Yıllarda Türkiye'de Sosyal Sınıflar ve Bölüşüm* [Social Classes and Distribution in Turkey in the 1980s], Ankara: İmge Kitabevi Yayınları.

Bovenkerk, F. and Yeşilgöz, Y. (1999). The Turkish Mafia, *Crime, Law & Social Change*, 31 (1), 80–5.

——— (2004). The Turkish Mafia and the State, in C. Fijnaut and L.Paoli (eds), *Organized Crime in Europe: Concepts, Patterns and Control Policies in the European Union and Beyond*, Dordrecht: Springer, pp. 585–601.

Bozarslan, H. (2007). Alevism and the Myths of Research: The Need for a New Research Agenda, in P.J. White and J. Jongerdeen (eds), *Turkey's Alevi Enigma: A Comprehensive Overview*, Leiden: Brill, pp. 3–16.

Bozkurt, S. and Yalman G. (no date). Case Study: AKP Governments and the Social and Labour Market Policy Transformations in Turkey in the 2000s [Online]. Available at: http://www.emergingcountries.org/pdf/labour%20market.social%20policy.Turkey.pdf [Accessed 13 October 2013].

Braun, F. (1988). *Terms of Address: Problems of Patterns and Usage in Various Languages and Cultures*, Berlin, New York, Amsterdam: Mouton de Gruyter.

Brenner, N. and Theodore, N. (2002). Cities and the Geographies of 'Actually Existing Neoliberalism', *Antipode*, 34 (3), 349–79.

Bruinessen, Van M. (1995). *Kürdistan Üzerine Yazılar*, İstanbul: İletisim Yayınları.

——— (1996). Kurds, Turks and the Alevi revival in Turkey, *Middle East Report*, 200, 7–10.

Bryman, A. (2001). *Social Research Method*, New York: Oxford University Press.

Buğra, A. (1998). The Immoral Economy of Housing in Turkey, *International Journal of Urban and Regional Research*, 2 (2), 303–17.

——— (2007). Poverty and Citizenship: An Overview of the Social–Policy Environment in Republican Turkey, *International Journal of Middle East Studies*, 39 (1), 33–52.

Buğra, A. and Keyder, Ç. (2006). The Turkish Welfare Regime in transformation, *Journal of European Social Policy*, 16 (3), 211–28.

Buğra, A. and Sınmazdemir, T. (2005). Yoksullukla Mücadelede İnsani ve Etkin bir Yöntem: Nakit Gelir Desteği. Unpublished paper, Boğaziçi University Social Policy Forum [Online]. Available at http://www.spf.boun.edu.tr/docs/STGP_Bugra.pdf [Accessed 03 October 2013].

Carmichael, F. and Ward, R. (2001). Male Unemployment and crime in England and Wales, *Economics Letters*, 73 (1), 111–15.

Castles, S. and Miller, J.M. (2003). *The Age of Migration: International Population Movements in the Modern World*, New York: The Guilford Press.

Castells, M. (1997). *The Power of Identity*, Oxford: Blackwell Publishers.

Central Bank of Turkish Republic (2000). Estimating the Underground Economy in Turkey [Available Online]. Available at: http://www.tcmb.gov.tr/research/discus/dpaper43.pdf [Accessed 29 January 2014].

Chant, S. (1994). Women, Work and Household Survival Strategies in Mexico, 1982–92: Past Trends, Current Tendencies and Future Research, *Bulletin of Latin American Research*, 13 (2), 203–33.

Cizre, Ü. (eds), (2008). *Secular and islamic politics in Turkey: the making of the Justice and Development Party*, New York: Routledge.

Clinard, M.B. (1966). *Slums and Community Development: Experiments in Self-Help*, Toronto: Collier MacMillan.

Clough, P. and Nutbrown L. (2002). *A Student's Guide to Methodology: Justifying Enquiry*, Los Angeles, London: Sage.

Cohen, A. (1998). *The Symbolic Construction of Community*, London: Routledge.

Coşar, N. and Demirci, S. (2009). Incorporation into the World Economy: From Railways to Highways (1850–1950), *Middle Eastern Studies*, 45 (1), 19–31.

Crompton, R. (1993). *Class and Stratification: An Introduction to Current Debates*, Cambridge: Polity Press.

Çeçen, A.A., Doğruel, A.S. and Doğruel, F. (1994). Economic Growth and Structural Change in Turkey 1960–88, *International Journal of Middle East Studies*, 26 (1), 37–56.

Çelik, A.B. (2003). Alevis, Kurds and Hemşehris: Alevi Kurdish revival in the nineties, In J. Joost and P.J.White (eds), *The Alevi enigma: a comprehensive overview*, Leiden, Brill, pp. 141–57.

——— (2010). Muhafazakar Sosyal Politika Yönelimi: Hak Yerine Yardım Yükümlülük Yerine Hayırseverlik, *İstanbul Üniversitesi Siyasal Bilgiler Dergisi*, 42, 63–81.

Çetintaş, H. and Vergil, H. (2003). Türkiye'de Kayıt Dışı Ekonominin Tarihi, *Doğuş Üniversitesi Dergisi*, 4 (1), 15–30.

Çınar, M. (1994). Unskilled urban migrant women and disguised employment: Home-working women in Istanbul, Turkey, *World Development*, 22 (3), 369–80.

Davis, M. (2007). *Planet of Slums*, London and New York: Verso.

Dedeoğlu, Saniye. (2008). *Women Workers in Turkey Global Industrial Production in Istanbul*, London, New York: Tauris Academic Studies.

Delaney, C. (1991). *The Seed and the Soil: Gender and Cosmology in Turkish Village Society*, Berkeley and Los Angeles: University of California Press.

Demirtaş, N. (2009). *Social Spatialization in a Turkish Squatter Settlement: The Dualism of Strategy and Tactic Reconsidered*, Frankfurt: Peterlang.

Demirtaş, N. and Şen, S. (2006). Varoş Identity: The redefinition of low income settlements in Turkey, *Middle Eastern Studies*, 43 (1), 87–106.

Deniz, M.B. (2010). *Grassroots Action Against Gecekondu Renewal Projects: The Case of Istanbul Başıbüyük and Ankara Dikmen Vadi*, Unpublished: Boğaziçi University, MA.

DİE (State Institute of Statistics) (1999). *Ücretler Gelir ve Gelir Dağılımları*, Ankara.

Dinçer, İ. (2011). The Impact of Neoliberal Policies on Historic Urban Space: Areas of Urban Renewal in İstanbul, *International Planning Studies*, 16 (1), 43–60.

Dinerstein A.C. and Neary, M. (2001). *The Labour Debate: An Investigation into the Theory and Reality of Capitalist Work*, Hants, Vermont: Ashgate Publishing House.

Drakakis-Smith, D. (1987). *The Third World City*, New York: Methuen & Co.

Duben, A. (1982). The Significance of Family and Kinship in Urban Turkey, in Ç. Kağıtçıbaşı et al. (eds), *Sex Roles, Family and Community in Turkey*, Indiana University Turkish Studies, pp. 73–99.

Dubetsky, A. (1976). Kinship, primordial ties and factory organization in Turkey: An Anthropological View, *International Journal of Middle Eastern Studies*, 7 (3), 433–51.

——— (1977). Class and Community in Urban Turkey, in C.A.O. Van Nieuwenhuijze (eds), *Commoners, Climbers and Notables*, Leiden: E.J. Brill, pp. 360–72.

Duyar-Kienast, Umut. (2005). *The Formation of Gecekondu Settlements in Turkey: The Case of Ankara*, Munich: Litverlag.

Dündar, Ö. (2001). Models of Urban Transformation: Informal Housing in Ankara, *Cities*, (18) 6, 391–401.

Ecevit, Y. (1998). Küreselleşme, Yapısal Uyum ve Kadın Emeğinin Kullanımında Değişmeler, in F. Özbay (eds), *Küresel Pazar Açısından Kadın Emeği ve İstihdamındaki Değişmeler* [The Change in Woman Labour and Employment from the Perspective of Global Market], İstanbul: İnsan Kaynağını Geliştirme Vakfı Yayını, pp. 31–78.

——— (2007). Yoksulluğa Karşı Feminist Bir Strateji İçin. *Amargi*, 6, 14–7.

Edlund, J. (1999). Trust in government and welfare regimes: Attitudes to redistribution and financial cheating in USA and Norway. *European Journal of Political Research* 35 (3), 341–70.

Eller, J.D. (1999). *From Culture to Ethnicity to Conflict: An anthropological perspective on international ethnic conflict*, Michigan: The University of Michigan Press.

Elson, D. (1991). Male bias in macro economics:the case of structural adjustment, in D. Elson, (eds), *Male Bias in The Development Process*, Manchester: Manchester University Press, pp. 164–90.

Erder, S. (1996). *Ümraniye İstanbul'a Bir Kent Kondu*, İstanbul: İletişim Yayınları.

——— (1997). *Kentsel Gerilim*, Ankara: Uğur Mumcu Araştırmacı Gazetecilik Vakfı Yayınları.

——— (1999). Where do you hail from? Localism and Networks in İstanbul, in Ç. Keyder (eds), *İstanbul Between the Global and the Local*, Lanham: Rowman and Littlefield Publishers, pp. 161–72.

Erdoğan, N. and Bora, T. (eds), (2007). *Yoksulluk Halleri Türkiye'de Kent Yoksulluğunun Toplumsal Görünümleri* [Social Reflections of Urban Poverty in Turkey], İstanbul: İletişim Yayınları.

Erendil, A. (2003). 'Made in Turkey', Threads: Newsletter of the Clean Clothes Campaign 16 [Online]. Available at: http://www.workerolympics.org/about-us/323 [Accessed 04 June 2010].

Erman, T. (1997a). Squatter (gecekondu) Housing versus Apartment Housing: Turkish Rural- to-Urban Migrant Residents' Perspectives, *HABITATINTL*, 28 (1), 91–106.

——— (1997b). The Meaning Of City Living For Rural Migrant Women And Their Role In Migration: The Case of Turkey, *Women's Studies International Forum*, 20 (2), 263–73.

——— (1998). Becoming 'Urban' Or Remaining 'Rural': The Views Of Turkish Rural-To-Urban Migrants On The 'Integration' Question, *International Journal of Middle East Studies*, 30, 541–61.

——— (2001). The Politics of Squatter (Gecekondu) Studies in Turkey: The Changing Representations of Rural Migrants in the Academic Discourse, *Urban Studies*, 38 (7), 983–1002.

Erman, T. and Eken, A. (2004). The 'Other of the Other' and 'unregulated territories' in the urban periphery: Gecekondu violence in the 2000s with a focus on the Esenler Case, İstanbul, *Cities*, 21 (1), 57–68.
Erman T. and Göker, E. (2000). Alevi Politics in Contemporary Turkey, *Middle Eastern Studies*, 36 (4), 99–118.
Eroğlu, Ş. (2009). Patterns of income allocation among young poor *Gecekondu* households in Turkey: overt mechanisms and women's secret kitties, *The Sociological Review*, 57 (1), 58–80.
——— (2010). The irrelevance of Social Capital in Explaining Deprivation: A Case Study of Turkish Gecekondu Households, *Tijdschrift voor Economische en Sociale Geografie*, 101 (1), 37–57.
——— (2011). *Beyond the Resources of Poverty: Gecekondu Living in the Turkish Capital*, Surrey: Ashgate Publishing Limited.
Ertan, M. (2012). Türk Sağının Kızılbaş Algısı, in T. Bora and G.G. Öztan, (eds), *Türk Sağı: Mitler, Fetişler, Düşman İmgeleri* [Turkish Right: Myths, Fetishes and Images of Enemy], İstanbul: İletişim Yayınları, pp. 203–42.
Espine-Andersen, G. (1990). *The Three Worlds of Welfare Capitalism*, Cambridge: Polity Press.
Fischer, C. (1976). *The Urban Experience*, New York: Harcourt Brace Jovanovich.
Fliche, B. (2005). The *hemşehrilik* and the village: the stakes of an association of former villagers in Ankara, *European Journal of Turkish Studies*, 2 [Online]. Available at: http://ejts.revues.org/385 [Accessed 08 October 2012].
Flick, U. (2007). *Using Visual Data in Qualitative Analysis*, London, California, New Delhi, Pekin: SAGE Publications.
Fraser, N. (1987). Women, Welfare and The Politics of Need Interpretation, *Hypatia*, 2 (1), 103–21.
Gal, S. and Irvine, J.T. (1995). The boundaries of languages and disciplines: How ideologies construct difference, *Social research*, 967–1001.
Gans, H.J. (1962). *Urban Villagers: Group and Class in the Life of Italian-Americans*, New York: The Free Press (Macmillan Co., Inc.).
Gedik, A. (1997). Internal Migration in Turkey, 1965–85: Test of Conflicting Findings in the Literature, *Review of Urban & Regional Development Studies*, 9 (2), 170–9.
Gilbert, A. (1994), *The Latin American City*, London: Latin American Bureau.
Gilley, B. (2006). The Determinants of State Legitimacy: Results for 72 Countries, *International Political Science Review*, 27 (1), 47–71.
Goldstein, D.M. (2005). Flexible Justice: Neoliberal Violence and 'Self-Help' Security in Bolivia, *Critique of Anthropology*, 25 (4), 389–411.
Gökçe, B. (2007). *Türkiye'nin Toplumsal Yapısı ve Toplumsal Kurumlar*, Ankara: Savaş Yayınları.
Grasmick, H.G. (1973). Social Change and Modernism in the American South. *American Behavioral Scientist*, 16 (6), 913–33.
Greenwood, M.J. (1997). Internal Migration in Developed Countries, in M.R Rosenzwieg and O. Stark (eds), *Handbook of Population and Family Economics*, Amsterdam: Elsevier B.V., pp. 647–720.
Gupta, K.A. (1979). Travails of a Woman Fieldworker, in M.N. Srinivas et al. (eds), *The Fieldworker and the Field: Problems and Challenges in Sociological Investigation*, New Delhi: Oxford University Press, pp. 103–15.
Güzey, Ö. (2009) Urban Regeneration and increased competitive power: Ankara in an era of globalisation, *Cities*, 26 (1), 27–37.

——— (2012). Türkiye'de Kentsel Dönüşüm Uygulamaları: Neo-liberal Kent Politikaları, Yeni Kentsel Aktörler ve Gecekondu Alanları, *Ideal Kent* 7, 64–84.

Habitat II (1997). *The Istanbul Declaration and the Habitat Agenda with subject index*, United Nations Conference on Human Settlements (Habitat II), İstanbul, 3–14 June 1996.

Halperin, R. (1998). *Practicing Community: Class Culture and Power in an Urban Neighbourhood*, Austin: University of Texas Press.

Hale, W. (1999). Turkey's domestic political landscape: A glance at the past and the future, *The International Spectator: Italian Journal of International Affairs*, 34 (1), 27–46.

Hale, W. and Özbudun, E. (2010). *Islamism, Democracy and Liberalism in Turkey: The Case of the AKP*, New York: Routledge.

Hammersley, M. and Atkinson, P. (1995). *Ethnography: in Practice*, Second Edition, Routledge: London and New York.

Harvey, D. (1989). From Managerialism to Entrepreneurialism: The Transformation in Urban Governance in Late Capitalism, *Geografiska Annaler, Series B, Human Geography*, 71 (1), 3–17.

——— (2009). *Social Justice and City*, Oxford: Blackwell Publishers.

Hattatoğlu, D. (2007). Küreselleşme, Yeni Emek Biçimleri, Yoksulluk ve Kadınlar, *Amargi*, 6, 8–21.

Hemmasi, M. and Prorok, C.V. (2002). Women's migration and quality of life in Turkey, *Geoforum*, 33 (3), 399–411.

Hersant, J. and Toumarkine, A. (2005). Hometown organisations in Turkey: an overview, *European Journal of Turkish Studies*, 2 [Online]. Available at: http://ejts.revues.org/397 [Accessed 30 November 2010].

Human Rights Watch (2012). Turkey: Coup Trial Offers Chance for Justice, Human Rights Watch [Online]. Available at: http://www.hrw.org/news/2012/04/04/turkey-coup-trial-offers-chance-justice [Accessed 26 February 2013].

Hunter, D.R. (1964). *The Slums: Challenge and Response*, London: Collier MacMillan.

Hürriyet Daily News (2008). *Turkey still awaits to confront with generals of the coup in Sep 12, 1980*, 9 October 2008 [Online]. Available at: http://www.hurriyet.com.tr/english/home/9884161.asp?scr=1 [Accessed 26 February 2013].

Ijaz, A. and Abbas T. (2010). The impact of intergenerational change on the attitudes of working-class South Asian Muslim parents on the education of their daughters, *Gender and Education*, 22 (3), 313–26.

Inglehart, R. and Norris, P. (2003). *Rising Tide: Gender Equality and Cultural Change*, New York: Cambridge University Press.

International Labour Organization (2012). Global Employment Trends 2012, Internal Labour Office, Geneva [Online]. Available at: http://www.ilo.org/wcmsp5/groups/public/@dgreports/@dcomm/@publ/documents/publication/wcms_171571.pdf [Accessed 07 December 2012].

Işık, O. and Pınarcıoğlu, M.M. (2002). *Nöbetleşe Yoksulluk: Gecekondulaşma ve Kent Yoksulları: Sultanbeyli Örneği* [Poverty in Turn], İstanbul: İletişim Yayınları.

İçduygu, A., Sirkeci, I. and Aydingun, I. (1998). Türkiye'de İçgöç ve İçgöçün İşçi Hareketine Etkisi, in A. İçduygu, I. Sirkeci and I. Aydıngün (eds), *Türkiye'de İçgöç* [Internal Migration in Turkey], Istanbul: Tarih Vakfı Yayınları, pp. 205–44.

Jennings, W., Farall, S. and Bevan, S. (2012). The Economy, crime and time: An Analysis of recorded property crime in England & Wales 1961–2006, *International Journal of Law, Crime and Justice*, 40 (3), 192–210.

Jessop, B. (2002). Liberalism, Neoliberalism and Urban Governance: A State-Theoretical Perspective, *Antipode*, 34 (3), 452–72.
Kalaycıoğlu, S. and Rittersberger-Tılıç, H. (2001). *Yapısal Uyum Programıyla Ortaya Çıkan Yoksullukla Başetme Stratejileri*, Unpublished paper presented at 7, Ulusal Sosyal Bilimler Kongresi, 21–23 November 2001, Ankara.
Kanaiaupuni, S.M. (2000). Reframing the Migration Question: An Analysis of Men, Women and Gender in Mexico, *Social Forces*, 78 (4), 1311–47.
Kandiyoti, D. (1988). Bargaining with Patriarchy, *Gender and Society*, 2 (3), 274–90.
Karpat, K. H. (1976). *The Gecekondu: Rural Migration and Urbanization*, Cambridge: Cambridge University Press.
——— (2003). *Türkiye'de Toplumsal Dönüşüm, Kırsal Göç, Gecekondu ve Kentleşme* [Social Transformation, Rural Migration, Gecekondu and Urbanization in Turkey], Ankara, Turkey: İmge Kitabevi.
——— (2004). The Genesis of the Gecekondu: Rural Migration and Urbanization (1976), European Journal of Turkish Studies, 1 [Online]. Available at: http://ejts.revues.org/54 [Accessed 20 October 2011].
Kaya, Y. (2008). Proletarianization with polarization: Industrialization, globalization and social class in Turkey, 1980–2005. *Research in Social Stratification and Mobility*, 26 (2), 161–81.
Kazgan, G. (1966). *Tarım Ekonomisi ve İktisadî Gelişme* [Agricultural Economy and Economic Development], İstanbul: İstanbul Üniversitesi İktisat Fakültesi Yayınları.
Keleş, R. (2010). *Kentleşme Politikası* [Urbanization Politics], Ankara: İmge Yayınları.
Kehl-Bodrogi, K. (2007). Atatürk and the Alevis: A Holy Alliance?, in P.J. White and J. Jongerdeen (eds), *Turkey's Alevi Enigma: A Comprehensive Overview*, Leiden: Brill, pp. 53–70.
Kelly, L., Burton, S. and Regan, L. (1994). Researching Women's Lives or Studying Women's Oppression? Reflections on what Constitutes Feminist Research, in M. Maynard and J. Purvis (eds), *Researching Women's Lives from a Feminist Perspective*, London, Bristol: Taylor and Francis, pp. 27–48.
Kendir, H. (2003). 'Küreselleşen Tarım ve Türkiye'de Tarım Reformu', *Praksis*, 9, 277–300.
Kentkur (2001). *Mamak Belediyesi Ege Kentsel Dönüşüm Projesi Revizyon Nazım İmar Planı Açıklama Raporu*, Ankara: Kentkur.
Keyder, Ç. (1987). *State and Class in Turkey*, London, New York: Verso.
——— (2005). Globalisation and Social Exclusion in Istanbul, *International Journal of Urban and Regional Research*, 29 (1), 124–34.
Kılınç, K. (2012). Imported but not delivered: the construction of modern domesticity and the spatial politics of mass housing in 1930s Ankara, *The Journal of Architecture*, 17 (6), 819–46.
Kıray, M. (1970). *Squatter housing: Fast depeasantization and slow workerization in underdeveloped countries*, Unpublished paper presented at Research Committee on Urban Sociology of the 7th World Congress of Sociology, 14–19 September 1970, Varna.
——— (2003). Kentleşme Yazıları, Second Edition, İstanbul: Bağlam Publishing.
Kitzinger, J. (1994). The Methodology of Focus Groups: The Importance of Interaction between Research Participants, *Sociology of Health & Illness*, 16 (1), 103–21.

Kitzinger, C. and Wilkinson, S. (1996). Theorizing Representing the Other, in S. Wilkinson and C. Kitzinger (eds), *Representing the Other: A Feminism and Psychology Reader*, London: Sage.

Koray, M. (1993). Employment and Unemployment in Turkey, *International Journal of Manpower*, 12 (5), 15–21.

Korte, C. and Ayvalıoğlu, N. (1981). Helpfulness in Turkey: Cities, Towns and Urban Villages, *Journal of Cross-Cultural Psychology*, 12 (2), 123–41.

Kristen, C. and Granato, N. (2007). The Educational Attainment of the second generation in Germany: Social Origins and ethnic inequality, *Ethnicities*, 7 (3), 343–66.

Kurtoğlu, A. (2005). Mekansal bir Olgu Olarak Hemşehrilik ve Bir Hemşehrilik Mekanı Olarak Dernekler, *European Journal of Turkish Studies*, 2 [Online]. Available at: http://ejts.revues.org/375 [Accessed on 07 April 2012].

Kurul, N. (2012). Turkey under AKP Rule: Neoliberal Interventions into the Public Budget and Educational Finance, in K. İnal and G. Akkaymak (eds), *Neoliberal Transformation of Education in Turkey: Political and Ideological Analysis of Educational Reforms in the Age of the AKP*, New York: Palgrave Macmillan, pp. 83–94.

Küçük, M. (2008). Türkiye'de Sol Düşünce ve Aleviler, in T. Bora and M. Gültekingil (eds), *Modern Türkiye'de Siyasi Düşünce*, Volume 8 Sol [Political Thought in Modern Turkey, Vol. 8 Left], İstanbul: İletişim Yayınları, pp. 896–935.

Kümbetoğlu, B. (1996). Gizli İşçiler: Kadınlar ve Bir Alan Araştırması, in S. Çakır and N. Akgökçe (eds), *Farklı Feminizmler Açısından Kadın Araştırmalarında Yöntem [Methodology in Women Studies from the Perspective of Different Feminisms]*, İstanbul: Sel Yayıncılık.

Lal, J. (1996). Situating Locations: The Politics of Self, Identity and 'Other' in Living and Writing the Text, in D. L. Wolf (eds), *Feminist Dilemmas in Fieldwork*, Colorado, Oxford: Westview Press, pp. 185–214.

Latapi, A.E. and Rocha, M.G. (1999). Crisis, restructuring and urban poverty in Mexico, *Environment and Urbanization*, 7 (1), 57–76.

Letherby, G. (2003). *Feminist Research in Theory and Practice*, Buckingham, Philadelphia: Open University Press.

Levine, N. (1973). Old Culture-New Culture: A Study of Migrants in Ankara, Turkey, *Social Forces*, 51 (3), 355–68.

Lloyd, P. (1979). *Slums of Hope? Shanty Towns of the third World*, Middlesex, New York, Victoria, Ontario, Auckland: Penguin Books.

Lucas, R.E.B. (1997). Internal Migration in Developing Countries, *Handbook of Population and Family Economics*, 1, 721–98.

Maclean, K. (2007). Translation in cross-cultural research: an example from Bolivia, *Development in Practice*, 17 (6), 784–90.

Mahmud, S. and Duyar-Kienast, U. (2001). Spontaneous Settlements in Turkey and Bangladesh: Preconditions of Emergence and Environmental Quality of Gecekondu Settlements and Bustees, *Cities*, 18 (4), 271–80.

Mangin, W. (1967). Latin American Squatter Settlements: A Problem and a Solution, *Latin American Research Review*, 2 (3), pp. 65–98.

Mardin, Ş. (2006). *Religion, society and modernity in Turkey*, New York: Syracuse University Press.

Martinelli, A. (2005). *Global Modernization: Rethinking the Project of Modernity*, London, California, New Delhi: SAGE Publications.

Mason, J. (2002). *Qualitative Researching*, London: Sage Publications.

Maynard, M. (1994). Methods, Practice and Epistemology, The Debate about Feminism and Research, in M. Maynard, J. Purvis (eds), *Researching Women's Lives from a Feminist Perspective*, London, Bristol: Taylor and Francis, pp. 10–26.

McAdam, S. (1999). The political Process and the Development of Black Insurgency; 1930–70, Chicago, IL: University of Chicago Press.

McDowall, D. (2004). *A Modern History of the Kurds*, Palgrave MacMillan, New York.

McIntosch J. and Munk, D.M. (2009). Social Class, family background and intergenerational mobility, *European Economic Review*, 53 (1), 107–17.

McKee, L. and O'Brien, M. (1983). Interviewing Men: Taking gender seriously, in E. Gamarnikow, D. Morgan, J. Purvis and D. Taylorson (eds), *The Public and the Private*, London: Heinemann, pp. 147–61.

Mellor, J. (2007). *Parallel Lives? Working Class Muslim and Non-Muslim Women at University*, Unpublished: University of York, PhD.

Ministry of National Education, Turkey (2012). *National Education Statistics Formal Education 2012–13*, Ministry of National Education [Online]. Available at: http://sgb.meb.gov.tr/istatistik/meb_istatistikleri_orgun_egitim_2012_2013.pdf [Accessed 20 May 2013].

Montell, F. (1999). Focus Group Interviews: A New Feminist Method, *NWSA Journal*, 11 (1), 44–71.

Mooney, G. and Neal, S. (2009). Community: themes and debates, in G. Moobey and S. Neal (eds), *Community: Welfare, Crime and Society*, New York: Open University Press, pp. 1–34.

Murakami, K. (2011). Negotiating Social Assistance: The Case of the Urban Poor in Turkey, Institute of Developing Economies (IDE) Discussion Paper No. 291.

Nalbantoğlu, G.B. (1997). Urban Encounters with Rural Turkey, in S. Bozdoğan and R. Kasaba (eds), *Rethinking Modernity and National Identity in Turkey*, University of Washington, D.C: Washington Press, pp. 192–210.

Narlı, N. (1999). The Rise of the Islamist Movement in Turkey, *Middle East Review of International Affairs*, 3 (3), 38–48.

Nelson, N. (1987). Rural-urban child fostering in Kenya: migration, kinship ideology and class, in Jeremy Eades (eds), *Migrant, Workers and the Social Order*, London and New York: Tavistock Publications, pp. 181–98.

Nesteruk, O., Marks, L. and Garrison, M.E.B. (2009). Immigrant Parents' Concerns Regarding Their Children's Education in the United States, *Family and Consumer Sciences Research Journal*, 37 (4), 422–41.

Oakley, A. (1981). Interviewing Women: a contradiction in terms, in H. Roberts (eds), *Doing Feminist Research*, London, Boston and Henley: Routledge & Kegan Paul, pp. 243–64.

Ochsen, C. (2010). Crime and labour Market Policy in Europe, *International Review of Law and Economics*, 30 (1), 52–61.

Oğuz, H.Ş. (2012). Alanda Bir Kadın, *Fe Dergi*, 4 (1), 1–64.

Öğretmen, İ. (1957). *Ankara'da 158 Gecekondu Hakkında bir Monografi* [A Monograph on 158 Gecekondus in Ankara], Ankara: Ajans Türk Matbaası.

Öniş, Z. (1997). The political economy of Islamic resurgence in Turkey: The rise of the Welfare Party in perspective, *Third World Quarterly*, 18 (4), 743–66.

Özar, Ş. and Ercan, F. (2004). Emek Piyasaları: Uyumsuzluk mu Bütünleşme mi? In N. Balkan and S. Savran (eds), *Neoliberalizmin Tahribatı: 2000'li yıllarda*

Türkiye [Destruction of Neoliberalism: Turkey in the 2000s], İstanbul: Metis, pp. 191–210.
Özbek, M. (2006). *Popüler Kültür ve Orhan Gencebay Arabeski* [Popular Culture and Orhan Gencebay's Arabesque], İstanbul: İletişim Yayınları.
Özcan, G.B. and Turunç, H. (2011). Economic Liberalization and Class Dynamics in Turkey: New Business Groups and Islamic Mobilization, *Insight Turkey*, 13 (3), 63–86.
Özdalga, E. (1999). Education in the Name of 'Order and Progress', Reflections on the Recent Eight Year Obligatory School Reform in Turkey, *The Muslim World*, 89 (3–4), 414–38.
Özler, I.Ş. (2000). Politics of the Gecekondu in Turkey: The political choices of urban squatters in national elections, *Turkish Studies*, 1 (2), 39–58.
Özmen Konutları. Photo Galleries, http://www.ozmenkonutlari.com/index.php?option=com_content&view=article&id=51&Itemid=73 [Accessed 12 March 2012].
Öztürk, M. (2004). Türk Sinemasında Gecekondular, *European Journal of Turkish Studies*, 1 [Online]. Available at: http://ejts.revues.org/94?&id=94&ref=http:/pdf/pdf/pdf/pdf/pdf/pdf/pdf/pdf/pdf/pdf/pdf/pdf/pdf/pdf/pdf/pdf/pdf/pdf/pdf/pdf/pdf/pdf/pdf/pdf/94?format=citation [Accessed 07 September 2010].
Özyeğin, G. (2001). *Untidy Gender: Domestic Service in Turkey*, Philadelphia: Temple University Press.
——— (2002). The Doorkeeper, The Maid and the Tenant: Troubling Encounters in the Turkish Urban Landscape, in D. Kandiyoti and A. Saktanber (eds), *Fragments of Culture: The Everyday of Modern Turkey*, London and New York: I.B.Tauris & Co Publishers, pp. 43–72.
Özuğurlu, A. (2005). Poverty or Social Production of Labour: Çöplük District, Unpublished: Middle East Technical University, PhD.
Pak, Sun Y. (2004). Cultural Policies and Vocational Religious Education: The Case of Turkey, *Comparative Education*, 40 (3), 321–41.
Parrenas, R.S. (2001). *Servants of Globalisation*, California: Stanford University Press.
Payne, G.K. (1984). Ankara, *Cities*, 1 (3), 210–14.
Pınarcıoğlu, M. and Işık, O. (2008). Not Only Helpless but also Hopeless: Changing Dynamics of Urban Poverty in Turkey, the Case of Sultanbeyli, İstanbul, *European Planning Studies*, 16 (10), 1353–70.
Pini, B. (2002). Focus Groups, Feminist Research and farm women: opportunities for empowerment in rural social research, *Journal of Rural Studies*, 18 (3), 339–51.
Pekdemir, M. (1988). Gecekondular ve Anti-Faşist Mücadele, *Sosyalizm ve Toplumsal Mücadeleler Ansiklopedisi*, [Encyclopaedia of Socialism and Social Movements], Volume 7, İstanbul: İletişim Yayınları, pp. 2346–7.
——— (2008). Devrimci Yol. in T. Bora and M. Gültekingil (eds), *Modern Türkiye'de Siyasi Düşünce*, Volume 8, Sol, İstanbul: İletişim Yayınları, pp. 743–79.
Petersen M.B., Slouthuus, R., Stubager, R. and Toheby, L. (2010). Deservingness versus values in public opinion on welfare: The automaticity of the deservingness heuristic, *European Journal of Political Research*, 50 (1), 24–52.
Petrol-İş (1996). *Year Book for 95–6*.
Portes, A. and Ruumbaut R.G. (2001). *Legacies: The Story of the Immigrant Second Generation*, Berkeley, CA: University of California Press.

Privatization Administration (no date). Privatization Endeavour in Turkey [Online]. Available at: http://www.oib.gov.tr/program/uygulamalar/privatization_in_turkey.htm [Accessed 29 January 2014].

Qin, D.B. (2006). Our Child Doesn't Talk to Us Anymore: Alienation in Immigrant Chinese Families, *Anthropology and Education Quarterly*, 37 (2), 162–79.

Sanchez-Jankowski, M. (2003). Gangs and Social Change, *Theoretical Criminology*, 7 (2), 191–216.

Sat, A. (2007). A Critique on Improvement Plans: A tool for Transformation of Squatter Housing Areas in Ankara, *METU Journal of the Faculty of Architecture*, 24 (2), 27–36.

Sayer, A. (2005). *The Moral Significance of Class*, Cambridge: Cambridge University Press.

Schnaiberg, A. (1970). Measuring Modernism: Theoretical and Empirical Explorations, *American Journal of Sociology*, 76 (3), 399–425.

——— (1971). The Modernizing Impact of Urbanization: A Causal Analysis, *Economic Development and Cultural Change*, 20 (1), 80–104.

Schofield, J.W. (2002). Increasing the Generalizability of Qualitative Research, in A.M. Huberman and M.B. Milles (eds), *The Qualitative Researcher's Companion*, London: Sage Publications, pp. 171–204.

Scott, R.B. (1968). *The Village Headman in Turkey: A Case Study*, Sevinç Matbaası: Ankara.

Sennett, R. (1998). *The Corrosion of Character: The Personal Consequences of Work in the New Capitalism*, W. W. Norton & Company Ltd: New York.

Sinclair-Webb, E. (2007). Sectarian Violence, the Alevi Minority and the Left: Kahramanmaraş 1978, in P.J. White and J. Jongerdeen (eds), *Turkey's Alevi Enigma: A Comprehensive Overview*, Leiden: Brill, pp. 88–215.

Ramazanoglu, C. and Holland, J. (2002). *Feminist methodology: Challenges and choices*, Sage.

Rittersberger-Tılıç, H. (1998). Alevi Revivalism, in T. Olsson, E. Özdalga and C. Raudvere (eds), *Alevi Identity: Cultural, Religious and Social Perspectives*, Istanbul: Swedish Research Institute, pp. 93–100.

Soytemel, E. (2013). The Power of Powerless: Neighbourhood based self-help networks of the poor in İstanbul, *Women's Studies International Forum* [Online]. Available at: http://dx.doi.org/10.1016/j.wsif2013.06.007 [Accessed 03 October 2013].

Stewart, F. (1992). Can Adjustment Programmes Incorporate the Interests of Women? In H. Afshar and C. Dennis (eds), *Women and Adjustment Policies in Third World*, London and Hampshire: MacMillan Press, pp. 13–45.

Szyliowicz, J.S. (1962). The Political Dynamics of Rural Turkey, *Middle East Journal*, 16 (4), 430–42.

Şahin, S. (2005). The Rise of Alevism as a Public Religion, *Current Sociology*, 53 (3), 465–85.

Şengül, H.T. (2001). *Kentsel Çelişki ve Siyaset: Kapitalist Kentleşme Süreçleri Üzerine Yazılar* [Urban Contradictions: Essays on Capitalist Urbanization Processes], İstanbul: Demokrasi Kitaplığı.

Şenses F., Taymaz E. (2003). Unutulan Bir Toplumsal Amaç: Sanayileşme: Ne Oluyor? Ne Olmalı, METU ERC Working Papers in Economics 03/01 [Online]. Available at: http://erc.metu.edu/menu/series03/0301.pdf [Accessed 23 April 2011].

Şentürk, D. (2012). Gecekondunun Penceresinden, *Feminist Politika* 13, 49.

Şenyapılı, T. (1981). A New Component in Metropolitan Areas: The 'Gecekondu Women, in N. Abadan Unat (eds), *Women in Turkish Society*, E. J. Brill: Leiden, pp. 194–218.

——— (1982). Economic change and the gecekondu family, in C. Kağıtçıbaşı (eds), *Sex roles, family, and community in Turkey*, Bloomington: Indiana University Turkish Studies 3, pp. 237–48.

——— (2004). *Barakadan Gecekonduya: Ankara'da Kentsel Mekanın Dönüşümü: 1923–60* [From Shantytown to Gecekondu: Spatial Transformation in Ankara 1923–60], İstanbul: İletişim Yayınları.

Tacoli, C. (1998). Rural-Urban interactions: a guide to the literature, *Environment and Urbanization*, 10 (1), 147–66.

Tansel, A. (2002). Determinants of school attainment of boys and girls in Turkey individual, household and community factors, *Economics of Education Review*, 21 (5), 455–70.

——— (2012). 2050'ye Doğru Nüfusbilim ve Yöneti: İşgücü Piyasasına Bakış. TUSİAD [Online]. Available at: http://www.tusiad.org/__rsc/shared/file/Isgucu-Piyasasina-Bakis-.pdf [Accessed 01 December 2012].

Tarhan, B.A. (2006). Ankara, Kent ve Modernleşme, in F. Cantek (eds), *Sanki Viran Ankara*, İstanbul: İletişim Yayınları, pp. 107–48.

Tas, H.I. and Lightfoot, D.R. (2005). Gecekondu Settlements in Turkey: Rural-Urban Migration in the Developing European Periphery, *Journal of Geography*, 104 (6), 263–71.

Taylor-Gooby, P. (2010). Opportunity and Solidarity, *Journal of Social Policy*, 40 (3), 53–470.

Tekeli, İ. and Okyay, T. (1977). *Dolmuşun Öyküsü*, Ankara: Çevre ve Mimarlık Bilimleri Derneği Yayınları.

Tekeli, İ. (2008). *Göç ve Ötesi* [Migration and Beyond], İstanbul: Tarih Vakfı Yurt Yayınları.

Tilly and Brown (1967). On Uprooting, Kinship and the Auspices of Migration, *International Journal of Comparative Sociology*, 8 (2), 139–64.

Todaro, M.P. (1992). *Economics for a developing world: an introduction to principles, problems and policies*, London, New York: Longman.

Turan, M. (2007). Başkentin Gecekonduları: Kentsel Dönüşüm Projelerinin Arka Bahçeleri, *Ruşen Keleş'e Armağan: Kent ve Planlama [For Ruşen Keleş: City and Planning]*, İmge Kitabevi Yayınları: Ankara, pp. 389–404.

Turgut, P. (2006). Bülent Ecevit: Political pragmatist and working-man's-cap populist who was five times Prime Minister of Turkey, The Independent [Online]. 07 November 2006. Available at: http://www.independent.co.uk/news/obituaries/bulent-ecevit-423240.html [Accessed 19 April 2012].

TUIK [Turkish Statistical Institute] (2009). Gençlerin İşgücü Piyasasına Geçişi Araştırma Sonuçları 2009, TUIK [Online]. Available at: http://www.tuik.gov.tr/PreHaberBultenleri.do?id=8373 [Accessed 01 December 2012].

Turkish Development Bank (2012). Kalkınma Sürecinde Tarım Sektörü: Gelişmeler, Sorunlar, Tespitler Ve Tarımsal Politika Önerileri, Vol. II [Online]. Available at: http://www.kalkinma.com.tr/data/file/raporlar/ESA/GA/2004-GA/GA-04-07-20_Kalkinma_Surecinde_Tarim_Sektoru_CiltII.pdf [Accessed 29 January 2014].

Türk-İş (2012). Türk-İş Araştırması: Açlık ve Yoksulluk Sınırı Temmuz 2012. Türk-İş [Online]. Available at: http://www.yol-is.org.tr/TR/belge/1-245/

turk-is-arastirmasi-temmuz-2012-aclik-ve-yoksulluk-sini-.html#icerik [Accessed 11 October 2012].

United Nations Human Settlements Programme (2003). *The Challenge of Slums: Global Report on Human Settlements 2003*, London, Sterling VA: Earthscan Publication.

Velayati, M. (2011). *Islam, Gender and Development: Rural-urban Migration of Women in Iran*, Lexington Books.

Vinay, J.P. and Darbelnet, J. (2004). A Methodology for Translation, in L. Venuti, (eds), *The Translation Studies Reader*, 2nd edition, New York, Oxon: Routledge, pp. 128–38.

Wacquant, L. (2000). Logics of Urban Polarization: The View from the Below, in R. Crompton, F. Devine, M. Savage and J. Scott (eds), *Renewing Class Analysis*, Oxford: Blackwell Publishers, pp. 107–19.

——— (1999). Urban Marginality in the Coming Millennium, *Urban Studies*, 36 (10), 1939–47.

Walsham, G. (1995). The emergence of interpretivism in IS research, *Information systems research*, 6 (4), 376–94.

Ward, P.M. (1976). The Squatter Settlement as Slum or Housing Solution: Evidence form Mexico City, *Land Economies*, 52 (3), 330–46.

Wedel, H. (2001). *Siyaset ve Cinsiyet: İstanbul Gecekondularında Kadınların Siyasal Katılımı* [Politics and Gender: Political Participation of Women in İstanbul Gecekondus], İstanbul: Metis Yayınları.

White, J.B. (2002). *Islamist mobilization in Turkey: A study in vernacular politics*, Washington: University of Washington Press.

——— (2004). *Money Makes Us Relatives: Women's Labour in Urban Turkey*, 2nd edition, New York and London: Routledge.

Williams, M. (2000). Interpretivism and Generalization, *Sociology*, 34 (22), 209–24.

Willmott, P. and Young, M. (1976). *Family and Class in a London Suburb*, London: New English Library.

Willmott, P. (1986). *Social Networks, Informal Care and Public Policy*, London: Policy Studies Institute.

Wilson, G. and Baldassare M. (1996). Overall 'Sense of Community' in a Suburban Region: The Effects of Localism, Privacy and Urbanization, *Environment and Behaviour* 28 (1), 27–34.

Wolcott, P. and Çağıltay, K. (2001). Telecommunications, Liberalization and the Growth of the Internet in Turkey, *The Information Society*, 17 (2), 133–41.

Wolf, D.L. (1996). Situating Feminist Dilemmas in Fieldwork, in D.L. Wolf (eds), *Feminist Dilemmas in Fieldwork*, Colorado, Oxford: Westview Press, pp. 1–56.

Wolf, E. (1966). Kinship, Friendship and Patron-Client Relations in Complex Societies, in M. Banton (eds), *The Social Anthropology of Complex Societies*, London: Tavistock Publications, pp. 1–22.

Wood, E.M. (1998). *Retreating from Class: The New 'True' Socialism*, London, New York: Verso Books.

World Bank (2005). *Turkey: Joint Poverty Assessment Report: Volume 1, Main Report*, World Bank Human Development Sector Unit, Europe and Central Asia Region [Online]. Available at: http://www-wds.worldbank.org/servlet/WDS ContentServer/WDSP/IB/2005/10/12/000012009_20051012161856/Rendered/PDF/296190rev0v1.pdf [Accessed 14 March 2013].

——— (2013). *Towards Universal Coverage: Turkey's Green Card Program for the Poor: UNICO Studies Series 18*, The World Bank [Online]. Available at: http://

www-wds.worldbank.org/external/default/WDSContentServer/WDSP/IB/2013/02/04/000333037_20130204152023/Rendered/PDF/750120NWP0Box300for0the0Poor0TURKEY.pdf [Accessed 14 March 2013].

Yalçıntan, M.C and Erbaş, A.E. (2003). Impacts of 'Gecekondu' on the Electoral Geography of Istanbul, *International Labor and Working Class History*, 64, 91–111.

Yalman, G. (2009). *Transition to Neo-Liberalism: The Case of Turkey in the 1980s*, İstanbul Bilgi University Press: İstanbul.

Yasa, I. (1966). *Ankara Squatter Families*, Ankara: Ministry of Health and Social Welfare.

Yavuz, F., Keleş, R. and Geray, C. (1978). *Urbanism: Problems, Applications and Policy*, Ankara: Ankara University Press.

Yeldan, E. (2005). Assessing the Privatization Experience in Turkey: Implementation, Politics and Performance Results, Report submitted to Economic Policy Institute Washington DC [Online]. Available at: http://www.bilkent.edu.tr/~yeldane/EPI_Report2005_Yeldan.pdf [Accessed 02 February 2012].

Yıldırmaz, S. (2010). Kente Yönelen Köylüler: Kırsal Yapının Dönüşümü, Göç ve Gecekondu, in B. Şen and A. E. Doğan (eds), *Tarih, Sınıflar ve Kent* [History, Classes and City], Ankara: Dipnot Yayınları, pp. 398–464.

Yılmaz, M. (2011). *An Inquiry into different urban transformation models in the context of rent and property transfer: The case of Mamak District*, Unpublished: Middle East Technical University. MS.

Yoltar, Ç. (2009). When the Poor Need Health Care: Ethnography of State and Citizenship in Turkey, *Middle Eastern Studies*, 45 (5), 769–82.

Yonucu, D. (2008). A Story of a Squatter Neighbourhood: From the place of the 'dangerous classes' to the 'place of danger', *Berkeley Journal of Sociology*, 52, 50–72.

Zürcher, Eric, J. (2004). *Turkey: A Modern History*, London & New York: I.B.Tauris.

INDEX